The Responsibility to Protect in International Law

This book tracks the development of the emerging international legal principle of a responsibility to protect over the past two decades. It explores the influential version of the principle introduced by the International Commission on Intervention and State Sovereignty in 2001 and compares it with more recent interpretations of the responsibility to protect. It reviews the dangers and inconsistencies inherent in all of these variants, but focuses in particular on the reading of the norm advocated by the United Nations through its human protection agenda. The author demonstrates that the evolving responsibility to protect principle can be recruited to support a wide range of irreconcilable projects, from those of cosmopolitan constitutionalism to those of hegemonic international law. However, despite the dangers posed by this susceptibility to conceptual hijacking, Oman argues that the responsibility to protect, like human rights, is an essential modern emancipatory formation. To remedy its dangerous malleability, the author advocates a distinctive interpretation of the responsibility to protect designed to limit its cooptation by liberal anti-pluralist and hegemonic international law agendas. Oman outlines the key features of such a minimalist conception, and explores its fit with the RtoP version of the responsibility to protect promoted in recent years by the UN. The author argues that two crucial features missing from the UN reading of the principle should be developed in future: an acknowledgement of the role of nonstate actors as bearers of the responsibility to protect, and a recognition of the principle's legal character. Both of these aspects of the principle offer means to democratize the international law-making enterprise.

Natalie Oman is Assistant Professor of Legal Studies at University of Ontario Institute of Technology. She has published in the areas of international law and human rights, philosophy of law, Indigenous legal issues and ethics.

Routledge Research in International Law

For a full list of titles in this series, visit https://www.routledge.com/Routledge-Research-in-International-Law/book-series/INTNLLAW

Available:

Transnational Terrorist Groups and International Criminal Law
Anna Marie Brennan

Confronting Cyberespionage Under International Law
Oğuz Kaan Pehlivan

Russian Discourses on International Law
Sociological and Philosophical Phenomenon
Edited by P. Sean Morris

Backstage Practices in Transnational Law
Lianne J.M Boer and Sofia Stolk

International 'Criminal' Responsibility
Antinomies
Ottavio Quirico

The Future of International Courts
Regional, Institutional and Procedural Challenges
Edited by Avidan Kent, Nikos Skoutaris and Jamie Trinidad

The Far-Right in International and European Law
Natalie Alkiviadou

International Law and Revolution
Owen Taylor

The Responsibility to Protect in International Law
Philosophical Investigations
Natalie Oman

The Responsibility to Protect in Libya and Syria
Mass Atrocities, Human Protection, and International Law
Yasmine Nahlawi

The Responsibility to Protect in International Law

Philosophical Investigations

Natalie Oman

Routledge
Taylor & Francis Group
LONDON AND NEW YORK

First published 2019
by Routledge
2 Park Square, Milton Park, Abingdon, Oxon OX14 4RN

and by Routledge
605 Third Avenue, New York, NY 10017

First issued in paperback 2021

Routledge is an imprint of the Taylor & Francis Group, an informa business

Publisher's Note
The publisher has gone to great lengths to ensure the quality of this reprint but points out that some imperfections in the original copies may be apparent.

British Library Cataloguing-in-Publication Data
A catalogue record for this book is available from the British Library

Library of Congress Cataloging-in-Publication Data
Names: Oman, Natalie, 1964- author.
Title: The responsibility to protect in international law / Natalie Oman.
Description: Abingdon, Oxon ; New York, NY : Routledge, 2019. | Based on author's thesis (doctoral - Osgoode Hall Law School, 2012) issued under title: A philosophical investigation of the responsibility to protect in international law. | Includes bibliographical references and index.
Identifiers: LCCN 2018056472| ISBN 9781472423948 (hardback) | ISBN 9781315553535 (ebook)
Subjects: LCSH: Responsibility to protect (International law)
Classification: LCC KZ4082 .O46 2019 |
DDC 341.5--dc23
LC record available at https://lccn.loc.gov/2018056472

ISBN 13: 978-1-03-208324-7 (pbk)
ISBN 13: 978-1-4724-2394-8 (hbk)

Typeset in Galliard
by Taylor & Francis Books

Tien ta foy

Contents

Acknowledgements

This book has benefited from the support of a web of generous colleagues. Deep thanks are owed in particular to Eyal Benvenisti, Obiora Okafor, Craig Scott, Jenny Nedelsky, Stepan Wood, Sasha Baglay, Jen Rinaldi, Tom McMorrow, Rachel Ariss, and Alison Kirk. Participation as a visiting scholar on the European Research Council's *Sovereigns as Trustees of Humanity* project, led by Eyal Benvenisti, provided me with the a rich environment of intellectual exchange in which to develop and test elements of the argument of Chapter 5 on sources of international law, and I am grateful for the camaraderie and support of the talented members of the project's 2015 research team who worked with me at the Buchmann Faculty of Law at Tel Aviv University.

This book would not have been completed without the patience and faith of my daughter, Arra Isabeau Etsu. I thank her and my extraordinary parents, Anne Nesbitt and David William Sinclair, for their unstinting support and love. Thanks are also due and overdue to all of the dear friends who have both encouraged and commiserated with me. Among their number are Terezia Zoric, Kim Wong, Eyal Chowers, Claire Wilkshire, Dave Jackman, Michelle Peacock, Scott Bartlett, Kyle Rees, Toni Stafford, and Rachel Marshall. I also thank my sister, Leslie Oman, for coming through in the clutch more than once.

Versions of elements of the argument have appeared as articles, and I am grateful to the various publishers for permission to include extracts from these works: to Taylor & Francis for "Hannah Arendt's 'Right to Have Rights': A Philosophical Context for Human Security," published in *Journal of Human Rights* on 10 August 2010, available online: www.tandfonline.com/doi/full/10.1080/14754835.2010.501262; to the *Canadian Journal of Law and Jurisprudence* for "The 'Responsibility to Prevent': A Remit for Intervention?" published in the *Canadian Journal of Law and Jurisprudence* in July 2009, available online: https://doi.org/10.1017/S0841820900004732; and to the *European Journal of International Law* for "Human Rights and Human Rights Protection Norms as General Principles of International Law," forthcoming.

Abbreviations and acronyms

AJIL	*American Journal of International Law*
BNA	basic needs approach
BRICS	Brazil, Russia, India, China, and South Africa
Can. TS	Canada Treaty Series
COW	Correlates of War Project
ECH	elementary considerations of humanity
EJIL	*European Journal of International Law*
EU	European Union
ICISS	International Commission on Intervention and State Sovereignty
ICC	International Criminal Court
ICJ	International Court of Justice
ICJ Rep.	International Court of Justice, Reports of Judgments, Advisory Opinions and Orders
ICTR	International Criminal Tribunal for Rwanda
ICTY	International Criminal Tribunal for the Former Yugoslavia
IDRC	International Development Research Centre
ILC	International Law Commission
ILM	International Legal Materials
ILR	International Law Reports
INGO	international nongovernmental organization
IO	international organization
GA	(United Nations) General Assembly
LNTS	League of Nations Treaty Series
NATO	North Atlantic Treaty Organization
NGO	nongovernmental organization
NILR	*Netherlands International Law Review*
OASTS	Organisation of American States Treaty Series
OAU	Organization of African Unity
P5	permanent five members of the UN Security Council
PCIJ	Permanent Court of International Justice
PDPT	purely domestic poverty thesis
Res.	Resolution
RG	*riconoscimento giuridico di esigenze della coscienza pubblica*

R2P	*The Responsibility to Protect* (ICSS Report)
SC	Security Council
SCR	Security Council Resolution
SCOR	Security Council Official Records
SD	sustainable development
Ser.	Series
TWAIL	Third World Approaches to International Law
UN	United Nations
UNGAOR	United Nations General Assembly Official Records
UNTS	United Nations Treaty Series

* * *

A word on the responsibility to protect and the struggle to save syllables: there are a sometimes-bewildering range of acronyms employed to refer to varying perspectives on the responsibility to protect norm. The variants discussed in this book include:

R2P	responsibility to protect (ICISS version)
RP	responsible protection (China's unofficial perspective on the responsibility to protect)
RtoP	responsibility to protect (UN acronym employed to distinguish the 2005 World Summit-guided version of the responsibility to protect)
RwP	responsibility while protecting (Brazil's 2011 interpretation of the responsibility to protect)
UN-R2P	term used in this book to refer to the UN's more fully-developed interpretation of the responsibility to protect dating from the late 2010s, following introduction of the RwP and RP perspectives

Abbreviations and acronyms

AJIL	*American Journal of International Law*
BNA	basic needs approach
BRICS	Brazil, Russia, India, China, and South Africa
Can. TS	Canada Treaty Series
COW	Correlates of War Project
ECH	elementary considerations of humanity
EJIL	*European Journal of International Law*
EU	European Union
ICISS	International Commission on Intervention and State Sovereignty
ICC	International Criminal Court
ICJ	International Court of Justice
ICJ Rep.	International Court of Justice, Reports of Judgments, Advisory Opinions and Orders
ICTR	International Criminal Tribunal for Rwanda
ICTY	International Criminal Tribunal for the Former Yugoslavia
IDRC	International Development Research Centre
ILC	International Law Commission
ILM	International Legal Materials
ILR	International Law Reports
INGO	international nongovernmental organization
IO	international organization
GA	(United Nations) General Assembly
LNTS	League of Nations Treaty Series
NATO	North Atlantic Treaty Organization
NGO	nongovernmental organization
NILR	*Netherlands International Law Review*
OASTS	Organisation of American States Treaty Series
OAU	Organization of African Unity
P5	permanent five members of the UN Security Council
PCIJ	Permanent Court of International Justice
PDPT	purely domestic poverty thesis
Res.	Resolution
RG	*riconoscimento giuridico di esigenze della coscienza pubblica*

R2P	*The Responsibility to Protect* (ICSS Report)
SC	Security Council
SCR	Security Council Resolution
SCOR	Security Council Official Records
SD	sustainable development
Ser.	Series
TWAIL	Third World Approaches to International Law
UN	United Nations
UNGAOR	United Nations General Assembly Official Records
UNTS	United Nations Treaty Series

* * *

A word on the responsibility to protect and the struggle to save syllables: there are a sometimes-bewildering range of acronyms employed to refer to varying perspectives on the responsibility to protect norm. The variants discussed in this book include:

R2P	responsibility to protect (ICISS version)
RP	responsible protection (China's unofficial perspective on the responsibility to protect)
RtoP	responsibility to protect (UN acronym employed to distinguish the 2005 World Summit-guided version of the responsibility to protect)
RwP	responsibility while protecting (Brazil's 2011 interpretation of the responsibility to protect)
UN-R2P	term used in this book to refer to the UN's more fully-developed interpretation of the responsibility to protect dating from the late 2010s, following introduction of the RwP and RP perspectives

Introduction

This book argues that the "responsibility to protect" is a moral, political, and legal principle, and that it is the product of an emerging transnational narrative justifying political and legal obligation.

This narrative is the "new story" that we have not yet learned, a story that aspires to make sense of these obligations in the face of our plural and sometimes irreconcilable worldviews. Precisely because of a growing global awareness of the diversity of ethical outlooks, many of us find ourselves no longer able to subscribe to the traditional metaphysical and religious justifications that have grounded obedience to political and legal authorities in the past.[1] Thus, human rights and popular sovereignty soared to prominence in recent decades as the seemingly indispensable global criteria of legitimacy in this fledgling narrative.[2] With the worldwide spread of human

1 Of course, some respond to the fact of plurality by cleaving more closely to those customary convictions, and one manifestation of this has been the success of calls for a return to past certitudes in political contests and platforms across Europe, North America, and the Middle East in the 2010s. But even this impulse is expressed using the key concepts of the emerging transnational narrative described below.

2 An appreciation of the legitimating function of human rights and popular sovereignty permeates global public discourses of the late twentieth and early twenty-first century, including those of the protestors who filled China's Tiananmen Square and Czechoslovakia's Wenceslas Square in 1989 and the streets of Sidi Bouzid and Egypt's Tahrir Square in 2011. For evidence of Chinese, Czechoslovakian, Tunisian and Egyptian protestors' commitment to the view that human rights and popular sovereignty ground legitimacy, see for example Charter 08, online at Charter 08 www.charter08.eu/2.html; Declaration of Charter 77, online at http://chnm.gmu.edu/1989/archive/files/declaration-of-charter-77_4346bae392.pdf; William H. Luers, "Czechoslovakia: Road to Revolution" (1990) 69 *Foreign Affairs* 77 at 86–89; and "Cairo's Biggest Protest Yet Demands Mubarak's Immediate Departure" *The Guardian* (5 February 2011), online at www.globalrights.info/world/africa/1118-cairos-biggest-protest-yet-demands-mubaraks-immediate-departure-.pdf. Theoretical analyses of the legitimating role played by popular sovereignty and human rights appear in Jürgen Habermas' account of the co-originality of popular sovereignty and human rights (see for example, his *Between Facts and Norms*, trans. by William Rehg (Cambridge, Mass.: MIT Press, 1996), at chap. 3 and 151; "Remarks on Legitimation Through Human Rights," in *The Postnational Constellation*, ed. and trans. by Max Pensky (Cambridge, Mass.: MIT Press, 2001), 113 at 118; and *The Divided West*, ed. and trans. by Ciaran Cronin (Cambridge, UK: Polity Press, 2006), at 130, 140–141); and also Michael Hardt and Antonio Negri, *Multitude* (New York: Penguin, 2004), at xvi–xvii, and Richard A. Falk, *The*

rights culture in the years following the adoption of the *United Nations Charter*, these two norms have become, not just the benchmarks of a specifically western form of legitimating these obligations,[3] but to the surprise of many, the reference points for validating such obligations across cultures and beyond states. Although frequently contested in their definition and execution, human rights and popular sovereignty now provide the grammar of self-justification for politico-legal communities worldwide.

Human rights and popular sovereignty play this pivotal role because they offer guarantees of the "non-coercive, non-exploitative interaction"[4] necessary for law to be regarded as *self-given*. The sense of "oughtness" or "bindingness" of norms that we associate with law depends upon the presence of just this feature, which Jean-Jacques Rousseau described as "obedience to the law one has prescribed for oneself" (and which, along with his successors in the republican philosophical tradition, he equated with liberty).[5] Implicit in the forms of interaction compatible with a sense of the self-givenness of law is, I will argue, the unreflective attribution of moral standing to every other member of the web of relationships in which each of us is embedded (whether those connections are emotional, transactional, social, or political). It is this attribution, now extended to a community of global reach, which—once it becomes conscious—compels our recognition of our mutual *responsibility to protect.*

The normalization of expectations of human rights and popular sovereignty, coupled with this extension of moral regard, create the conditions for the emergence of a form of the responsibility to protect that exhibits *legal* normativity in response to failures of global governance. Lest this account sound too idealistic—a cardinal sin in the realm of academic legal theorizing—let me note at the outset that I do not subscribe to the argument that it is feasible to "update" international law such that it would become "radically distinct from empire and pure power politics,"[6] as the preceding paragraphs might suggest. What I claim instead is that the interpretation of the responsibility to protect I advocate here is animated by self-reflexive norms that can effectively constrain the principle's cooptation for purposes that contradict the humanitarian goals invoked to justify its existence.

These collected papers, written over the nearly two decades since the responsibility to protect's rise to public attention, focus on the theoretical underpinnings

Costs of War: International Law, the UN, and World Order After Iraq (New York: Routledge, 2008), at 84–86.

3 Habermas, "Remarks on Legitimation," *ibid.* at 118. In this 2001 essay, Habermas cautioned that these criteria of legitimate governance could be applied only to western-style constitutional democracies, a caveat that I argue below is increasingly inapplicable.

4 Jutta Brunée and Stephen J. Toope, "International Law and Constructivism: Elements of an Interactional Theory of International Law" (2000) 39 *Columbia Journal of Transnational Law* 19 at 51.

5 Jean-Jacques Rousseau, *On the Social Contract or Principles of Political Economy* in *On the Social Contract,* ed. and trans. by Donald A. Cressy (Indianapolis, Ind.: Hackett Publishing, 1983), 17 at 27.

6 Jean L. Cohen, "Whose Sovereignty? Empire Versus International Law" (2004) 18 *Ethics & International Affairs* 1 at 3.

of the norm and its companion concept, human security. They reflect upon the trajectory of the norm's development as its operationalization and implementation have de-emphasized certain elements of its original formulation, and critically assess the implications of these exclusions for the responsibility to protect's coherence and intercultural legitimizability. Taken together, the chapters aim to fill lacunae in the existing literature by exploring the linked concepts of the responsibility to protect and human security from an interdisciplinary perspective, drawing upon the theoretical resources of philosophy, legal theory, and political science. As the argument that follows will demonstrate, it is only by employing an interdisciplinary approach of this sort that the limitations, dangers, and possibilities of these evolving legal and international policy concepts become fully apparent.

Scope

This book takes as its starting point the conception of the responsibility to protect introduced by the International Commission on Intervention and State Sovereignty (ICISS) in 2001.[7] ICISS was established following the 1999 bombing campaign conducted by the North Atlantic Treaty Organization (NATO) in Kosovo. NATO's intervention was a response to Serbian troop movements in early 1999 that were believed to presage an imminent ethnic cleansing or genocide attempt against ethnic Kosovars by the Serbian government. Previous atrocities in Rwanda and Srebreniça and state failure in Somalia had induced a profound crisis of confidence in the post-Cold War capacity of the international community to prevent such intra-state disasters from unfolding, and domestic pressure had made it untenable for many NATO governments *not* to act. There was no agreement among the permanent members of the Security Council of the United Nations (UN) on a course of action. NATO, therefore, proceeded to intervene without Council authorization, which in the reckoning of many commentators was a violation of the UN Charter.

In the wake of these events, ICISS was commissioned to determine the state of international law and historical practice in situations where catastrophic threats to populations arise. ICISS's conclusions thematize and develop a concept employed by Francis M. Deng and Roberta Cohen in their work on internal migrants: "sovereignty as responsibility."[8] On the ICISS reading, the *responsibility to protect* is a crystallizing principle of international law mandating a range of forms of coercive intervention in states for human protection purposes. The principle is recommended by ICISS as an alternative to a much more politically contentious *right* of humanitarian intervention. It is meant to legalize sovereignty-impinging actions by the international community of states in response to substantial threats to the human rights and physical safety of populations, specifically, "large scale loss of life … with genocidal intent or not, which is

7 ICISS, *The Responsibility to Protect* (Ottawa, Canada: International Development Research Centre, 2001).

8 See Cohen and Deng, *Masses in Flight: The Global Crisis of Internal Displacement* (Washington, DC: Brookings Institution Press, 1998).

the product either of deliberate state action, or state neglect or inability to act, or a failed state situation; or … large scale 'ethnic cleansing.'"[9]

The responsibility to protect is justified by ICISS in terms of what is assumed to be a shared interest in human security. It is the universal claim of human security upon our moral sensibilities as human beings that serves as the philosophical basis for the emerging legal norm. No workable substitute for this posited claim has been devised in subsequent efforts to articulate the responsibility to protect's major features. As the interpretive community around the norm grew and an attenuated version of the responsibility to protect was adopted by the 2005 World Summit, the human security claim initially remained the unremarked foundation of the responsibility to protect. Later, as the diplomatic aim of achieving consensus among state members guided deliberation under UN auspices, there was a de-emphasis of human security's role, in deference to resistance among some states to the conditional understanding of sovereignty which the conceptual relationship implies.[10] As a result, the logical coherence of contributions to the development of the norm offered by Brazil, China, and more latterly, the UN, has been compromised.

To date, most of the public discussion of a right of humanitarian intervention, and almost all analyses of the responsibility to protect, have taken for granted the conventional conceptual terrain of international law. My argument seeks to identify some of the unexamined premises that determine that terrain's limits, such as a possessive individualist ontology,[11] and a state-centric and legal centrist vision of legitimate authority. It traces these boundaries in order to show why the assumption of a linear evolution of cosmopolitan norms has proven unfounded, and to encourage speculation about the possibility of alternative legal forms that de-couple territoriality and sovereignty at the local and transnational levels. I argue that such forms would better serve the professed ends of a responsibility to protect than the state-centric vision endorsed by proponents of ICISS's or the UN's particular accounts of this principle. By sacrificing a naturalized, absolutist status for the state, such an expansion of the legal imaginary can use the idea of a responsibility to protect to articulate "the conditions and contours" of a field of justice that recognizes the systemic inequalities structuring the existing international legal, political, and economic

9 ICISS, *Responsibility to Protect*, at 32.

10 States of the Non-Aligned Movement and the Group of 77 have signalled concern about the proposition that sovereignty could be subject to assessment by outside actors at various points in the norm's evolution. The historical experience of nineteenth century tests of "civilization" to which many of their members were subject is an important determinant of this wariness. Russia, China, and the USA have expressed opposition to the infringement of UN Charter Article 2(7)'s guarantee of non-interference in matters "essentially within the domestic jurisdiction of states" that a fulsome understanding of human security would sanction (*Charter of the United Nations*, 26 June 1945, Can. TS 1945 No. 7).

11 Possessive individualism is a term coined by C.B. Macpherson to describe the market assumptions built into the ontology of modern liberal democratic theory. It regards humans as primarily rational and appropriative utility-maximizers and consumers. See, e.g., *The Life and Times of Liberal Democracy* (Oxford: Oxford UP, 1977) at 43.

orders.[12] These are the inequalities that generate or exacerbate the very humanitarian crises that the responsibility to protect was designed to alleviate.

Organization

The argument in support of these conclusions and prescriptions is presented in the form of a series of thematically-linked essays. Chapter 1, "A Philosophical Underpinning for a State's 'Responsibility to Protect,'" provides a general introduction to the responsibility to protect principle and its provenance. It outlines the challenges and possibilities posed by the principle's grounding in the contentious concept of human security. It is, indeed, the condition of human security that is safeguarded by the responsibility to protect in early interpretations of the norm. Human security is assessed in terms of the achievement of fundamental elements of human flourishing—although which elements are fundamental and how their achievement is to be measured have proven controversial. The chapter demonstrates the particular usefulness of an Aristotelian understanding of human flourishing for ensuring the logical coherence of this chain of reasoning by drawing upon the work of Martha Nussbaum and Amartya Sen in the debate over the standards of legitimacy of international human rights.

Chapter 2, "Intercultural Judgement and The Role of a *Sensus Communis*," investigates the necessary features of a viable theory of intercultural judgement. Such a theory would provide an adequate account of the conditions of intercultural legitimacy for judgements about conflicts in which fundamental and culturally-informed normative convictions are at stake, such as those concerning the nature of human flourishing and related accounts of human security. This chapter seeks to survey and build upon the theories of judgement explicit or implicit in the work of Immanuel Kant, Charles Taylor, Hannah Arendt, Lisa Disch, Seyla Benhabib, Jennifer Nedelsky, Jürgen Habermas, and Thomas Morawetz, in order to sensitize readers to the kinds of philosophical standards that an interculturally legitimizable responsibility to protect would have to meet. To avoid dilettantism, this investigation is necessarily approached from within the western philosophical tradition that is my own particular home. While seeking to map some of the limits of that tradition, it does not and cannot aim to be exhaustive, but rather to act as a suggestive stimulus to further conversation.

In the rush to address the conventional security concerns arising from the events surrounding the 2001 destruction of the World Trade Centre, the concept of human security was endorsed as a good by a variety of elite actors and institutions, most notably those associated with the reform agenda of former UN Secretary-General Kofi Annan and the early human protection agenda of his successor, Ban Ki-moon. In Chapter 3, "Hannah Arendt's 'Right to Have Rights' and Human Security," I explore the implications and opportunities that arise from the fact that this initial affirmation occurred in the absence of a clear and

12 I owe this apt phrase to Wendy Brown, "Suffering the Paradoxes of Rights" in Wendy Brown and Janet Halley, eds., *Left Legalism/Left Critique* (Durham: Duke UP, 2002), 420 at 432.

consistent definition of the concept of human security itself. While the content of human security has remained subject to a range of interpretations, the concept has moved rapidly along the continuum of normativity toward the pole of legality in company with its symbiote concept, the responsibility to protect. But by leaving the definition of human security open-ended in order to avoid dissensus, proponents of the concept have failed to provide an interculturally legitimate grounding for the responsibility to protect, and moreover have facilitated the projection of a non-existent consensus upon accounts of human flourishing devised by great powers with vested interests in coercive intervention. In this chapter, I argue that Hannah Arendt's idea of a right to have rights is the conceptual ancestor of contemporary human security policies, and that her approach offers important insights regarding human security's philosophical implications and its pitfalls and limitations. At the same time, Arendt's work on the right to have rights also provides crucial guidance for human security advocates about the necessary shape that an interculturally legitimate vision of human security would have to take. Only such an enriched view could adequately underpin a proactive agenda for "root cause" prevention of the domestic conditions associated with atrocity crimes—genocide, war crimes, crimes against humanity, and ethnic cleansing.[13]

Chapter 4, "The Scope of the 'Responsibility to Prevent' Atrocity Crimes: A Remit for Intervention?" explores a worry shared by many students of the legal history of colonialism. This is the fear that the responsibility to protect might be coopted by advocates of a "liberal anti-pluralist"[14] reading of international law.[15] Authors in this latter camp have included Anne-Marie Slaughter, Robert Kagan, Timothy Garton Asch, Michael Ignatieff, Fernando Téson, and John Rawls. All have held variants of the view that the international community is divided into: 1) state members of a modernized "Family of Nations" consisting in liberal democratic polities, and 2) outlaw states that fall outside the purview of the immunities and protections accorded sovereign states within international law. I argue here that a powerful account of the differences between these latter states—former colonies and satellites of great powers—and the

13 Following the 2005 World Summit, the range of triggering circumstances for coercive intervention associated with the development of the responsibility to protect under UN auspices has been narrowed to the four atrocity crimes listed here (*World Summit Outcome Document*, GA Res. 60/1, UNGAOR, 60th Sess., UN Doc. A/RES/60/1 (24 October 2005), online at www.who.int/hiv/universalaccess2010/worldsummit.pdf, at para. 138).

14 This term was coined by Gerry Simpson to describe an approach to membership in international political community that emphasizes conformity to liberal values, with exclusionary effect. It is contrasted with a "liberal pluralist" perspective which prioritizes tolerance of diversity and is (more) inclusionary in its effects. See Simpson's *Great Powers and Outlaw States* (Cambridge, UK: Cambridge University Press, 2004), at 76–78.

15 For examples of expressions of this concern, see Richard Falk, "Kicking the Intervention Habit," Opinion, Al Jazeera English (10 March 2011), online at http://english.aljazeera.net/indepth/opinion/2011/03/201138143448786661.html; Marwan Bishara, "West Overzealous on Libya," Opinion, Al Jazeera English (18 March 2011), online at http://english.aljazeera.net/indepth/opinion/2011/03/2011318132217965513.html.

predominantly western states whose publics take human rights culture for granted has captured the imagination of international politico-legal elites. This story differentiates between western European-descended political communities and the "others" in terms of their commitments to (a particular reading of) democratic governance, human rights, and human security. The responsibility to protect, often promoted as a means of securing the preceding three goods, has become an important element in this narrative of difference and hierarchy.[16] This chapter centres upon a subsidiary element of the responsibility to protect termed (confusingly) the "responsibility to prevent." It argues that the prescriptions associated with the responsibility to prevent by ICISS rest upon a set of prevailing assumptions about the root causes of threats to human security that are not tenable or not proven. These assumptions both rely upon and reinforce the dualistic narrative of lawful and outlaw states that has dominated foreign policy-making in western countries for the first decades of the twenty-first century. The chapter further shows how ICISS's model of institutionalizing preventive intervention on humanitarian grounds is susceptible to cooptation by the democracy promotion project frequently associated with the liberal peace thesis. It highlights the absence of intercultural agreement about grounds for a muscular interpretation of a responsibility to prevent (i.e., one that includes one-size-fits-all root cause, structural prevention); and in so doing, it offers support for the consensus that has emerged around limiting the preventive scope of the responsibility to protect principle at this time.[17] The chapter consequently recommends continuing sensitivity to these concerns in the exercise of UN influence on the development of atrocity crime prevention policies by regional focal points networks.

Chapter 5, "The International Legal Character of the Responsibility to Protect," offers the first half of a detailed examination of the nature of the responsibility to protect's normativity. In its earliest articulation, the principle is described by ICISS as possessing a moral, political, and legal character. In the wake of the 2005 World Summit, the UN's diplomatic efforts to consolidate state support for the norm led to official

16 Obiora Okafor has detailed the way that this story was coupled with what he calls the "newness claim"—the thesis that the circumstances following the 9/11 attacks on U.S. soil were so extraordinary that they required a deviation from fundamental international legal norms—in order to justify derogations from prohibitions against the use of force and torture (See his "Newness, Imperialism, and International Legal Reform in Our Time: A TWAIL Perspective" (2005) 43 *Osgoode Hall Law Journal* 171 at 172–173).

17 The minimalist recommendations that endorsed in this chapter share some features with the version of the responsibility to protect doctrine affirmed by the 2005 World Summit. While both advocate that the responsibility to protect encompass a more limited set of legal elements than the ICISS reading of the principle, there are important differences between the recommendations developed in this chapter and those of the World Summit. These include the World Summit's lack of support for a "code of conduct" mandating that permanent member (P5) states abstain from Security Council debates on proposed actions mandated by the responsibility to protect, the weakening of the obligatory aspect of the responsibility and removal of criteria for its exercise, and the *World Summit Outcome Document*'s commitment to legal centrism. (Further differences regarding the philosophical underpinning of the responsibility to protect and the legal pluralist approach to its exercise that I advocate are developed in the concluding chapter.)

pronouncements that emphasized its moral and political force, and downplayed or even denied its international legal character. This chapter demonstrates that the responsibility to protect's normativity is indisputably legal, and that this legal nature is most compellingly characterized as that of a general principle of international law. Although like other international legal principles (such as the proscription against the use of force), the responsibility to protect may have a *parallel* legal source in customary international law, the demonstration of the norm's bona fides as a general principle of the *human rights and human rights protection* class in this chapter makes it unnecessary to engage in the debate over whether it meets the evolving criteria of a customary international legal norm. Instead, the chapter concentrates on two tasks. First, it demonstrates that the process of *riconoscimento giuridico di esigenze della coscienza pubblica* or "legal recognition of the demands of public conscience"[18] is a source of general principles of international law. (General principles of international law comprise one of the five categories of international legal sources acknowledged in the authoritative list that appears in Article 38(1) of the *Statute of the International Court of Justice.* [19]) Second, it shows that the responsibility to protect is an example of a sub-category of general principles I term the human rights and human rights protection class.

It is this international legal quality that offers the best hope of invoking the responsibility to protect successfully in order to compel assistance from the great power states in humanitarian crises when their traditionally-conceived national interests play a minor role. Future development of the principle must take into account this legal nature, and explore the possibilities inherent in its possible multiple sources of origin in international law.

Chapter 6, "Distant Strangers and Our Responsibility to Protect," completes the investigation into neglected aspects of the principle's fundamental character initiated in the previous chapter, by examining its moral dimension.[20] In general, discussions of the moral force of the responsibility to protect have been tainted by explicit or implicit association with the dualistic and hierarchical vision of a morally and culturally superior "saviour" class of states empowered to act to variously control or protect an inferior class of "savage" and "victim" states and/or sub-national entities (outlined in Chapter 4).[21]

18 This process was first identified by Italian jurist and scholar Giuseppe Sperduti in his *Lezioni di diritto internazionale* (Milano: A. Giuffrè, 1958).

19 *Statute of the International Court of Justice*, 26 June 1945, Can. TS 1945 No.7 (entered into force 4 October 1945), Article 38.

20 The third, *political* aspect of the responsibility to protect is not a subject of examination here, as the interests of both the would-be interveners and the likely subjects of intervention have been reiterated repeatedly in public debates over humanitarian intervention in the past two decades. (In general, interveners seek a means of legitimating coercive actions that protect what they perceive to be their national security and fulfil the expectations of their home publics, while avoiding a clearcut obligation to intervene. Potential intervenees tend to want the class of situations subject to intervention to be sharply circumscribed; this tendency was exacerbated by the events following the UN Security Council-authorized intervention in Libya for human protection purposes in 2011.)

21 Makau Mutua, "Savages, Victims and Saviors: The Metaphor of Human Rights" (2001) 42 *Harvard International Law Journal* 201.

Here, I take up the question of agency in order to offer a tentative account of an interculturally legitimizable moral foundation for the responsibility to protect that aims to avoid the pitfalls of this dualistic vision. The state-centric and legal centrist qualities of the ICISS interpretation of the principle, which are reiterated in all subsequent state-sponsored accounts of the norm to date, do not engage with the possibility of regarding nonstate actors as potential bearers of the responsibility to protect. But the logic of the original ICISS claim—that a state's failure to fulfil its responsibility to protect its own population results in the devolution of that responsibility onto other states—entails that individual persons must be bearers of the responsibility to protect in their own right. It is only in virtue of this individually-borne responsibility that the moral and political dimensions of the obligation come to be vested in the states which represent them. And as noted previously, no satisfying alternative basis for the responsibility to protect has been espoused by the UN or other state members of the interpretive community such as Brazil or China.

I point to Onora O'Neill's work on obligations to geographically and temporally distant strangers[22] to illustrate how this attribution of responsibility to individuals fits with our unreflective assignment of moral standing to distant others in our everyday practices.[23] In turn, the equal respect and concern that is implied by our (often unexamined) normative presuppositions concerning distant others are actualized in the "demands of public conscience"[24] that are the product of the proliferating processes of global deliberation and opinion-formation made possible by new technologies of communication. These evolving processes are constituting a "weak public" sphere of global scope—"weak" in the sense that the public's "deliberative practice consists exclusively in opinion formation and does not also encompass [institutionalized] decision making," but nonetheless, not *ineffective.* [25] Evidence of the potency of this growing instantiation of the "community of humanity" lies in the very process of international legal norm-recognition outlined in the preceding chapter.

This concluding chapter ties together central themes from earlier chapters in order to highlight the practical implications of the aspirational reading of the responsibility to protect advocated in these pages. One inescapable conclusion of this survey is that the responsibility to protect can be recruited to support a remarkable range of projects, including those of cosmopolitan constitutionalism—in both its liberal pluralist and liberal anti-pluralist incarnations[26]—and of hegemonic international law—in both its unilateral and multilateral variants. I show

22 Onora O'Neill, *Bounds of Justice* (Cambridge, Mass.: Cambridge University Press, 2000).

23 This expression of moral concern suggests a possible basis on which to develop an interculturally shared vision of human flourishing capable of grounding a positive solidarity.

24 Sperduti, *Diritto internazionale*, at 69.

25 Nancy Fraser, "Rethinking the Public Sphere," in Craig Calhoun, ed., *Habermas and the Public Sphere* (Cambridge, Mass.: MIT Press, 1992), 109 at 132; cited in Hauke Brunkhorst, *Solidarity* (Cambridge, Mass: MIT Press, 2005), at 137.

26 Simpson, *Great Powers*, chap. 3.

here how the alternative account of the responsibility to protect proposed in preceding chapters would serve to limit the extent to which the principle can be recruited to further liberal anti-pluralist and hegemonic international law agendas. At the same time, I take note of the ways in which the UN's evolving "UN-R2P" reading of the responsibility to protect has partially succeeded in this same task by confining the scope of the principle to four specific crimes (genocide, ethnic cleansing, war crimes, and crimes against humanity) and by dropping the language of procedural (and in practice, often low-intensity) democracy promotion associated with the original ICISS goal of root-cause prevention. I show how this partial UN reinterpretation of the responsibility to protect reduces the risk, identified in previous chapters, of invasive cultural, social, political, and economic engineering justified in the name of the responsibility to protect (and simultaneously eliminates the urgency of the need for an intercultural consensus on a rich conception of human flourishing capable of legitimating such root cause prevention). I outline how this UN-sponsored theoretical revision is coupled with efforts to encourage a responsibility to protect "lens" through an increasingly articulated framework of internal consultation and information-sharing about potential threats to human security among UN bodies, as well as between those bodies and regional actors through the regional focal points networks.[27] However, as the alternative reading of the responsibility to protect principle outlined here indicates, the current UN interpretation of the doctrine remains partial, failing to address not only the implications of its compelling moral nature and binding legal character, but missing, as yet, the opportunity to use the principle as a vehicle for the democratization of international law itself.

The main message of this final chapter is that the role of the responsibility to protect in international law and politics remains unsettled. Its proponents now have the opportunity to develop the principle in a way that looks ahead to the increasing polycentrism and legal pluralism portended by the disaggregation of states and reactive resurgence of competing regional hubs. At such a moment, the best immediate use of the responsibility to protect may be as a prod to democratic reform of the Security Council itself, by raising the spectre of a legal source for action in fulfilment of the responsibility to protect outside of Council authorization. In the longer term, recognition of the responsibility to protect as a general principle of international law could play a leading part in the project of imagining the shared normative terrain of a "democracy across borders."[28]

27 Edward Luck, "The United Nations and the Responsibility to Protect" (August 2008), online at www.stanleyfoundation.org/publications/pab/LuckPAB808.pdf, at 6.

28 I owe this phrase to James Bohman, *Democracy Across Borders* (Cambridge, Mass.: MIT Press, 2007).

1 A philosophical underpinning for a state's "responsibility to protect"

This chapter grapples with the ethical implications of the humanitarian crises that have multiplied during the era of global disorder and realignment precipitated by the end of the Cold War. These catastrophic events have wracked countries of the economic south that have lost or gained strategic importance to the great powers (Somalia, Rwanda, Sierra Leone, Sudan, Libya, Democratic Republic of Congo, Syria, Myanmar, Central African Republic, Venezuela), the political communities of the dismantled Soviet Union and Yugoslavia that are no longer fully subject to the disciplinary action of their former metropoles (Chechnya, Bosnia, Kosovo, Ukraine), and peoples who lack state status of their own (Kurds, Yazidis, the Maya of Guatemala).

These humanitarian crises have played out (and continue to unfold) against a backdrop of increasing transnational economic interdependence, instantaneous communication, and the rise of social media as a powerful tool for shaping political opinion. They have contributed to the moral certitude of proponents of a global "human rights culture," and to the rise of a nativist and populist resistance to human rights in states around the world (including many prominent past champions of international human rights law). All of these factors have fuelled an intense debate over the possibility of legitimating international intervention for humanitarian purposes in situations where states are unable or unwilling to act to prevent or alleviate humanitarian catastrophes, or may in fact be the perpetrators of large-scale human rights violations against their own citizens. With the terrorist attack on the World Trade Center in 2001, the focus of this debate shifted to the subsidiary question of whether military intervention in the pursuit of regime change (where it was anticipated that the new regime would be a democratic one) could itself be justified as a form of humanitarian intervention.

This chapter is concerned primarily with the first and more fundamental of these debates, and will grapple with it in the following form: Is it possible to develop a philosophical framework for intervention on humanitarian grounds that is interculturally legitimizable?

Intercultural legitimacy matters for at least two reasons. The first springs from the fact that there has been a growing acknowledgement of the fundamentally *situated* character of human agency since the mid-twentieth century. The intensification of intercultural contacts that has accompanied the large-scale movements of refugees and immigrants in recent decades has made it apparent to more and more people that each human culture furnishes the universe in different ways. This increasing attention to our situatedness has resulted in a valorization of the uniqueness of specific cultural, gender, and racial standpoints, and to a lesser degree, those associated with class, religion, and physical ableness. This phenomenon is the impulse behind identity politics, the movement that has been largely responsible for the celebration of previously denigrated identities, as evinced, for example, in multiculturalism policies. But identity politics is also the source of the concomitant claim that the *legitimacy* of social and political judgements depends upon their inclusivity, achieved, at a minimum, via broad consultation with representatives of diversely situated social, cultural, and/or national groups. Such groups will assess the merits of specific public choices with reference to the standards of value arising from their own cultural-linguistic background understandings, among other normative criteria.

As a result of the impact of identity politics, the sense has grown that the legitimacy of governments' policy agendas depends upon the existence of both a procedure for consulting diversely-situated parties and widespread, substantive agreement that policy is rooted in shared values. And this felt need for process and substantive legitimacy applies increasingly to non-citizens potentially affected by interventionary foreign policy choices, as well. The perceived legitimacy at home of a state's interventionary actions abroad now depends in part on the existence (or the perception of the existence) of local endorsement among the intended (mostly other-cultural) subjects of the intervention.[1]

Further, as has been well-recognized in the burgeoning literature on peacebuilding, it is fundamentally important that civilian and former combatant populations regard the terms of any form of humanitarian aid purportedly undertaken on their behalf—whether military or non-military—as locally legitimate.[2] In the absence of local legitimacy, efforts to rebuild a country's physical infrastructure, political and economic structures, and civil society will be seriously and perhaps fatally impeded. As a matter of political and practical necessity then, those who wish to intervene coercively or cooperatively on humanitarian grounds need legitimacy internally and externally in order to gain cooperation and to preserve and enhance the binding power of the international legal order.

These are the observations that inform the following sketch of a philosophical foundation for the responsibility to protect, the approach to intervention on humanitarian grounds first identified by the International Commission on Intervention and State Sovereignty (ICISS).[3]

1 See Katarina Tomaševski, *Responding to Human Rights Violations, 1946–1999* (The Hague: Martinus Nijhoff, 2000), at chap. 12 for a nuanced discussion of the ambiguous impact of this felt need for normative support.

2 See, e.g., Ian S. Spears, "Debating Secession and the Recognition of New States in Africa" (2004) 13 African Security Review 35; Carrie Manning, "Local Level Challenges to Post-Conflict Peacebuilding" (2003) 10 *International Peacekeeping* 25.

3 ICISS, *The Responsibility to Protect* (Ottawa, Canada: International Development Research Centre, 2001).

The responsibility to protect

ICISS was established to address the problem of reconciling demands for legal recognition of a right of humanitarian intervention with the existing or possible structure of the international legal order. The Commission was created in the wake of the 1999 NATO military intervention in Kosovo, undertaken without Security Council authorization. The illegality of that action at the time it was executed was a source of concern to many of those involved,[4] and it was the assailability of that intervention's legitimacy that inspired Lloyd Axworthy, then-minister of Foreign Affairs for the Canadian government, and other international diplomatic and NGO actors to push for the creation of the Commission.

The December 2001 ICISS report introduced two important correctives and one decisive innovation into the intervention debate. First, it abjured an exclusive focus upon military intervention for humanitarian purposes, re-establishing intervention involving the physical crossing of state borders (usually the intended referent of the term "humanitarian intervention") as one extreme of a spectrum that continues through economic and diplomatic isolation and finally extends to the prosaic and varied efforts to influence that typify the foreign policy practices of all states. The report underscored the importance of regarding military intervention as a last resort that can only be employed in a manner proportionate to the human rights violation or humanitarian crisis in question. Second, the report stressed the priority of the task of preventing humanitarian crises in order to minimize the need for considering coercive intervention. But the report's main contribution lay in its innovative reconceptualization of the challenge posed to state sovereignty by cross-border intervention.

The ICISS report's authors argued that states bear *primary* responsibility for the protection of the people under their care. However, when states fail to make good faith attempts to fulfil this responsibility, it devolves upon the international community of states to protect populations at risk from domestic threats such as severe state repression and collapse, insurgencies, and civil strife. Through these simple premises, ICISS endorses a paradigm shift that sought to change the terms of the debate over intervention and provides a theoretical foundation for focusing upon the human needs of individuals to proponents of intervention on humanitarian grounds. The report's authors offered a means of escaping the political deadlock associated with efforts to establish an international legal right of intervention by framing the issue of intervention in terms of a responsibility to protect. This conceptual judo aimed to dramatically diminish the

4 For a counter-argument that the NATO action in Kosovo may have been implicitly authorized by the Security Council via a series of resolutions that pre-dated the intervention, see Christine Gray, "From Unity to Polarization: International Law and the Use of Force against Iraq" (2002) 13 *European Journal of International Law* (*EJIL*) 1. Craig Scott provides an alternative attribution of legality to the Kosovo action, that rests on the claim that SC Res. 1244 (1999), which incorporated the terms of the peace settlement between NATO and Yugoslavia in its text, could be viewed as constituting retroactive endorsement of the NATO intervention by the Council ("Interpreting Intervention" (2001) 39 *Canadian Yearbook of International Law* 333 at 353).

apparent relevance of the issue of the sanctity of state sovereignty, essentially by recognizing that sovereignty itself has been redefined in practice.

In performing this reinterpretation of the concept of sovereignty, the ICISS panel acted in accordance with a significant body of legal scholarship that regards the exclusivity and inviolability of sovereignty as legal fictions.[5] The ICISS report's advocacy of what might be conceived as a kind of civil law duty to rescue on the part of states relies heavily upon the argument that the legal and political concept of sovereignty has undergone a significant transformation, and that that shift has been insufficiently acknowledged in the interpretation of public international legal instruments. The ICISS report's authors framed their attempt to document and advocate this redefinition of sovereignty as just one instalment in an ongoing process of evolving reinterpretation. By thematizing this strand of existing practice concerning sovereignty in the context of humanitarian crises, the report sought to influence the jurisgenerative processes of international law formation in this area:

> [w]hile there is not yet a sufficiently strong basis to claim the emergence of a new principle of customary international law, growing state and regional organization practice as well as SC [Security Council] precedent suggest an emerging guiding principle—which in the Commission's view could properly be termed "the responsibility to protect."[6]

The responsibility to prevent

The ICISS report's authors described the responsibility to protect as encompassing three constituent elements: 1) the responsibility to prevent humanitarian catastrophes, 2) the responsibility to react to such events when they occur, and 3) the responsibility to rebuild after intervention. This suite of responsibilities is borne primarily by the individual state whose population is at risk, and lies residually with state-members of the international community.[7] On the Commission's interpretation, the burden of responsibility on outside states is enhanced and in some circumstances even transferred, when

5 See, e.g., Nicholas Onuf, "Intervention for the Common Good" in G.M. Lyons and M. Mastanduno, eds., *Beyond Westphalia?* (Baltimore, MD: Johns Hopkins University Press, 1995) 43; Friedrich Kratochwil, "Sovereignty as *Dominium*" in G.M. Lyons and M. Mastanduno, eds., *Beyond Westphalia?* (Baltimore, MD: The Johns Hopkins University Press, 1995) 21; W. Michael Reisman, "Sovereignty and Human Rights in Contemporary International Law" (1990) 84 *American Journal of International Law* (*AJIL*) 866 at 867–868.

6 ICISS, *Responsibility to Protect*, at 15.

7 The "international community" is a contested term. In this book, it refers to entities that participate in decision-making processes that aim to contribute to global governance in some fashion. These can include, for example, NGOs, international organizations, nonstate peoples' representative organizations, state governments, corporate and hybrid actors involved in transnational governance of matters that would traditionally fall under the rubric of public policy-making (e.g. self-regulation in the forestry and other natural resource sectors). However, because this definition is more encompassing than traditional ones that attribute membership in the international community to states alone (or perhaps to states plus certain international organizations such as the UN and International Monetary Fund), a limiting phrase like the one used above will

the home-state fails to fulfil its obligation to ensure its population's *human security* through incapacity, inaction, or as the perpetrator of policies that threaten to cause an imminent crisis.

The limited space devoted in the report to discussion of a responsibility to prevent belies its fundamental importance to the argument of the report as a whole. ICISS took its inspiration for the discussion of "root cause" prevention efforts from Article 55 of the UN Charter, which recognizes that "the creation of conditions of stability and well-being which are necessary for peaceful and friendly relations among nations" requires solutions to international economic, social, and health problems, cooperation in international, cultural, and educational affairs, and universal respect for human rights.[8] By adopting a broad definition of peace and security based on this Article, ICISS implied that a legal basis for Security Council intervention on preventive grounds could be developed under Chapter VII of the Charter. ICISS downplayed the possibility of non-cooperative root cause intervention, emphasizing the importance of cultural sensitivity ("it is important that developed countries be aware of the cultural barriers that may inhibit the interpretation of information ... and that they ... examine closely their own policies for evidence of their potential negative impact on developing countries") and the desirability of "maximum possible cooperation between helpers and those helped."[9] The report provided a general list of political, economic, legal, and military reforms that could fall under the rubric of root cause prevention, emphasizing that poverty, political repression, and uneven distribution of resources are predisposing factors that are widely recognized as contributing to the likelihood of armed conflict.

The international consultations conducted by ICISS revealed that even the states that expressed the most adamant opposition to the idea of legalizing coercive intervention affirmed the desirability of such action in certain extreme situations. ICISS set out to define the limits of these exceptional circumstances in which the responsibility to react is relatively undisputed with as much precision as possible. By outlining six criteria for military intervention—right authority, just cause, right intention, last resort, proportional means, and reasonable prospects—the report aimed to provide an uncontroversial basis for international agreement about the kinds of situations in which intervention is acceptable, and to limit the potential for abuse of a prospective intercultural legal norm authorizing coercive intervention for human protection purposes. But while the authors clearly identified preventive responsibility as the foundational aspect of the responsibility to protect, they failed to define the parameters of acceptable *pre*-crisis intervention in similar detail.

The explanation for this omission likely lies in the differing impact of cultural relativism on the problems of reactive intervention and preventive intervention.

be employed here to indicate to the reader when one of these more parsimonious definitions is under discussion.

8 *Charter of the United Nations*, 26 June 1945, Can. TS 1945 No. 7.

9 ICISS, *Responsibility to Protect*, at 23.

The task of summarizing the general agreement that already existed around the authorization of reactive intervention in exigent, "conscience-shocking" situations was complex but manageable for the ICISS commissioners, largely because culturally relative values are *not* at issue in these cases. The kinds of threats to human security and international peace and security that are classified as sufficient causes of coercive intervention by ICISS are so extreme that the Commission's consultations encountered little objection to them.

However, the more nebulous root cause threats to human security identified by the Commission *do* involve profound issues of culturally relative standards of value, both with respect to the particular types of situations that should be regarded as requiring intervention and with respect to the limits on intervention itself. But it may be possible to set aside the controversy over cultural relativism here by focusing instead upon the intuitions underlying the attribution of an obligation of care to states. By thinking once again about *what* it is that states could be construed as having a responsibility to protect, we can come to a better understanding of *why* we might regard it as important for states to perform this protective function.

The discussion of the responsibility to prevent is framed as the fulcrum on which the Commission's argument turned. It is in these pages that ICISS had the opportunity to explain the shared moral commitment that grounds and brings coherence to the responsibility to protect doctrine and the recommendations of the report as a whole. And yet, here the report falls short. In order to provide a consistent, interculturally defensible basis for ICISS's interpretation of the responsibility to protect principle, three things had to be accomplished in the analysis of the responsibility to prevent. The first was to clearly identify which positive features of human life states are being assigned the responsibility for fostering under the umbrella of human security (e.g., freedom of intellectual inquiry, good bodily health, etc.). The second was to explain why these features of human life matter more than others, with arguments that have traction in multiple cultural traditions. And the third was to provide an account of why we should impute to states a special responsibility for protecting those features.

The report may be hinting at an answer to these questions with its reference to Article 55 of the UN Charter, but this general reference to human rights is surely insufficient as the sole shared basis for both a reconceptualization of state sovereignty and the thoroughgoing pre-crisis social engineering activities listed under the rubric of preventive intervention. The long-term impact of ICISS's expansive reading of the responsibility to protect hangs upon our ability to find convincing answers to these fundamental questions begged by the report's authors. I argue below that it is possible and necessary to outline a philosophical foundation for the responsibility to protect that offers such answers in a form that could be persuasive to a broad cross-section of the world's political and cultural communities.

In what follows, I sketch the bare bones of one such philosophical framework for a state's responsibility to protect, building on the neo-Aristotelian development ethics of Martha Nussbaum and Amartya Sen. It offers an account of human flourishing that could serve as an interculturally defensible basis for ICISS's assertion that states bear a responsibility to protect that should be interpreted as a responsibility to ensure human security. In so doing, this argument helps to flesh out and justify ICISS's broad definition of human security as "the security of people—their physical safety, their economic and social well-being, respect for their dignity and worth as human beings, and the protection of their human rights and fundamental freedoms."[10] It also has the potential to offer a basis for discriminating among the many possible measures of pre-crisis (preventive) intervention in a culturally-sensitive way.

The capabilities approach

Development economics is concerned with the economics of development in the countries of the global south. This area of study emerged in concert with the achievement of independence by former colonial states in Africa and Asia during the 1960s, and was originally dominated by a utilitarian approach that focused on GNP as the logical indicator of the level of a state's development. However, beginning in the 1970s, an interdisciplinary coalition of development economists and other social scientists, along with activists and philosophers, began raising questions about the appropriateness of western measures of "development" for the less-industrialized countries of this region.[11]

As members of this dissenting network of academics and activists began to recognize that deprivation is a result of factors beyond inadequate income, they mounted critiques of the standard utilitarian approach to measuring and determining the goals of development. These critics argued that an approach to development that assigned primary importance to the GNP of a given state was simply defining the standard of living of that state's citizens in terms of the amount of purchased goods consumed by them. As a result of the efforts of this coalition of dissenters, it is now generally agreed among those involved in development economics that the traditional GNP-based approach to development constitutes an extremely crude way of trying to capture an individual's standard of living, and is more accurately regarded as a measure of what Amartya Sen dubs "opulence."

The traditional development economics view came to be seen as inadequate because it measures standard of living as determined by "the possession of specific goods and services that can be purchased with money," and is thus skewed insofar as it takes disproportionate account of the concerns of those in the upper socioeconomic strata of societies.[12] Those challenging development economics argued that what was actually needed in discussions about the priorities of development was a measure of *quality of life* rather than opulence.

10 *Ibid.*

11 The early history of this critical shift is outlined in Kenneth Aman, ed., *Ethical Principles for Development*, (Upper Montclair: Institute for Critical Thinking, 1991) and Martha C. Nussbaum and Jonathan Glover, eds., *Women, Culture and Development* (Oxford: Clarendon Press, 1995).

12 Jerome M. Segal, "The Economic Development Program," in *Ethical Principles for Development*, at 180.

In the course of advancing this critique of established development economics, a new school of thought was generated around the idea of "basic needs." This new approach mandated the creation of a development ethics to serve as the indispensable foundation for development economics.

One influential offshoot of this basic needs approach (BNA) is the *capabilities approach*, inspired primarily by the work of economist Amartya Sen. In the early 1980s, Sen began writing about the shortcomings of the BNA and highlighting in particular the extent to which the BNA still defined basic needs in terms of commodities. Sen suggested that a more useful way of looking at the issue would be to address individuals' basic "capabilities" rather than their basic needs.[13] For Sen, the animating question for development policy-makers must be: "What are the people of this country actually able to do and to be?" This question focuses on individuals' capabilities for human functioning, and compares the functioning of all the groups in the population to one another. The capabilities view examines individuals' needs for different resources in order to become capable of equal levels of functioning, rather than attributing value to resources in themselves, as the traditional approach, and to some extent the BNA, both do. It does not measure quality of life in terms of utility, where utility is construed as the satisfaction of subjective preferences, since one of Sen's key concerns was the extent to which preferences are not always a reliable indicator of quality of life as a result of their socially constructed character.

Nussbaum took up Sen's original notion of capabilities and developed it in collaboration with him by drawing upon her own work on the idea of human flourishing in Aristotelian moral theory and Marx's philosophical writings. Building on both of these sources, Nussbaum concurred with Sen's view that the goal of development policy and practice should be the enhancement of our *potential* (capabilities) for characteristically human functioning, rather than the accomplishment of any particular activities in themselves. Potential, rather than execution—i.e., functioning—is the proper goal of development policy on Nussbaum's view because it allows greater scope for maximizing individuals' choices about their own visions of a good human life.

In her early writings on this subject, Nussbaum devoted a great deal of attention to the task of reconciling the universal applicability of a general vision of human flourishing with a significant degree of sensitivity to cultural specificity, although one of her primary motivations was always to devise a comparative measure of the quality of life of individuals from different societies.[14]

In this early work, Nussbaum recognized clearly that any such list—essentially, a thumbnail sketch of the elements of a good human life—must necessarily build upon a particular understanding of what it is to be human. And drawing upon both the Aristotelian notion of human flourishing and a series of ongoing intercultural conversations, she self-consciously developed what she called a "thick, vague theory" of the good life to underpin her catalogue of characteristic human capabilities:

13 Amartya Sen, "More than 100 Million Women are Missing" (1990) 37 *New York Review of Books* 61.

14 Nussbaum and Glover, eds., *Women, Culture and Development*, at 5.

> The thick vague theory is not, in the sense that worries liberals, a metaphysical theory. That is, it is not a theory that is arrived at in detachment from the actual self-understandings and evaluations of human beings in society; nor is it a theory peculiar to a single metaphysical or religious tradition. Indeed, it is … both internal to human history and strongly evaluative. And its aim is to be as universal as possible, to set down the basis for our recognition of members of very different traditions as human across religious and metaphysical gulfs. The theory begins … from an account of what it is to be a human being.[15]

Nussbaum looked to the commonalities among myths and stories from many cultural traditions as a means of discovering continuities in the way that, across temporal and cultural and geographical distances, we "situate the human being in some way in the universe: between the beasts, on one hand, and the gods, on the other."[16] Based on this survey of both narrative and practice across cultures, Nussbaum suggested a preliminary list—"a summary of what we think so far, and … an intuitive approximation, whose intent is not to legislate, but to direct attention to certain areas of special importance"—that delineates key areas of common human experience. In fact, the aim of this exercise was to begin to map the limits and capabilities that are constitutive of humanness, from many different perspectives. Summarizing freely, this list reads roughly as follows:

1 being able to live to the end of a complete human life, as far as possible
2 being able to have bodily health
3 being able to avoid unnecessary pain and to have pleasurable experiences
4 being able to use the five senses, to imagine, think, and reason
5 being able to have attachments to things and people outside ourselves
6 being able to form a conception of the good and to engage in critical reflection about the planning of one's own life (practical reason)
7 being able to recognize and show concern for other human beings, to engage in various forms of familial and social interaction (affiliation)
8 being able to affiliate with other species and with nature
9 being able to laugh, play
10 being able to live one's own life and nobody else's
11 being able to live one's own life in one's very own surroundings and context

The rather specific conception of what it is to be human that this list implies is the foundation for Nussbaum's evolving accounts of good human functioning. At its best, it seeks to distinguish among the fundamental aspects of our diverse lived experiences and aspirations, to describe those commonalities, and then to

15 Martha C. Nussbaum, "Aristotelian Social Democracy" in R. Bruce Douglass, Gerald Wara, and Henry Richardson, eds., *Liberalism and the Good* (London: Routledge, 1990), at 203.

16 Martha C. Nussbaum, "Human Functioning and Social Justice: In Defense of Aristotelian Essentialism" (1992) 20 *Political Theory* 202 at 215.

prescribe based on those observations. It is honestly evaluative, privileging *practical reason* and *affiliation* not just as individual elements of the catalogue, but as architectonic aspects of human life that "infuse ... all the other functions and plan ... for their realization in a good and complete life."[17] This list takes sides; it sketches a particular vision of human life and proclaims that vision to be superior—more fulfilling of our potential for humanness than others. It is a starting-point for conversation, debate, and persuasion. And Nussbaum makes it clear in her early writings that she regards it as such.

However, as this list became more detailed over time, what began as an open-ended and flexible account of the defining capabilities of the human condition hardened into a more programmatic account of a constitutionalizable set of political principles. The thick vague theory of the good underlying the later list is less vague, and the intent of the list, originally conceived as a means of directing attention to areas of unique importance in human life, seems, contrary to Nussbaum's stated purpose above, to be legislative. As a result, the space that Nussbaum wanted to create in the early account for the paradigmatic Aristotelian activity of context-dependent ranking of goods is much less in evidence in this later work. The most striking changes in the list occurred in the (here mostly omitted) descriptions that accompany each of the elements.

The most potentially problematic change lies in the later description Nussbaum attaches to the category of "control over one's environment," in which she adjured the necessity of "having property rights on an equal basis with others; having the right to seek employment on an equal basis with others."[18] Her early view drew heavily upon her reading of Aristotle, and depicted a right to private property as only instrumentally, rather than foundationally useful.[19] In her 2000 paper, "In Defense of Universal Values," Nussbaum explained that she "expands the role of property rights" on the basis of what she came to regard as "the intimate relationship between property rights and self-definition."[20]

In the same paper, Nussbaum indicated that she regards the main changes in the later versions of the list as pertaining to bodily integrity, control over the individual's environment (property rights and employment opportunities) and dignity and non-humiliation. She says that the inspiration for these changes lay in a series of conversations she had concerning her list with a cross-section of people in India, and comments that "[o]ddly, these features of human 'self-sufficiency' and the dignity of the person are the ones most often criticized by Western feminists as 'male' and 'Western'."[21]

It is not apparent that the relationship between self-definition and property rights is a foundational one in human existence, as the inclusion of such rights on the list seems to assert. It rather seems possible that contingent historical

17 Nussbaum and Glover, eds., *Women, Culture and Development*, at 226–227.

18 Martha C. Nussbaum, *Women and Human Development* (Cambridge: Cambridge University Press, 2000), at 80.

19 See Nussbaum, "Aristotelian Social Democracy," at 231–232.

20 Martha C. Nussbaum, "In Defense of Universal Values" (2000) 36 *Idaho Law Review* 379 at 421.

21 *Ibid.* at 418.

circumstances have created economic, legal, and cultural conditions in which property rights can serve as a means of securing important prerequisites of human flourishing. Jack Donnelly's research on the special usefulness of human rights (including property rights) as a tool for combatting the forms of oppression unique to modern capitalism suggests one explanation for the phenomenon of non-western valorization of property rights identified by Nussbaum. And Rajeev Bharghava's work on the distortive effects of colonialism on indigenous Indian cultural and legal traditions offers complementary critical insights into why these elements of a stereotypically western liberal and individualistic vision of rights might play a prominent role in contemporary Indian society.[22]

I wonder if Nussbaum's later willingness to make more conclusive claims about the political implications of the capabilities she regards as defining features of the good life limits the intercultural legitimizability of her list to a greater degree than many sympathetic to her project might wish. The great appeal of Nussbaum's original formulation of an open-ended list was its potential contribution to the process of seeking "unforced consensus"—a term originally coined by Charles Taylor in his writings on international human rights standards. Such a consensus, whether in the field of development ethics or human rights, would include "[a]greement on norms, yes; but a profound sense of difference, of unfamiliarity, in the ideals, the notions of human excellence, the rhetorical tropes and reference points by which these norms become objects of deep commitment for us."[23] It is this sense of difference that serves as the inspiration for the moments of self- and cultural-transformation that Nussbaum continues to advocate, at least on the theoretical level, when she emphasizes the open-ended nature of her list of capabilities.

If Nussbaum's attempt to develop an exhaustive roster of human functional capabilities that accommodates all possibilities of what we recognize as human ways of being were interpreted in the open-ended way she seems at times to have originally intended, a great deal of room for cultural adaptability of the specific target levels of each functioning would be possible. Once a certain basic level of these functionings is achieved, individuals' choices about which capabilities to maximize take over, but up to that point, broad, even universalizable generalizations are possible. Choice would remain a key feature of this variant of her early theory insofar as we allow for a multiplicity of capabilities (that can be viewed as elements of a good human life) which can be ordered in a great variety of ways according to individuals' personal conceptions of the good and of culturally distinct ways of nurturing the development of those capabilities.

22 Jack Donnelly, *Universal Human Rights in Theory and Practice* (Ithaca, NY: Cornell University Press, 1989); Rajeev Bhargava, "How Should We Respond to the Cultural Injustices of Colonialism?" in Jon Miller and Rahul Kumar, eds., *Reparations: Interdisciplinary Inquiries* (Oxford: Oxford University Press, 2007), at 215.

23 Charles Taylor, "Conditions of an Unforced Consensus on Human Rights" in Joanne Bauer and Daniel A. Bell, eds., *The East Asian Challenge for Human Rights* (Cambridge: Cambridge University Press, 1999), at 124.

In Sen's work on this subject, he also surveys what he regards as the necessary relation between liberal democratic political structures and opportunities for human flourishing. In a nod to John Rawls, he describes his mature theory with the sobriquet "development as freedom," still defining freedom in terms of opportunities for human flourishing, but concentrating upon freedom understood in terms of civil and political rights and the liberal democratic political structures he came to view as their guarantor. Sen does not devote a great deal of attention to identifying what the central capabilities are, but instead examines five interconnected "instrumental" freedoms that he argues constitute both the means and ends of development, since they enable human beings to live "lives they have reason to value." They include: 1) political freedoms, 2) economic facilities, 3) social opportunities, 4) transparency guarantees, and 5) protective security. Sen emphasizes the "remarkable empirical connection that links freedoms of different kinds with one another."[24]

Both Nussbaum and Sen aim to respond to pressing matters of international public policy that they regard as broadly associated with the issue of development (such as malnutrition and gross systemic abuses of women's human rights) by finding some way of justifying what might be called "interference with the other" in terms that are acceptable to those interfered with. Nussbaum increasingly emphasized the importance of subscribing to a single universalizable list of human functionings and capabilities (rather than to a range of culturally-tailored lists as in her original account[25]) as a means of developing such a justification. This curtailment of the adaptability of her list, coupled with her later interest in specifying political requirements necessary for the fostering of certain capabilities, appear to have been in large part consequences of her growing involvement in the study of the particular problems faced by women in less-industrialized countries, and her belief that culture-specific customs constitute a fundamental obstacle to the improvement of women's job, education, and health access in many countries of the global south.

Despite the concerns I have raised about the tendency shared by Nussbaum and Sen to reduce the cultural adaptability of their accounts of human flourishing in their later work, their complementary theories have accomplished two valuable goals. They have made individuals and their varying needs for resources for flourishing an undeniable priority in the field of development economics through the influence their ideas have exercised upon the *Human Development Reports* produced by the United Nations Development Programme since 1993.[26] And both authors publicly and seriously wrestled with the previously unbroached issue of cultural sensitivity in development ethics, even when they argued strenuously for limits to such sensitivity in their later writings.

24 Amartya Sen, *Development as Freedom* (New York: Alfred A. Knopf, 1999), at 38, 31.

25 Martha C. Nussbaum, "Non-Relative Virtues: An Aristotelian Approach" (1988) 13 *Midwest Studies in Philosophy* 32 (a discussion of capabilities which suggests a much greater potential for culture-specific tailoring of the interpretation of specific capabilities).

26 See, e.g., *Human Development Reports: 1993, 1994, 1995, 1996, 1997* (New York: United Nations Development Programme).

These two goals are remarkably consonant with two of the primary aims of ICISS. The Commission's main conceptual innovation flows from its focus on the human security of individuals—that is, the attainment of the preconditions for flourishing. The wording of the ICISS report also makes it plain that the Commission was both politically and theoretically motivated to assert its respect for cultural specificity in strong terms. By adapting a philosophical framework based on the early account of human flourishing proposed by Nussbaum and Sen, a persuasive and logically consistent foundation for the responsibility to protect can be developed. There is good reason to believe that such a framework would be more philosophically adequate to two central tasks than the Commission's weak reference to an expanded concept of peace and security based on Article 55. The first task is explaining why states should bear the responsibility for fostering human flourishing, and the second is offering guidance in developing interculturally legitimizable criteria for limiting the scope of preventive intervention in particular cases.

The capabilities approach as a philosophical foundation for a state's responsibility to protect

The link between Nussbaum's and Sen's theories and a state's responsibility to protect rests largely upon the role that both authors assign to the state as the bearer of an obligation to ensure the achievement of at least a threshold level of human capabilities. Simply put, they both hold that this is what states are *for*.

This core idea is derived from Aristotle's understanding of the role of the polis in constituting a good human life. In grounding this claim, Nussbaum explicitly cites Aristotle's *Politics*: "It is evident that the best *politeia* is that arrangement according to which anyone whatsoever might do best and live a flourishing life"; and "[i]t is the job of the excellent lawgiver to consider, concerning a city and a class of human beings and every other association, how they will partake in the flourishing living that is possible for them" (Greek parenthetical interpolations omitted).[27] The promotion of the necessary conditions for human flourishing provides the primary defensible and just purpose for the existence of states.

> The basic intuition from which the capability [sic] approach starts, in the political arena, is that human capabilities exert a moral claim that they should be developed.... We believe that certain basic and central human endowments have a claim to be assisted in developing, and exert that claim on others, and especially, as Aristotle saw, on government.... In thinking of political planning we begin, then, from a notion of the basic capabilities and their worth, thinking of them as claims to a chance for functioning, which give rise to correlated political duties.[28]

27 Aristotle, *Politics*, 1324a23–5, 1325a7 quoted in Martha C. Nussbaum, "Nature, Function, and Capability: Aristotle on Political Distribution," WIDER Working Papers (Helsinki: World Institute for Development Economics Research, 1988), at 2.

28 Martha C. Nussbaum, *Sex and Social Justice* (New York: Oxford University Press, 1999), at 43.

It follows that a state's duty of protection is an obligation to safeguard the potential for human flourishing of its population. If we can identify a set of fundamental qualities shared by those citizens that inherently *call out* for development in order for human organisms to have a chance at becoming what they could ("[t]heir very being makes forward reference to functioning"[29]), then a state's failure to satisfy, or to attempt to satisfy, that need might well be considered to constitute adequate grounds for triggering the subsidiary responsibility of other states to ameliorate the situation. The moral claim that human capabilities are described as exerting here is not limited to domestic government or government as such; government is simply the agency on which that claim is exerted most strongly. What the intercultural investigations of Nussbaum and Sen lead them to conclude is, roughly, that many human societies do and should endorse the idea that the good for human beings consists in performing characteristically human functions well. The state and states bear primary responsibility for creating the conditions that make it possible for human beings to exercise the defining human functional capabilities. Nussbaum and Sen hold that we will have the opportunity to live more fully human lives if we pursue human flourishing, and that it is possible to identify the preconditions or basic elements of that flourishing.

Conclusions

This chapter has offered a brief sketch of a promising philosophical underpinning for the pioneering effort by ICISS to reconceptualize sovereignty in terms of a responsibility to protect. This survey of the applicability of Nussbaum and Sen's development ethics work to the justification of a state's responsibility to protect constitutes a preliminary demonstration of why the promotion of human flourishing—defined in terms of the existence of opportunities to achieve prescribed minimal levels of capability for human functioning—should become the proper end of any intervention justified on humanitarian grounds. The notion of human flourishing has the potential to be interculturally legitimizable because of its culturally adaptable, context-dependent features. Most notably, this neo-Aristotelian framework suggests a basis for developing specific interculturally-justifiable criteria for potentially invasive social and political engineering activities that are recommended by the ICISS report under the rubric of the responsibility to prevent root causes, and later framed in terms of structural prevention.

It's apparent from this brief overview that for the purpose of developing a philosophical basis for a state's responsibility to protect, the early versions of both Nussbaum and Sen's arguments are more useful than the more mature variants. The most important reason for this preference is the sense, very much informed by Charles Taylor's arguments concerning the desirability of "unforced consensus," in which it is not sufficient simply to identify the minimal elements of human flourishing, but (as Nussbaum herself initially held) that it is also crucial to do so in a way that meaningfully accommodates the range of human possibility and imagination that cultural diversity inspires. Such an approach would leave space for

29 *Ibid.*

the activity of strong evaluation in accordance with the standards of value to which the characteristic cultural-linguistic community/ies of which each of us is a member give rise, and for the related possibility of local legitimation.[30]

As noted above, the main danger of this approach is posed by the elision of liberal democratic political institutions and the conditions for human flourishing that occurs in the later interpretations of Nussbaum and Sen. The legitimacy of this neo-Aristotelian approach depends upon ensuring that states that "score" poorly on a comparative index of quality of life, or that lack formal liberal democratic institutions, are not simply assigned an inferior grade of statehood and classified as prospective or presumptive subjects of intervention. The point of turning to a comprehensive vision of human flourishing rather than, for example, to an expanded framework of human rights in order to underpin a state's responsibility to prevent is: 1) to formally recognize the significance of the functional capabilities that are being identified by an intercultural process of negotiation and discussion, and 2) to affirm the process of developing a shared but context-adaptable vision of human flourishing. By seeking a moving consensus that draws upon the background understandings of participants from a great variety of cultural-linguistic communities as the human flourishing approach proposes, we are forced to question not just other-cultural ways of understanding the meaning and distinctiveness of human forms of life, but to reflect critically upon our own.

30 The concept of strong evaluation refers to the activity of assessing the qualitative worth of one's desires and evaluations (Charles Taylor, "What is Human Agency?" in *Philosophical Papers: Human Agency and Language*, vol. 1 (Cambridge: Cambridge University Press, 1985)).

2 The role of a *sensus communis* in a theory of judgement

This chapter is devoted to a survey of possible forms that an interculturally applicable theory of judgement might take. Such a theory is the necessary underpinning of any interculturally legitimizable catalogue of key elements of human flourishing, such as those proposed in the writings of Martha Nussbaum and Amartya Sen and discussed in the previous chapter.

A theory of judgement also has an important role to play when we engage in practical reasoning about whether and how to implement the responsibility to protect during an unfolding crisis, or to pursue policies designed to further a particular ideal of human security. This is so because it is never possible to consult and deliberate with all of those potentially affected by these types of decisions. Such inclusive deliberation is a widely-felt need today as a consequence of the rise of a worldwide human rights culture, which has altered standards of impartiality. In a climate of radically plural worldviews, there is a need for justification; the specific conception of human flourishing that informs the way we rank competing goods in any particular case cannot be assumed as an ontological given, but must be understood as a shared aspiration. A theory of judgement helps us to critically assess our implicit assumptions as we search for a way to justify to ourselves and to others the legitimacy of the moral, political, and legal conclusions we reach about how to act, when those affected subscribe to substantially different hierarchies of goods.

The theories of judgement that I focus upon here originate in Immanuel Kant's theory of aesthetic judgement as outlined in his *Critique of Judgement*, and Hannah Arendt's reinterpretation of Kant's argument for the purpose of grounding her own theory of political judgement. Arendt's creative appropriation of Kant's theory of aesthetic judgement has been taken up by an assortment of contemporary political theorists and philosophers who are concerned with the legitimacy of moral and political judgement in multicultural environments. Ronald Beiner, Seyla Benhabib, Iris Marion Young, Lisa Disch, and Jennifer Nedelsky (among notable others) have all developed variants of the theory of judgement that Arendt left unfinished at the time of her death.

The appeal of Arendt's work for these theorists lies mainly in two interrelated features that draw upon Kant's original theory in distinctive ways. The first is the "claim of agreement" that Arendtian judgements make upon other members of a judging community which enjoys a "subjective" universality and necessity. The usefulness of such a claim of agreement is self-evident for theorists who are grappling with the inescapable contemporary problem of judgement in multicultural settings. In trying to answer questions like—how do you make interculturally valid judgements? Or, perhaps more modestly—how can you justify your judgements in a world of plural values and perspectives?—Arendt's interpretation of Kant offers significant promise precisely because it purports to retain, in some form, these compelling qualities of subjective universality and necessity.

The second feature of Arendt's unfinished neo-Kantian theory of judgement that serves the needs of many contemporary theorists is her incorporation of a mechanism for representative consultation of multiple perspectives in the process of judging. Kant's argument concerning the fundamentally *social* character of a judgement of taste is transmuted by Arendt into the assertion that political and moral judgements require an act of imaginative conversation with others involved in and affected by such judgements which she sometimes characterizes as "going visiting." Arendt's emphasis upon the importance of dialogue (uniquely construed, it must be admitted) is seen as particularly valuable by those whose work is influenced by Jürgen Habermas' theory of communicative action—who include at a minimum discourse theorists, scholars working in the area of deliberative democracy and their closest critics, as well as many of those making use of constructivist theory. Arendt uses her interpretation of Kant's theory of aesthetic judgement to justify the requirement in her own theory of moral-political judgement that judgements be constituted via a process of conversation that tests the assumptions of each judging individual—and this aspect of her work has been employed as a useful conceptual tool by philosophers and social and political theorists for exploring the problem of how members of diverse democratic polities can reach agreements and sustain effective and responsive governments.

Note on the history of the appeal of these two qualities

These two qualities that form the heart of the appeal of Arendt's and Kant's theories—the special advantage they seem to offer in persuading others to agreement, and their active acknowledgement of the social nature of judgements—are attractive to a particular group of contemporary theorists for an important reason. Both are rooted in a specific vision of the relationship between human ontology and the nature of language which dates back to the ancient Greeks, and has been most recently and influentially revived under the rubric of Habermas' theory of communicative action.

Aristotle described human beings as distinguished by two characteristics: their gregariousness and their possession of the faculty of language. But in ancient Greek, the word for language—*logos*—is polysemic: it is also the word for reason. And so, Aristotle asserts, human beings are fundamentally "political" creatures because their humanity is generated through speaking and reasoning with others about what is good and evil, ugly and beautiful—acts that can only occur among the community of peers that inhabits a *polis*. Only "a beast or a god" could live outside a *polis* for this reason.[1] For Aristotle, to live a "good" or flourishing human life meant to participate with one's peers in the public process of decision-making about the right means and ends to be pursued by them jointly, as members of the *polis*, in order to shape the conditions and choices of their lives as citizens.[2]

Habermas shares with Aristotle the conviction that human beings are intersubjectively constituted as individuals through mutual recognition. Habermas' theory of communicative action (sometimes referred to as universal pragmatics or discourse morality) begins with the assumption that the most fundamental form of human activity is communicative action oriented toward reaching mutual understanding with other human beings. Understanding depends upon "reciprocal comprehension, shared knowledge, mutual trust, and accord with one another."[3] Agreement is based on recognition of what Habermas identifies as three universal validity claims that every speech act makes, implicitly or explicitly: a claim to the truth of what is said (or assumed); a claim to the "rightness" of the linguistic utterance in the given context, or of the underlying norm; and a claim to the speaker's truthfulness. So for Habermas, everyday linguistic interchange is a process of raising and recognizing validity claims.

The assessment of those claims' validity draws upon the explicit and implicit shared background understandings of what Habermas refers to as the lifeworld, the prereflective and implicit knowledge about "how to go on"[4] that goes, for the most part and always at the deepest level, unthematized. The background knowledge of the lifeworld exercises a "world-constituting function" in virtue of three features—its immediacy, its totalizing character, and its holism—which together mean that "I ... as my body, find myself always already occupying an intersubjectively shared world."[5]

In everyday linguistic interaction ("naive" communicative action), we generally take for granted that the reasons supporting the validity claims raised are good ones; however, when this assumption is brought into doubt, disagreement over the moral

1 Aristotle, *The Politics*, ed. and trans. by Ernest Barker (Oxford: Oxford University Press, 1946), at I.ii, §10, 11, 14.

2 This ideal of democratic participation has served as a continuing inspiration for political philosophers, particularly republican thinkers such as Hannah Arendt. One of the consequences of this ongoing influence has been the problematic privileging of the agonistic form of speech in which ancient Greek political debates occurred in western academic and political practice; the form of this privileging that appears in Habermas' work have been subjected to thoughtful criticism by other inheritors of this same tradition, such as Iris Marion Young in *Justice and the Politics of Difference* (Princeton, NJ: Princeton University Press, 1990) and Seyla Benhabib in *Situating the Self* (Cambridge, UK: Polity Press, 1992).

3 Jürgen Habermas, *On the Pragmatics of Communication*, ed. by Maeve Cooke (Cambridge, MA: MIT Press, 1998), at 23.

4 A useful phrase employed by Ludwig Wittgenstein to convey roughly the same notion. See for example, his *Philosophical Investigations*, trans. by G.E.M. Anscombe, 3rd ed. (New York: Macmillan Publishing Co., 1958), at §154, 155.

5 Habermas, *Pragmatics of Communication*, at 244.

norms underlying our judgements occurs, and routine communicative action is disrupted. Several options are then available to the interlocutors, but Habermas concentrates on the situation in which participants choose to continue their communicative activity at a more reflective level through argumentative speech in order to seek agreement. This process of examination entails the problematization of various aspects of the background knowledge of the lifeworld that had been regarded by (some or all) participants in the speech situation as unreflectively true up to that point. In order to generate moral norms that will be recognized as binding upon (i.e., could win the assent of) all those to whom they apply, this form of communicative action also requires a series of "idealizing suppositions"; these facilitate the conduct of discourse despite their counterfactuality in most real-life speech situations. Key suppositions are that all competent and potentially affected parties are entitled to participate on equal terms, that no relevant argument is excluded, and that interlocutors are motivated only by the force of the better argument. These idealizing presuppositions define an ideal communication community that functions as a regulative ideal, but they are based upon the necessary practical presuppositions of all argumentation oriented toward reaching understanding, Habermas asserts. Everyday speech displays similar, if imperfectly realized, reciprocity expectations and symmetry conditions since "only moral rules that could win the assent of all affected as participants in a practical discourse can claim validity."[6] This is why the idealizing presuppositions based upon these everyday practices define the structure of rational discourse. By adopting rational discursive argumentation as the procedure for resolving moral disputes, we gain a "guarantee [of] openness and equal inclusion, uncoerciveness, and transparency and … help bring the better argument into play."[7] By requiring "a self-critical attitude and an empathetic exchange of interpretive perspectives," the conditions of rational discourse create circumstances in which participants will be "affected by … the rational motives of *others*," with the result that all will "take [others'] understanding of themselves and of the world just as seriously as [their] own."[8]

Habermas argues that guided by such demanding conditions of communication, agreement reached in discourse ("idealized rational acceptability") is capable of constituting valid moral norms that merit universal recognition, insofar as such agreement is *consensual*, and affirms that the norm in question is *equally in the interest of all affected*. Consequently, Habermas claims, in the contemporary world "the idea of justice has been sublimated into the concept of the impartiality of a discursively attained agreement";[9] "what is just is assessed … in terms of the conditions for impartial judgement formation [the conditions outlined above]."[10] In other words, Habermas holds that in a world of plural values in which a single shared worldview is absent, the validity of moral norms can only be assessed in

6 Jürgen Habermas, *Justification and Application*, trans. by Ciaran P. Cronin (Cambridge, MA: MIT Press, 1993), at 50.
7 Jürgen Habermas, *Truth and Justification*, ed. and trans. by Barbara Fultner (Cambridge, MA: MIT Press, 2003), at 270.
8 *Ibid.*
9 *Ibid.* at 248.
10 *Ibid.* at 262.

terms of faithfulness to the *procedure* that produces them, where the elements of that procedure are dictated by our shared human nature as intersubjectively-constituted individuals.

For this reason, Habermas' interpretation of the relationship between human ontology and language has been taken up by many contemporary theorists. It offers a means of coping with the dilemma posed by plural values in diverse national and global communities that acknowledges our social individuality—our rootedness in particular cultures, ethnicities, and religions—and yet avoids the typical pitfall of such an acknowledgement: value-relativism. Instead, it endorses a "post-metaphysical" and deontological, procedural solution to the problem of establishing the validity of moral norms: a solution that is itself presented as a product of the very processes that lead to our intersubjective constitution as human beings.

Kant's theory of aesthetic judgement

In order to assess the merit and consistency of the claims of Arendtian theories of judgement, it's useful to trace the origins of those theories by providing an overview of Kant's argument itself. In his first and second *Critiques* concerning pure reason and practical reason, Kant describes a system of critical philosophy involving the faculties of reason, understanding, and judgement, which each "legislate" for distinct realms of human experience. The faculty of reason legislates *a priori* for freedom in the supersensible or noumenal realm; the faculty of understanding legislates *a priori* for nature as an object of sense in the phenomenal world. In his *Critique of the Faculty of Judgement* Kant discusses the way in which judgement functions as a third faculty of the mind that acts as a link between these realms. *Judgement* mediates between the concepts of nature and of freedom by making possible the transition from the conformity to law in accordance with nature to the final purpose in accordance with freedom. It does so by means of the concept of a guiding principle: that of the "purposiveness," or directedness, of nature.[11]

The faculty of judgement brings together universal concepts and particular sense-intuitions worked over by the imagination, and thereby makes possible our empirical knowledge of the world. In determinant judgements the universal that subsumes particular representations yet-to-be-found is given; in reflective judgements, a particular is given for which the universal concept must be found. The function of reflective judgements is "to establish the unity of all empirical principles under higher ones, and hence to establish the possibility of their systematic subordination."[12] The principle of reflective judgement is the purposiveness of nature; "that is, nature is represented by means of this concept *as if* an understanding contained the ground of the unity of the variety of its empirical laws" [emphasis added].[13]

11 Immanuel Kant, Introduction, *Critique of Judgement*, trans. and with an introduction by J.H. Bernard (New York: Hafner Publishing, 1051), at IX.
12 *Ibid.* at IV.
13 *Ibid.*

Reflective judgements must assume that

> that which in the particular (empirical) laws of nature is from the human point of view contingent, yet contains a unity of law in the combination of its manifold into an experience possible in itself—a unity not indeed to be fathomed by us, but yet thinkable.[14]

Thus, such judgments proceed as if there existed a systematic unity under merely empirical laws, although human beings are unable to comprehend or prove such unity.

According to Kant, aesthetic judgements[15] that concern the beautiful and the sublime in nature and art are a variety of reflective judgement ideally-suited to the illumination of this principle, for:

> they belong to the cognitive faculty alone and point to an immediate reference of this faculty to the feeling of pleasure or pain according to some principle *a priori*, without confusing this with what may be the determining ground of the faculty of desire, which has its principles *a priori* in concepts of reason.[16]

Kant defines an aesthetic judgement of taste as pleasure inspired by the mere perception of an object of nature or a work of fine art when that object seems to "fit" our perceptive capacities.[17] In a judgement of taste, the faculty of intuitions—the imagination—is subsumed under the faculty of concepts—the understanding—"so far as the former *in its freedom* harmonizes with the latter *in its conformity to law*."[18] The judgement of taste rests on the immediate satisfaction inspired by this free play of the representative faculties in which the form of the object is compared undesignedly with the indeterminate concept of the understanding. The impression of harmony that we gain from contemplating beautiful objects of nature or fine art is described by Kant as an *a priori* regulative idea—thus, the theory of aesthetic judgement links the realms of nature and of freedom.

The question that Kant employs to lend structure to his discussion of aesthetic judgements is: "How are judgements of taste possible?"[19] In order to answer this question, Kant analyzes the judgement of taste according to the table of categories laid out in the first *Critique*: he describes the beautiful in terms of the four moments of relation, quantity, quality, and modality. He begins with the observation that "all interest presupposes or generates a want, and, as the determining ground of assent, it leaves the

14 *Ibid.* at V.

15 I follow current convention in rendering Kant's term "aesthetical" judgement as "aesthetic" except when quoting him directly.

16 Immanuel Kant, Preface, *Critique of Judgement*, at 5.

17 Lewis White Beck, ed. Editor's Introduction: *Critique of the Faculty of Judgement*, in *Kant Selections*, The Great Philosophers, Paul Edwards, general ed. (New York: Macmillan Publishing, 1988), at 335.

18 Kant, *Critique of Judgement*, at §35.

19 *Ibid.* at §36.

judgement about the object no longer free."[20] As a means of ensuring that taste in the beautiful is a *free* satisfaction, Kant stipulates that no interest of sense or of reason influences our assent. Kant argues that once we regard the beautiful as the object of a disinterested satisfaction, it follows that the beautiful must be regarded as the object of a *universal* satisfaction:

> For the fact of which everyone is conscious, that the satisfaction is for him quite disinterested, implies in his judgement a ground of satisfaction for all men. For since it does not rest on any inclination of the subject (nor upon any other premeditated interest), but since the person who judges feels himself quite *free* as regards the satisfaction which he attaches to the object, he cannot find the ground of this satisfaction in any private conditions connected with his own subject, and hence it must be regarded as grounded on what he can presuppose in every other person.[21]

Therefore, although judgements of taste are singular in respect of logical quantity, they carry with them an "aesthetical quantity" of universality.

Because the judgement of taste is based on the relation of the form of a representation of an object to the feeling of pleasure or pain, rather than on the reference of a representation to the cognitive faculty, the judgement of taste may only postulate the *possibility* of a generally valid aesthetic judgement.[22] Although aesthetic judgements "make a rightful claim upon everyone's assent" no rule can be formulated according to which every person could be forced to concur with a particular judgement of beauty. Thus, the state of mind in the free play of the imagination and the understanding constitutes the "subjective universal communicability" of the mode of representation in a judgement of taste.

Oddly, perhaps, for the contemporary reader, Kant holds that aesthetic satisfaction is inspired by objects which are purposive in their forms, but have no comprehensible function or purpose:

> An object, or state of mind, or even an action is called purposive ... merely because its possibility can be explained and conceived by us only so far as we assume for its ground a causality according to purposes, i.e. in accordance with a will which has regulated it according to the representation of a certain rule. There can be, then, purposiveness without purpose, so far as we do not place the causes of this form in a will, but yet can only make the explanation of its possibility intelligible to ourselves by deriving it from a will.[23]

The consciousness of the formal purposiveness in the play of the subject's cognitive powers *is* the pleasure in a representation of a beautiful object, but because "it

20 *Ibid.* at §5.
21 *Ibid.* at §6.
22 *Ibid.* at §8.
23 *Ibid.* at §10.

contains a determining ground of the activity of the subject … in respect of cognition in general, without however being limited to any definite cognition," it contains only a form of the *subjective* purposiveness of a representation.[24] Objective purposiveness can be cognized only through a definite concept which refers the manifold of intuition to a definite purpose; a judgement of taste is based on a merely formal purposiveness, "a purposiveness without purpose."[25]

Judgements of taste are based on a feeling of pleasure inspired by the representation of an object in the observer, rather than on a concept of what beautiful objects look like: a judgement of taste claims that everyone *ought* to give his or her approval to the beautiful object because of a subjective principle which Kant regards as "a common sense," and not because of a theoretical objective necessity. "This common sense is assumed … simply as the necessary condition of the universal communicability of our knowledge, which is presupposed in every logic and in every principle of knowledge that is not sceptical."[26] We presuppose an indeterminate norm of common sense which is assumed as subjectively universal, and therefore necessary for everyone. Thus, a judgement of taste takes on the character of an objectively universal judgement, with the caveat that we do not claim an unconditioned necessity for the judgement, but only claim that everyone *ought* to give their assent. In sum, a judgement of taste is "a conformity to law without a law; and a subjective agreement of the imagination and understanding … subsist[ing] along with the free conformity to law of the understanding (which is also called purposiveness without purpose)."[27]

Arendt's theory of judgement

In taking up Kant's theory of judgements of taste as a model for her own theory of moral-political judgement, Arendt claims simply to be making evident the nascent political content of what she describes as Kant's "nonwritten political philosophy."[28] (And indeed, the two qualities that Kant identifies as distinctive of political judgement—disinterestedness and universality—are the same two features that define aesthetic judgement for him.[29]) Arendt claims to regard what many view as her own distinctive theory of judgement as simply an interpretation (albeit a rather liberal one) of Kant's critique of judgement, and her lectures on Kant's third *Critique* provide crucial insights into her position.

In Arendt's early writings, she regards political action as the activity of a plurality of actors performing together in a public space, and judgement, "the most political of

24 *Ibid.* at §12.
25 *Ibid.* at §15.
26 *Ibid.* at §21.
27 *Ibid.* at §22.
28 Hannah Arendt, *Lectures on Kant's Political Philosophy*, ed. by Ronald Beiner (Chicago, IL: University of Chicago Press, 1982), at 19.
29 See Ronald Beiner, "Interpretive Essay," in Arendt, *ibid.* at 124.

man's mental abilities,"[30] seems to consist for her in the deliberation that is intrinsic to such political action.

> Human beings can act as political beings because they can enter into the potential standpoints of others; they can share the world with others through judging what is held in common, and the objects of their judgements as political beings are the words and deeds that illuminate the space of appearances.[31]

In her later work, she develops a theme exemplified in the final sessions of her *Lectures on Kant's Political Philosophy*: the redemptive potential of judgement understood as a means of bestowing meaning.[32]

In numbers Twelve and Thirteen of her *Lectures*, Arendt explores several key elements of the Kantian faculty of judgement that play a prominent role in her understanding of moral-political judgement. Arendt uses Kant's observations concerning human *sociability* as the basis for her ontological claim that human beings are socially constructed. For Arendt, sociability is "the very origin … of man's humanity." The faculty of judgement "presupposes the presence of others"[33] and "when one judges, one judges as a member of a community."[34] This insight is captured by Kant, Arendt believes, in his conception of the *sensus communis*, or common sense.

In making an aesthetic judgement (or, Arendt wants to argue, a moral-political judgement according to her own definition), we consult our *sensus communis* in order to distance ourselves from all private interest in the judgement, and achieve a generality or universality of outcome. The *sensus communis* is like the "internal," private sense of taste according to Arendt, insofar as it senses not an object but a sensation, and is intrinsically discriminatory (producing an "it-pleases-or-displeases-me" reaction that is immediate).[35] But via an act of imagination, objects no longer present to us—the objects of judgement—are re-presented, allowing us the distance of reflection that is necessary to achieve disinterestedness and right judgement. Disinterestedness for Kant and Arendt consists in disregarding our subjective private conditions, or self-interest, "abstracting from the limitations which contingently attach to our own judgement."[36] In this way our *sensus privatus* is transformed into a *sensus communis*, for it emerges that the nonsubjective element introduced by the process of reflection is intersubjectivity. Because I judge as a member of a community, my judgements always reflect upon others and "take … their possible judgements

30 Hannah Arendt, "Thinking and Moral Considerations," in Responsibility and Judgement, ed. by Jerome Kohn (New York: Schocken Books, 2003), at 188.
31 Beiner, "Interpretive Essay," at 93.
32 *Ibid.* at 138–139.
33 Arendt, *Lectures on Kant's Political Philosophy*, at 74.
34 *Ibid.* at 72.
35 *Ibid.* at 64.
36 *Ibid.* at 43.

into account."[37] In consulting what I imagine might be the judgements of others, I reflect on the approbability or disapprobability of my initial it-pleases-or-displeases-me reaction based on the criterion of that initial choice's communicability or publicity.

Thus, the *sensus communis* makes possible enlarged thought—putting oneself in thought in the place of everyone else to achieve a "general standpoint"—and enlarged thinking makes possible communicability or publicness: "one can communicate only if one is able to think from the other person's standpoint; otherwise one will never meet him, never speak in such a way that he understands."[38] So the distinguishing virtue of the faculty of judgement for Arendt is *impartiality*, which is obtained both by abstracting from my own self-interest and particular situation and by taking the viewpoints of others into account.

In summary, Arendt's interpretation of Kant's theory of judgement offers two great strengths, both flowing from the unique role of the *sensus communis.* The *sensus communis* makes it possible to enlarge one's mentality by considering multiple points of view, so the *procedure* for judging mandated by the *sensus communis* ensures a form of inclusivity of all members of a relevant public. And further, because the *sensus communis* is "what judgement appeals to in everyone," judgements of this sort possess a "special validity" for members of a judging community. What Arendt means by this term is not, of course, that it is possible to compel agreement with right judgements, but that it *is* possible to appeal to the "community sense" of other members of a community in order to invoke the special validity of the judgement for those members. The person "wooing" or "courting" agreement under these circumstances thus enjoys a special persuasive advantage.

Arendtian theories of judgement: Disch, Benhabib, and Young

The subtle variations among the interpretations of Arendt's theory of judgement in the writings of Lisa Disch, Seyla Benhabib, and Iris Marion Young illuminate the differences among the theoretical approaches to which each is committed: respectively, deliberative democracy, discourse theory (in many ways the progenitor of deliberative democratic theory and now considered one of its sub-fields), and emancipatory politics. Each of these authors employs Arendt's conception of enlarged mentality as a means of achieving impartiality and in some measure, of gaining a persuasive edge over members of a particular public. For these authors, impartiality achieved by means of an Arendtian procedure serves as a way of taking account of diversity and ensuring inclusivity in a democratic polity without embracing the conceit of an "objective" standpoint.

Lisa Disch

Lisa Disch argues that the technique of enlarged thinking pioneered by Arendt for achieving critical understanding cultivates a state of mind she describes as "situated

37 *Ibid.* at 67.
38 *Ibid.* at 74.

impartiality." Disch focuses on the metaphor of *storytelling* invoked by Arendt to explain her interpretation of the methodology for judging that she believes inheres in Kant's conception of judgements of taste. Disch is particularly interested in Arendt's conviction that enlarged thinking is the means for fostering the impartiality necessary for aesthetic judgements of taste. Such thinking involves "comparing your judgement with the possible rather than the actual judgements of others ... by putting ourselves in the place of any other man, by abstracting from the limitations which contingently attach to our own judgement."[39]

In *Eichmann in Jerusalem*, Arendt famously employs a methodology of historiographic storytelling that eschews a conventional linear narrative and the Archimedean authorial viewpoint that this implies. She instead makes explicit her necessarily situated and specific moral stance on the material she discusses, without closing off other analytic pathways or normative conclusions for her reader. Disch's investigation of Arendt suggests that Arendt developed her own unique approach for cultivating intersubjective understanding as a result of the combined influences of her methodological innovations in historiography and her reading of Kant's conviction that the validity of judgements of taste depends upon the presumption that others would assent to those judgements. Arendt describes the technique she devised for achieving a form of non-abstract impartiality as "going visiting" and "thinking without banisters." Disch employs the term "situated impartiality" to distinguish the condition of mind that Arendt's method aims to foster from enlarged thinking, its Kantian inspiration.

Arendt describes the task of the individual who seeks to "visit" the standpoint of a particular other in the introduction to her biography of Rahel Varnhagen: "What interested me solely was to narrate the story of Rahel's life as she herself might have told it."[40] Elizabeth Minnich summarizes Arendt's approach in that early work as seeking "some act of mind that could move her both in and out of Varnhagen's life in a way that neither Rahel, caught within her own story, nor others, standing outside of it, could achieve. She decided to think *with* Rahel Varnhagen, and neither *as* nor *about* her."[41]

In her later writings, Arendt took the kernel of this idea of thinking with and incorporated it into her notion of going visiting. Visiting is Arendt's refinement of Kant's idea of taking the standpoint of every man; it involves imagining "how I would feel and think" if I were in the place of all others with an interest in, for example, a particular political choice to be made. Arendt is not advocating that I imagine what it is like to *be* another person, however; she cautions:

39 Kant, *Critique of Judgement*, at 136.

40 Hannah Arendt, *Rahel Varnhagen*, rev. ed. (New York: Harcourt Brace Jovanovich, 1974), at xv.

41 Elizabeth Minnich, "To Judge in Freedom: Hannah Arendt on the Relation of Thinking and Morality," in Gisela T. Kaplan and Clive S. Kessler, eds., *Hannah Arendt: Thinking, Judging, Freedom* (Sydney, Australia: Allen & Unwin, 1989), at 135.

> I must warn you here of a very common and easy misunderstanding. The trick of critical thinking does not consist in an enormously enlarged empathy through which one can know what actually goes on in the mind of all others. To think, according to Kant's understanding of enlightenment, means *Selbstdenken*, to think for oneself.... To accept what goes on in the minds of those whose "standpoint" (actually, the place where they stand, the conditions they are subject to, which always differ from one individual to the next, from one class or group as compared to another) is not my own would mean no more than to passively accept their thought, that is, to exchange their prejudices for the prejudices proper to my own station.[42]

And so, Disch argues, in order to go visiting "you must travel to a new location, leave behind what is familiar, and resist the temptation to make yourself at home where you are not"[43] while still acting and thinking in your own identity; only in this way can we preserve and learn from plurality without giving in to the passivity of uncritical prejudice.

Unlike the universalizing Kantian account of enlarged thinking in which "one raises one's idiosyncratic preference for an object to a critical judgement by *abstracting* from one's own contingent situation to arrive at the standpoint of *any* observer,"[44] Arendt's method involves considering diverse opinions in order to better situate my own standpoint. For her, "impartiality is obtained by taking the viewpoints of others into account; impartiality is not the result of some higher standpoint that would then actually settle the dispute by being altogether above the melée."[45] Instead, as Disch explains,

> impartiality involves telling oneself the story of an event or situation from the plurality of perspectives that constitute it as a public phenomenon. This critical vantage point, not from outside but from within a plurality of contesting standpoints, is ... "situated impartiality."

For Disch, the judgement made possible by such a standpoint is "neither objective and disinterested nor explicitly identified with a single particularistic interest."[46]

Seyla Benhabib

Seyla Benhabib takes up the work that Arendt had intended to pursue in her unwritten third volume of *The Life of the Mind* by using Arendt's account of thinking from the standpoint of others as the basis for a moral theory. Benhabib

42 Arendt, *Lectures on Kant's Political Philosophy*, at 43.
43 Lisa Jane Disch, *Hannah Arendt and the Limits of Philosophy* (Ithaca and London: Cornell University Press, 1994), at 159.
44 Lisa Jane Disch, "More Truth Than Fact: Storytelling as Critical Understanding in the Writings of Hannah Arendt" (1993) 21 *Political Theory* 665 at 686.
45 Arendt, *Lectures on Kant's Political Philosophy*, at 42.
46 Disch, "More Truth than Fact," at 666.

regards Arendt's conception of enlarged thinking as an attempt to reconcile the conflict in the western philosophical tradition between the pull of contextual judgement, advocated most famously by Aristotle, with the allure of a universal morality, usually associated with Kant.[47] Benhabib uses Arendt's appropriation of Kant's work on judgement as the basis for her own notion of "symmetrical reciprocity"—the condition of judgement that she argues is the basis of moral respect between persons.

In *Situating the Self*, Benhabib develops a model of symmetrical reciprocity as moral conversation. Benhabib's central claim is that attempts to reach agreement among diversely situated agents require the cultivation of a capacity for reversing perspectives. In exercising this capacity through Arendtian acts of imagination, I "anticipate … communication with others with whom I know I must finally come to some agreement."[48]

Benhabib asserts that this method of seeking understanding across difference employs the very skills that we use unreflectively in everyday exchanges. Following Arendt, she explains,

> in conversation, I must know how to listen, I must know how to understand your point of view, I must learn to represent to myself the world and the other as you see them. If I cannot listen, if I cannot understand, and if I cannot represent, the conversation stops, develops into an argument, or maybe never gets started.[49]

Thus, enlarged thinking requires that I use my imagination to extend and exceed my experience, creating a simulated dialogue with others who could be my partners in conversation. The purpose of such an imagined conversation for Benhabib is to allow me to think from the standpoints of others. However, Benhabib does not forget Arendt's warning against confusing "going visiting" with an exercise in empathy. As for Arendt, her focus is restricted to "merely making present to oneself what the perspectives of others involved are or could be, and whether I could 'woo their consent' in acting the way I do."[50]

Benhabib finds support in Arendt's account of the understanding necessary for political judgement for her own notion of symmetrical reciprocity and the communicative ethical theory that hinges upon it:

> Judgement involves the capacity to represent to oneself the multiplicity of viewpoints, the variety of perspectives, the layers of meaning which constitute a situation…. This "enlarged mentality" can be described precisely as exercising the reversibility of perspectives which discourse ethics enjoins.[51]

47 Seyla Benhabib, *Situating the Self* (New York: Routledge, 1992), at 126.
48 *Ibid*. at 137.
49 *Ibid*. at 52.
50 *Ibid*. at 137.
51 *Ibid*.

So we see that both Benhabib and Disch interpret Arendt as prescribing a method that amounts to a sophisticated form of "putting oneself in the place of another" in order to build understanding across difference. The arguments of these two authors emphasize that while I imagine myself in your place, I—myself in my own evolving identity—ought to think about what *your place* is like. This view is distinct from the tendency among deliberative democratic theorists to regard the act of putting myself in your place as being primarily about *myself* (this orientation is, of course, seldom overtly acknowledged). By attending to the other's moral-equality-in-difference in this way, a form of positive solidarity is generated that is based on a recognition of her in terms she might use to describe herself. Iris Marion Young pushes this tendency even further in her deconstruction of Arendt's notion of enlarged thinking.

Iris Marion Young

Young reads Arendt's interpretation of enlarged thinking very differently than does Benhabib, and she draws sharply contrasting conclusions concerning both the nature of the intersubjective relationships that it gives rise to and the essence of Arendtian impartiality.

While endorsing Benhabib's efforts to remedy discourse morality's neglect of concrete particular others in their specific narrative situations by means of a theory of moral judgement, Young feels that Benhabib does not go far enough in taking account of the unique nature of each individual's situatedness in a particular standpoint determined by the contingent interplay of the individual's class, gender, sexual orientation, gender expression, ableness, and religious, ethnic, and racialized identities. (Young also regards Disch as subject to this criticism, but concentrates her critical commentary on Benhabib's argument.) Young takes issue with just those statements of Benhabib's that suggest that moral respect requires that we regard others as holding positions which are reversible and symmetrical with our own. She argues along *with* Disch, Benhabib, and Arendt that empathy is not the route to building understanding with others for the purpose of reaching legitimate moral and political judgements. But she distinguishes herself from the first two authors, and perhaps Arendt as well, by suggesting that being able to adopt the others' standpoints imaginatively is an insufficient, dangerous, and ultimately impossible means of pursuing understanding in the service of judgement.[52]

Young argues that human beings' standpoints are irreducibly asymmetrical because of the vagaries of personal history and social positioning. Ignoring this fact by equating moral respect with reversibility of perspectives and symmetry (via identification with divergently situated others) threatens to further entrench existing unequal power relations by assigning a false legitimacy to public, seemingly inclusive, processes of decision-making. When we suppose that others' perspectives are symmetrical and reversible with our own, we also tend to assume

52 Young develops her critique in the context of her theory of communicative democracy, designed to serve as an alternative to theories of deliberative democracy that are in turn conceived as correctives to interest-based democratic theories.

that they are similar to our own, and thus fully comprehensible to us. This assumption tends to impede communication, discouraging us from listening for evidence of the incommensurability of our experiences and situations.

The interpretation of Arendt's injunction to "put oneself in the place of another" that is endorsed by both Benhabib and Disch as a means to achieving enlarged thought inspires some of Young's most vehement criticism for this very reason:

> [W]hen people obey the injunction to put themselves in the position of others, they too often put *themselves*, with their own particular experiences and privileges, in the positions they see the others in. When privileged people put themselves in the position of those who are less privileged, the assumptions derived from their privilege often allow them unknowingly to misrepresent the other's situation.
>
> [...]
>
> When members of privileged groups imaginatively try to represent to themselves the perspective of members of oppressed groups, too often those representations carry projections and fantasies through which the privileged reinforce a complimentary image of themselves. The idea of reversing perspectives assumes that the perspectives brought to a situation are equally legitimate. Where structured social injustice exists, this may not be true.... [A]sking the oppressed to reverse perspectives with the privileged in adjudicating a conflict may itself be an injustice and an insult.[53]

So for Young, the moral respect that helps to validate moral and political judgements does *not* require reversibility and sympathy (identification with divergently situated people) as Benhabib's understanding of enlarged thought suggests. On Young's view, Arendt's goal of fostering enlarged thinking is better achieved by attending to the asymmetry and irreversibility of participants' perspectives.

She identifies two main reasons for this claim. The first is that "publicity in Arendt's sense is maintained only if the plurality of perspectives that constitutes it is preserved,"[54] and the assumption of reversibility destroys, or at least compromises the integrity of, that originary plurality. The second, and most compelling advantage she believes that Arendt's interpretation offers is that it possesses a greater claim to objectivity. She observes that

> when we try to represent a multiplicity of viewpoints to ourselves, we have merely aggregated a series of subjective and self-regarding perspectives, rather than adopting a new, more objective thinking derived from them all. If we represent to ourselves all the perspectives, we still have not represented *that upon which* these are perspectives [emphasis mine].[55]

53 Iris Marion Young, "Asymmetrical Reciprocity" in *Intersecting Voices* (Princeton, NJ: Princeton University Press, 1997), 38 at 48, 45.

54 *Ibid.* at 58.

55 *Ibid.* at 57.

The objectivity that Young believes asymmetrical reciprocity makes possible is dependent upon publicity, which entails both attention to the standpoints of the people involved in the public activity of communication, and attention to the public world itself that we constitute together as "a creative product of the dialogue among our multiple perspectives, but [one that is] distinct from them because it is an objective relation between us."[56] Young supports the accuracy of this view of Arendtian objectivity by citing Arendt's famous metaphor for the *sensus communis*:

> To live together in the world means essentially that a world of things is between those who have it in common, as a table is located between those who sit around it. The world, like every in-between, relates and separates men at the same time.[57]

I take the connotations of Young's argument to be that by failing to explicitly include discussion of the role played by reflecting upon the relations among our various perspectives in coming to an enlarged mentality, Benhabib and Disch pay insufficient attention to the "table" that simultaneously connects and separates us, and to our multiple perspectives on it. In doing so, Young implies, they miss a key aspect of "sociability" itself: the constitutive activity of engaging in second-order determinations of approbation or disapprobation—strong evaluations rooted in our shared background understandings.

For Young, asymmetrical reciprocity gives us access to "the public world that lies between us." It is the account of this shared web of social relations "that surrounds us and within which we act"[58] revealed to us by Young's Arendtian approach to enlarging our thought that creates the opportunity for such strong evaluation.

* * *

The characterization of the impartiality that makes enlarged thinking possible for Young is closely akin to the idea of impartiality captured in this passage by Susan Drummond: "the original position is not abandoned for an impartial, general point of view: it is elaborated to include an understanding of the ways that partial points of view affect other partial points of view."[59] On Young's view, speaking with and listening to *all* actual others affected by a given public deliberation would be the substance of such an impartiality, while she regards *imagining* those others' standpoints as antithetical to the achievement of the goal of redistribution of power that animates her communicative democratic theory. But in defining her understanding of enlarged thinking in this way, Young relinquishes the practical—although arguably fraught—advantage offered by Arendt's imaginative procedure. In large polities, despite technological advances available in

56 *Ibid.* at 58.
57 Hannah Arendt, *The Human Condition* (Chicago, IL: University of Chicago Press, 1958), at 52, cited in Young, "Asymmetrical Reciprocity," at 58.
58 Young, *ibid.*
59 Susan Drummond, *Incorporating the Familiar* (Montréal, Canada: McGill-Queens, 1997), at 150.

industrialized countries, it has proven extremely difficult to create mechanisms for speaking with and listening to every citizen that are not subject to charges of unequal accessibility. This is not to deny the intuitive appeal of the aspiration, but the implication of Young's argument seems to be that it is necessary to suspend judgement and deny judgement's legitimacy until that process is complete. I am unconvinced that the benefit to be derived from such a denial is very substantial; and as we will see in the subsequent discussion of Jennifer Nedelsky's methodology for enlarging thought to encompass multiple communities of judgement, there is reason to regard the suspension-of-judgement strategy as dubious as well.

The validity of judgements

The sensus communis *and the issue of universality*

In the past half-century the growing acknowledgement in western academic and political circles of the fundamentally situated character of human agency has resulted in a valorization of the uniqueness of specific cultural, gender, sexual identity and racialized identity standpoints (and to a lesser degree, those associated with class, religion, and physical ableness). This phenomenon is the source of the impulse behind identity politics, which has been largely responsible for the celebration of previously denigrated ascriptive identities, and for the concomitant political and theoretical attention that has been accorded to the claim that legitimacy depends upon inclusivity, achieved, at a minimum, via broad consultation with representatives of diversely situated social groups. Disch, Benhabib, and Young all explored Arendt's procedure for taking account of diversity as a first step in achieving Kantian impartiality in order to secure this type of legitimacy for their own theories.

But this valorization of diversity and situatedness simultaneously problematizes the former touchstones of objectivity and neutrality that formed the constituent elements of the "view from nowhere"[60] that was once thought to guarantee the universality of moral and political judgements. So claims about the justness of an action or a legal precept are now widely regarded as requiring a new theoretical basis if they are to apply in any general way to people drawn from disparate backgrounds. The challenge is to avoid nihilism while acknowledging the fact of human situatedness and the cultural (at least) relativism that flows from that irreducible particularity. Consequently, the "special validity" possessed by Arendtian judgements for members of (appropriately constituted) judging communities holds a potentially powerful appeal. Roughly speaking, judgements that can invoke a version of Kant's *sensus communis* are thought by Arendt to be able to make "claims of agreement" that are generally, if not universally, applicable.

60 See Thomas Nagel, *The View from Nowhere* (Oxford: Oxford University Press, 1986) on the pitfalls of the ideal of disengaged reason that has characterized western philosophical thinking since the time of the ancient Greeks.

But few of Arendt's contemporary interpreters have seriously considered what the content of an updated version of Kant's *sensus communis* might be. It is no longer tenable to assume, as Kant did, that the structure of human cognitive faculties alone serves as a reasonable foundation for claims of a subjective universal validity of judgements. But alternative accounts of what it is a community needs to share in order for judgements to make a claim of agreement upon its members *are* possible.

In what follows, four possible alternatives to defining the *sensus communis* will be sketched. We will move from an approach I call "empty essentialism" inspired by Charles Taylor's work, to a consideration of the meaning behind Rousseau's infamous phrase "to persuade without convincing," through an overview of Jennifer Nedelsky's analysis of Arendtian "communities of judgement," and finally to a brief reflection on the possibilities inherent in Thomas Morawetz's Wittgensteinian account of "deliberative practices." In exploring the question—What does a judging community need to share in order for a claim of agreement to obtain among its members?—we will trace a path from what might be described as the most ontologically grounded to the least ontologically fundamental of the explanations considered.

Empty essentialism—Taylor and Gadamer on fusing horizons

Charles Taylor has sketched what could be regarded as an alternative content for the *sensus communis* in his reworking of Hans-Georg Gadamer's conception of the fusion of horizons.[61]

One of Gadamer's unique contributions to the theory of intersubjective understanding lies in his definition of "prejudice" (*Vorurteil*). He begins with the assertion that "we belong to history."[62] Prejudice and preconception are constitutive of our being because we "stand always within tradition" and "it is always part of us."[63] When we interpret an ancient text or historical action, we are only able to achieve some degree of understanding by drawing upon and examining our prejudices, which serve as a kind of depository for the effective-historical residue of the object of our research. In this sense, the condition of being prejudiced is actually the prerequisite of the possibility of understanding.

On Gadamer's view, retrospective understanding depends upon the acquisition of the proper historical standpoint through a "fusion of horizons."[64] Historical consciousness is "only something laid over a continuing tradition," so the horizon

61 See Natalie Oman, "Paths to Intercultural Understanding: Feasting, Shared Horizons, and Unforced Consensus," in Catherine Bell and David Kahane, eds., *Intercultural Dispute Resolution in Aboriginal Contexts* (Vancouver, BC: UBC Press, 2004), 70, at 81–81.

62 Hans-Georg Gadamer, "The Rehabilitation of Authority and Tradition" in Kurt Mueller-Volmer, ed., *The Hermeneutics Reader*, trans. Garrett Barden and John Cumming (New York: Continuum, 1985), 261 at 261.

63 *Ibid.* at 265.

64 Hans-Georg Gadamer, "The Principle of Effective History," in Mueller-Volmer, ed., *The Hermeneutics Reader*, 267 at 270.

of the contemporary interpreter is actually just a circumscribed portion of a single continuum of shared orientations that is accessible to her by means of hermeneutical reflection. The process of understanding involves what Gadamer describes as a fusing of the horizons of the interpreter and her object of study, as the historical horizon is simultaneously projected and removed.[65]

This interpretive technique is often regarded as a catch-all for addressing any variety of breakdown or failure of intersubjectivity, but its intended and best use is as a model for the kind of interpretation required to develop an understanding of an historical text or action. Gadamer's account of a fusion of horizons is premised upon the fact that the interpreter and the phenomenon which she seeks to understand are part of the same historical continuum (in the sense that the effective-history of the phenomenon is constitutive of the prejudices of the interpreter); as a result, it is doubtful that this approach can generate authentically *inter*-cultural understanding, insofar as individuals from cultures with very different conceptual schemes or worldviews will clearly not share membership in a single tradition in any meaningful sense.

Taylor offers a distinct account of the fusion of horizons model which, because it rests upon a broader interpretation of the common tradition requirement than Gadamer's theory, could be employed to "update" Kant's version of the *sensus communis* in order to generate interculturally valid claims of agreement. Taylor argues that the intractable socio-biological conditions of human experience in combination with human linguisticality give rise to a set of "inescapable questions" that are constant across cultures (how we relate to fellow members of our society and to the ensemble of humankind, to time, to the cosmos, and to the absolute or some sense of the divine) which the framework understandings of every human culture must address more or less explicitly.[66] These inescapable ontological circumstances demand that each cultural frame defines in some sense its members' "moral predicament" in relation to these questions, and this serves as a sufficient basis for intercultural understanding to be a real possibility. This form of "empty essentialism"[67] satisfies the same requirement for commonality that a shared tradition fulfils in Gadamer's argument. However, because this version of the fusion of horizons argument reworks the foundation for intercultural understanding, it is free of the weakness that compromises the applicability of Gadamer's interpretation to the general endeavour of building all varieties of intercultural understanding.

Taylor's version of the fusion of horizons argument is designed to avoid the pitfalls of cultural relativism, while retaining an appreciation of the social constitution of each individual's identity. Taylor holds that understanding occurs through the development of a "language of perspicuous contrast"; as such a language evolves through dialogue

65 *Ibid.* at 273.

66 Charles Taylor, "Modernity, Faith, and Morality" (paper presented in the Sprole Lecture Series, Faculty of Religious Studies, McGill University, Montréal, Canada, Winter 1992) [unpublished].

67 By this term I mean to indicate a view that defines human nature in terms of open-ended categories, rather than a specific set of uniform qualities.

between participants in different cultures, it comes to encompass the range of possibilities of meaning available to both, and so fuses the horizons of understanding of those engaged in the conversation. This language would be something more, and thus different, than either of the original languages, "a language in which we could formulate both their way of life and ours as alternative possibilities in relation to some human constants at work in both."[68]

The viability of such a language of perspicuous contrast depends for Taylor on the existence of that core of common orientations or perpetual problems whose culturally-specific solutions are available for comparison. And this intercultural common ground also serves as the foundation for "claims of agreement" that could adjudicate among different cultures' commonsense understandings of various aspects of their worlds.

Taylor rejects the proposition associated with cultural relativism that understanding simply amounts to adopting the agent's point of view or unreflectively accepting the terms of her self-description (a position which Taylor explicitly identifies with Peter Winch). Rather, Taylor argues that (social scientific) understanding consists in the development of a theoretical account that will "make the agent's doings clearer than they were to him."[69] He suggests that such an account will make it possible to apply the desirability characterizations of the subject culture correctly, to employ "key words" in the same way that bearers of that culture do, and to explain details of cultural practices and institutions.[70] The more fully it facilitates these activities, the better the account.

Adjudication among interpretations plays a further role in this model of intercultural understanding, insofar as the development of this species of meta-language is understood by Taylor to open up the possibility of evaluating particular aspects of the original two construals of the world as better or worse, or more or less appropriate. From an original condition of mutual incomprehension, two culturally-distinct interlocutors slowly cobble together a language of perspicuous contrast which encompasses the original two languages and allows each of their users not only to grasp the foreign conceptual scheme of the other by means of "illuminating contrast,"[71] but also to compare specific features of these schemes in terms of their ability to satisfy context-dependent criteria.[72]

This account of the process of fusing horizons seems to offer an alternative way of understanding Arendtian enlarged thinking. The shared background understandings that help to comprise fused horizons for Taylor could plausibly be viewed as the content of the interlocutors' *sensus communis*, serving as a universalizable basis for intercultural judgements.

68 Charles Taylor, "Understanding and Ethnocentricity," in *Philosophy and the Human Sciences*, vol. 2, *Philosophical Papers* (Cambridge: Cambridge University Press, 1985), 116, at 125.
69 *Ibid.* at 118.
70 *Ibid.* at 119, 121, 123.
71 Clifford Geertz, "From the Native's Point of View" in *Local Knowledge* (New York: Basic Books, 1983), 55 at 57.
72 Taylor, "Understanding and Ethnocentricity," at 128, 129.

Rousseau—to persuade without convincing

In his *Social Contract*, Jean-Jacques Rousseau tries to define a highly circumscribed community of judgement—citizens of the society of the general will—whose members would share a set of background understandings of such depth and uniformity that they could communicate in silence while seeking the general will. Each would abstract from his own private self-interest and search within his own heart for the inner voice of *conscience* that would guide him to the general will which "considers only the general interest,"[73] while yet obeying only "a law he prescribes for himself." In the period of transition to this condition of moral liberty, Rousseau contemplates the possibility that the public counsel of an ideal-type figure he referred to as the legislator might provide the citizens of such a society with indispensable assistance. But the mandate of this virtuous and formally powerless figure would simply be "to persuade without convincing" the members of the polity.

What does this mean? The answer lies in Aristotle's *Rhetoric*, in his account of the special topics relevant to the various audiences to which the genres of deliberative, forensic, and panegyric speech are directed. For Aristotle, rhetoric is "the faculty of discovering all the possible means of persuasion in any subject."[74] Although his Introduction certainly contains evidence that Aristotle was influenced by Plato's Socratic attack on rhetoric and *doxa* in the *Gorgias*, his ensuing account of rhetoric is far from uniformly condemnatory. As Aristotle indicates in his discussion of the special topics, *persuasion* appeals to something deeper than our culturally conditioned conventions of rational argumentation. Successful persuasion addresses itself to the implicit background understandings which underlie and give shape to the form of life that determines the relatively explicit criteria of discursive rationality. Persuasion in this sense is a process of appealing by various means to those less-thematized and articulable shared understandings—the elusive substance of what we could call a *sensus communis*—that we are inducted into by living and functioning within them, but also can come to know by actively and arduously working to expand our ability to practise enlarged thinking. So being open to being persuaded, rather than convinced (in the Habermasian sense) suggests an openness to claims of agreement founded upon a shared *sensus communis* that seems consistent with Rousseau's description of the process of seeking the general will. But Rousseau believes that in order for such claims of agreement to be subjectively valid for members of the community, citizens must share a cultural and social framework whose extreme homogeneity is itself the source of the possibility of moral and political transparency. However, the establishment of such a high degree of uniformity in the *sensus communis* is thought by Rousseau to require the surveillance of the institution he dubs "the censorship" and conditioning by a civil religion. At the same time, the very strength of the claim of

73 Jean-Jacques Rousseau, *Discourse on the Origin and Foundations of Inequality*, in *On the Social Contract*, trans. by Donald A. Cress (Indianapolis, IN: Hackett Publishing, 1983), bk. II, chap. iii, at 31–32.

74 Aristotle, *The "Art" of Rhetoric*, trans. by John Henry Freese (Cambridge, MA: Harvard University Press, 1926), at bk. I.

agreement that this homogeneity makes possible—a strength essential to the achievement of moral liberty for the citizenry—implies a degree of spiritual vulnerability that Rousseau believes would necessitate the harshest of measures against those who threatened it.[75]

Jennifer Nedelsky—communities of judgement

Jennifer Nedelsky tries to retain the tremendous practical advantage that springs from the ability "to persuade without convincing" by focusing more on the substance than the procedure of Arendt's account of enlarged thinking. Nedelsky develops Arendt's notion of "communities of judgement" as a means of trying to overcome the paralysis in matters of moral and political judgement that often accompanies a keen appreciation of the implications of cultural relativism.

For Nedelsky, attention to the identification of judging communities produces a conceptual tool that helps to explain the nature of our complex situatedness. By elaborating and testing examples of different types of judging communities ranging from women's support groups to religious communities, Nedelsky is able to explain the qualities that Young believes make our standpoints asymmetrical and irreversible within the conceptual terms of Arendt's theory itself. By pointing out that most people in most places in the modern world are members of multiple, often contesting communities of judgement, Nedelsky can account for the complexity of multifaceted identities within her theory of community-based judgement.[76]

The concept of "normative orders" from the theory of legal pluralism is useful in drawing out Nedelsky's point here. Just as legal pluralists observe that the norms that animate or regulate our behaviour in any given situation can be drawn from the variety of (sometimes incommensurable) legal orders that help to constitute our sense of right and wrong, Nedelsky argues that our memberships in numerous disparate or overlapping communities of judgement can provide us with a variety of sources of standards of beauty, ugliness, justice, and right behaviour.

Examples of such sources of normativity include the often distinct normative orders that are explicitly and implicitly endorsed by members of a nuclear family, a national constitution, and an indigenous land tenure system.[77] Nedelsky talks about the way that the shared memories of a community could form the basis for certain communal norms.[78]

75 I refer here to Rousseau's infamous discussion of the need for "forcing" dissidents "to be free," and in extreme cases, putting them to death (Rousseau, *Discourse on Inequality*, bk. I, chap. vii).

76 Jennifer Nedelsky, "Relations of Freedom and Law's Relations," (2012) 8 *Politics & Gender* 231.

77 See for example, John Borrows, *Recovering Canada: The Resurgence of Indigenous Law* (Toronto: University of Toronto Press, 2002), chap. 2, and Gisday Wa and Delgam Uukw, *The Spirit in the Land* (Gabriola, BC: Reflections, 1989, 1992).

78 See Jennifer Nedelsky, "Communities of Judgment and Human Rights," (2000) 1 *Theoretical Inquiries in Law* 1 at 32–33.

However, despite her interest in what might be termed "micro-" communities of judgement, Nedelsky is fully aware of the potential uses and abuses of a broadly-defined community of judgement along the lines of the world community discussed by Kant and Arendt in connection with the idea of a world-spectator (*Weltbetrachter*).[79] Nedelsky appreciates the lure of the Arendtian claim of agreement for those who wish, for example, to advocate international human rights. But she is also suspicious of the *raison d'état* implications of any universal claim of special validity.

She perceptively notes that the language of universality can be invoked to *deny* that the imposition of power is involved in a judgement since "the common sense of all mankind is offended" by the actions being condemned, citing contemporary human rights disputes and the Nuremberg trials as examples. (Upendra Baxi and Makau Mutua develop complex critiques of existing human rights regimes from similar starting points. Both reach the hesitant conclusion that universal claims of validity for existing international human rights standards remain useful because of the potentialities that the discourse of international human rights retains for facilitating resistance against colonizing impositions of power.[80])

> The invocation of the common sense of mankind thus cannot lift us out of the complexities of multiple, conflicting communities (and their power relations) and the ways in which they vastly complicate the workings of the enlarged mentality. Those who invoke the common sense of humanity as the basis for their institutions bear the burden of examining and revealing the standpoints they have actually considered in arriving at this claim of a universal standpoint.

79 Judgements are the purview of the spectator—notably the critic, the historian—because the most important condition of judgements is that of impartiality. ("The advantage the spectator has is that he sees the play as a whole, while each of the actors knows only his part, or, if he should judge from the perspective of acting, only the part of the whole that concerns him. The actor is partial by definition" (Arendt, *Lectures on Kant's Political Philosophy*, at 68–9).)

80 As Baxi frames the matter: "international human rights standards and norms empower peoples' movements and conscientious policy-makers everywhere to question political practices. That, to my mind, is an inestimable potential of human rights languages, not readily available in previous centuries. Human rights languages are all that we have to interrogate the barbarism of power, even when these remain inadequate to humanize fully the barbaric practices of politics" ("Voices of Suffering and the Future of Human Rights" (1998) 8 *Transnational Law & Contemporary Problems* 125 at 126–127). However, as Baxi observes, that usefulness is tempered by the "radical uncertainty" that must accompany our invocation of "human rights ideals, values, languages, standards, and even norms that address their 'universality'" (*The Future of Human Rights*, 2nd edn. (Oxford: Oxford University Press, 2002, 2006), at 116). While Makau Mutua is willing to allow cautious support for "a new multicultural human rights corpus" that could "play a role in changing the unjust international order and particularly the imbalances between the West and the Third World," he argues that such an understanding of human rights would have to move beyond the conventional script of "liberal nationalism and democratic internal self-determination" ("Savages, Victims, and Saviors" (2001) 42 *Harvard International Law Journal* 201 at 243).

> And their institutions bear the responsibility of fostering ongoing open exchange between those from different standpoints.[81]

* * *

By developing Arendt's notion of communities of judgement in order to better explain the multiplex nature of identities, Nedelsky puts herself in danger of undercutting the basis for the claim of special validity for moral and political judgements appealing to the *sensus communis* of such communities. The reading of the content of the *sensus communis* implied by her discussion of the multiplicity of such judging communities is so "thin" that we are left wondering whether members of such communities share enough in common to establish a subjective duty of assent at all. And how meaningful is the concept of community itself, once it becomes attenuated past a certain point? Further, is that attenuation really necessary when we have concepts that seem to do much of the same explanatory work—like the legal pluralist notion of a normative order—available to us?

Nedelsky has intimated that in order for judgements arrived at by members of multiple judging communities in conversation with one another to be regarded as legitimate in extreme cases, such as those concerning the prospect of military intervention, the achievement of consensus or something very close to it is important.[82] Arendt discussed moral and political judgements only in the context of a single judging community (to the best of my knowledge), and so it is not clear what her opinion on this issue would be. However, we do know that Arendt makes a concerted effort to point out that all we can ever hope to attain is *relative* impartiality, since although judgement "always reflects upon others ... [and] takes their possible judgements into account," at the same time "I obey a law given to myself regardless of what others may think of the matter."[83] It seems reasonable to infer that while Arendt might well have accepted that in the case of disagreement among members of multiple judging communities about, for example, a human rights norm, the judgement concerning that norm's acceptability would not have a general subjective validity—that is, it would not be able to make a claim of agreement upon members of the communities of judgement that were not largely supportive of it. However, Arendt's ruminations on the predicament of the individual whose own judgement conflicts with the *sensus communis* of her judging community in *Eichmann in Jerusalem*, [84] coupled with her attention to

81 Nedelsky, "Communities of Judgement," at 27–28.

82 Professor Nedelsky made this point in a verbal summary of her paper, "Communities of Judgement and Human Rights" (Paper presented at the Dilemmas of Global Justice Conference, Munk Centre for International Studies, University of Toronto, Canada, 5 April 2003). Her comments were extemporaneous, and suggestive only, so my commentary is provisional. (It is of some interest to note that this paper was delivered in the midst of the U.S.-British invasion of Iraq.)

83 Arendt, *Lectures on Kant's Political Philosophy* at 67, 68.

84 Hannah Arendt, *Eichmann in Jerusalem: A Report on the Banality of Evil*, revised and enlarged edition (New York: Penguin Books, 1994), 294–298. See also Hannah Arendt, *The Life of the Mind* (New York: Harcourt, 1971), 179–193.

the unavoidably proprietary nature of every individual's standpoint, suggest that she would certainly not regard non-conforming "personal" judgements as illegitimate. And so by extension, when an entire community's *sensus communis* yields a judgement that isn't endorsed by "competing" judging communities, it follows that Arendt would hold that the non-conforming judgement was legitimate for members of the originating community; but it would be invalid for, and unable to claim the agreement of, members of the other communities of judgement whose *communi sensu* did not support it.

But what would the practical implications for members of the community that produced the non-conforming judgement be? Since that judgement would have a general subjective validity for them, it would exercise a claim of agreement that would condition their choices about appropriate action. Suppose that the choices concerned possible action to prevent or halt large-scale, gross violations of human rights, like the 1994 genocide against Tutsis and those who tried to protect them in Rwanda, or the 1995 massacre of over 8,000 Bosniak men and boys that took place in the UN "safe area" of Srebreniça, or the 2013 chemical weapons attacks on hundreds of civilians in Syria? I believe that the implication of Arendt's argument is that if such a protective action were taken and it was not supported by the *sensus communis* of the larger community of "relevant" interlocutors —in this case, generally understood to include all those national judging communities represented by state governments at the UN—the action could not be regarded as (universally) valid. However, it could be regarded as *warranted* for those who acted (although whether the particular means chosen to execute the judgement were warranted is another question).[85] This is so because the respect that identity politics demands for the situatedness of other-cultural interlocutors is owed equally to my own situatedness as a member of a (for me) primary judging community.

There are certain kinds of judgements that by their nature must be regarded as universally applicable, and moral judgements in hard cases are exemplars of these.[86] In such cases, we express our judgements in universal assertions of the form: "children should not be compelled to serve as soldiers; kidnapping is wrong." To the extent that we are alive to our immersion in specific cultural contexts constituted by particular background understandings, we are likely to suppose that any such moral judgement can only be justified by relativistic or culture-specific reasons. So we typically *infer* the existence of the implicit "I

85 I want to make clear that I am thinking of truly exigent situations in which judgements about abuses of human rights are assembled as grounds for coercive intervention of some form, setting aside questions of political will and material capability for the moment. Very seldom does such a situation arise in which what seems to be a simple choice between the judgements of one community over another confronts us; as Nedelsky notes, in most cases, such an either/or choice among communities' judgements "will not work well, either for the psychological integrity of the judge (assuming some real connection to the conflicting communities) or for the institutional efficacy of rights-enforcing organizations"(Nedelsky, "Communities of Judgement," at 24).

86 The argument in support of this point draws on material from Oman, "Paths to Intercultural Understanding," at 84–85.

believe that" clause preceding the assertion; yet the universal force of the moral judgement is not blunted by the explicit inclusion of that clause. Thomas Morawetz explains Wittgenstein's appreciation of this point in *On Certainty*:[87]

> It is a fallacy to say that because my claims, as seen by *others*, are "merely" personal and because "my certainty is my own" [§174] I ought to (or can) subject my own ways of proceeding to the same kind of scrutiny and evaluation as I do the claims of others. This is nonsense: what could I use to check my picture of the world and my practices as a whole but my picture of the world and my practices?[88] The recommendation that I treat my own claims as merely personal is incoherent. It involves the misconception that I can stand impartial between my own ways of proceeding and those of others.
>
> [...]
>
> I can admit the possibility that I will come to think differently (that "my eyes" will be "opened" [§578]) but I cannot accommodate this standing possibility ("so far as one can know such a thing" [§623]) by disclaiming my own certainty.[89]

Arendt's theory of judgement supports the argument that my situatedness in a particular (inter-)cultural context—that is, as a participant in specific communities of judgement—must be assigned as much significance as the situatedness of an other with whom I am trying to build understanding in order to enlarge my thinking and develop a shared *sensus communis*. In hard cases, I cannot but draw upon the standards of value that constitute the ground of my own situatedness and define my notion of personhood (however these may have been transformed through experience and past episodes of going visiting). Therefore, in such cases, when I am unable to understand or recognize the legitimacy of a set of other-cultural standards of value, I have no choice but to employ my own in exercising moral judgement.[90] At the same time, I always hold open the possibility of self-transformation through the discovery of "experiences recalcitrant to my way of understanding" that may be encountered in the process of seeking a more encompassing *sensus communis* by enlarging my mentality.[91] This perpetual

87 Ludwig Wittgenstein, *On Certainty*, ed. and trans. by G.E.M. Anscombe and G.H. von Wright (Oxford: Basil Blackwell, 1969).

88 Nedelsky points out that Arendt's procedure for seeking an enlarged mentality provides an answer to this question (private communication (6 June 2003)). I can check my picture of the world and my practices by referring to what I take to be the picture of the world and practices employed by others; however, it seems plain that such a procedure will serve as only an imperfect mechanism for such a process, since it would certainly not suffice for me to "check my picture of the world and my practices *as a whole* [emphasis mine]."

89 Thomas Morawetz, *Wittgenstein and Knowledge* (Amherst, MA: University of Massachusetts Press, 1978), at 134.

90 Orson Scott Card provides an instructive examination of this issue in his novel, *Speaker for the Dead* (New York: Tom Doherty Associates, 1986).

91 Morawetz expands upon this point: "Men do not 'know the truth with perfect certainty' [*On Certainty*, §404] because there remains a series of impotent possibilities—

openness to the potentialities of dialogical interaction precludes zealotry or dogmatism in intercultural relationships.

Awkward as this point is to make, it's important to make it because part of Arendt's appeal is the promise her theory of judgement seems to hold for resolving the moral and political paralysis that a serious acknowledgement of the phenomenon of situatedness often induces. Her theory offers a procedure for grounding non-universalist judgements via the claim of agreement that the *sensus communis* makes possible. But the *way* that Arendt acknowledges situatedness also has implications for judgements that fall beyond the ambit of the kinds of judging communities that she concentrated on in her own writings, like the competing communities just alluded to.

In such a case, moral respect demands that I continue in moral conversation with representatives of other standpoints and actively engage in the process of attempting not only to enlarge my thinking by seeking to engage other standpoints through dialogue and (informed) imaginative acts, but also to increase the *scope* of my enlarged thought. Nedelsky's efforts to initiate a discussion of the concrete means that can be employed to expand both our capacity for enlarged thinking and the scope of our enlarged thought are very helpful on this point; for her these tasks comprise the primary political challenge of expanding the *sensus communis* to include members of new judging communities.[92] However, she does not neglect to caution against the constant danger of using the judgements of such an expanded *sensus communis* to justify *raison d'etat* policies (in just the way that invocations of human rights are sometimes used).[93]

But a caveat is required here, for this danger of condoning or assisting the forces of continuing colonization by advocating the pursuit of universalizable, intercommunally determined norms should not be interpreted as a sufficient basis for denying the partial legitimacy of intercommunal norms that *are* forged under unequal conditions of power. Although Nedelsky and Young would regard the redistribution of power among judging communities that such a process might make possible as a fundamental justification of the search for an enlarged mentality based on an expanded *sensus communis*, such a redistribution among *national* communities is not a necessary condition of the legitimacy of intercommunal norms negotiated at the international level.

possibilities because they cannot be discounted, because life is unpredictable, impotent because the awareness of their possibility is not the sort of thing I can weigh as evidence for or against any grounded beliefs" (*Wittgenstein and Knowledge*, at 135).

92 It is not plain to me that the current formulation of Nedelsky's argument concerning the enlargement of mentality offers explanatory or theoretical purchase superior to that of the Gadamerian-Taylorean theory of "fusing horizons." This is a significant issue that must be addressed in any less preliminary treatment of judgement theory.

93 See Katarina Tomasevski, *Responding to Human Rights Violations, 1946–1999* (The Hague: Martinus Nijhoff, 2000) chap. 12, for a meticulously documented account of the implicatedness of state sanctions-imposers in the generation of the human rights crises they seek to use international sanctions to manage.

The dual character of law as a phenomenon that creates spaces for resistance and for oppression is a theme that has been the subject of penetrating analyses by a variety of figures, including Makau wa Mutua, Upendra Baxi, and Jeremy Webber.[94] And influential critics/proponents of international legal norms associated with humanitarian intervention such as Martti Koskenniemi and Craig Scott make this same observation in their own ways.[95] All concur that the challenge in situations marked by the simultaneous existence of relations of force and relations of justice is "not to deny the role of power, but to understand how standards can emerge from an interaction that is fundamentally imperfect, and yet acquire normative force."[96]

Thomas Morawetz—deliberative practices

A final approach to reconceptualizing the *sensus communis* and consequently, the foundation for a claim of agreement for rightly-constituted judgements can be developed on the basis of Thomas Morawetz's critique of the application of Wittgenstein's metaphor of language games to the debate over constitutional interpretation that flourished in late twentieth century American legal theory.[97] Morawetz asserts that his own conception of a "deliberative practice" does better justice to the way judges understand their own processes of judgement and their attempts to justify those judgements to others. For Morawetz, a deliberative practice involves "discourse with the shared purpose of forming and defending judgements," and his examples of such practices include judicial decision-making, moral reasoning and aesthetic criticism—all debates that "refer to widely shared

94 Mutua, "Savages, Victims, and Saviors," Baxi, *The Future of Human Rights*, and Jeremy Webber, "Relations of Force and Relations of Justice: The Emergence of Normative Community Between Colonists and Aboriginal Peoples" (1995) 33 *Osgoode Hall Law Journal* 623 at 628–629.

95 Koskenniemi, *From Apology to Utopia* (Cambridge: Cambridge University Press, 2006) chap.7 and "The Pull of the Mainstream," book review of *Human Rights and Humanitarian Norms as Customary Law* by Theodor Meron (1990) 88 *Michigan Law Review* 1946 at 1959–1962; see also Scott, "Interpreting Intervention" (2001) 39 *Canadian Yearbook of International Law* 333 at 336–338.

96 Webber, "Relations of Force," at 629. In arguing that the norms that evolve under such conditions of inequality are not inherently illegitimate, Webber differs not only with Young and Nedelsky, but also with a fundamental assumption of Habermasian discourse morality—the directive that the legitimacy of moral norms that emerge from discourse must be *equally* in the interest of all participants.

Note, however, that Habermas is talking about universal moral norms. Webber too might agree that for an intercommunal norm to take on a "universal" legitimacy, it would require a greater semblance of equality. But I suspect he would argue that if such norms are construed as simply universal*izable*, the very process of negotiating their application (and transformation) to encompass more and more communities would ensure a greater degree of equality.

97 Morawetz, "The Epistemology of Judging," in Dennis Patterson, ed., *Wittgenstein and Legal Theory* (Boulder, CO: Westview Press, 1992), 1. Morawetz relies, as do I, on his previous analysis of Wittgenstein's notion of a practice here, which he developed in his *Wittgenstein and Knowledge*.

activities and/or institutions in civilized societies ... [that] extend over the history of civilization and seem intractable."[98]

Deliberative practices allow for the "inevitability" of diversity within shared ways of proceeding. Even when participants disagree, "they recognize the argumentative strategies of others. They share a sense of what reasons are relevant to the common discourse. However, this ability to anticipate the range of intelligible moves and responses that other participants will make is understood as fallible, and challenges to this aspect of what might, once again, be described as our *sensus communis* can be accommodated. "If a response is wholly unexpected and seems unintelligible or nonsensical, one can construct the kind of conversational bridges that would make it intelligible. Of course, conversations sometimes take surprising turns within the bounds of these constraints."[99] The possibility of building such bridges will clearly depend upon the degree to which the thinking and the scope for the thinking of the participants is "enlarged" and open to further enlargement.[100]

Each participant

> will have a characteristic way of reasoning that cuts across the several deliberative practices in which she participates and represents an interpretive orientation to the world, a way of sorting out the phenomena of experience and making sense of them.

But such strategies are not independent of each other: "a part of each participant's way of proceeding will be a strategy for incorporating or dismissing the favored strategies of others."[101] So each interlocutor will in some measure take account of the reasons adduced by others, recognizing and anticipating similar moves on the part of others as part of the practice itself.

What this amounts to is a competition among the diverse strategies that comprise the deliberative practice,

> as there is no natural order of precedence among categories of facts, among categories of reasons and justifications. For example, psychological explanations are not inherently more basic than political and economic explanations, nor is the reverse true. Appeals to the inherent features of a work of art are neither more nor less basic a mode of justification (in esthetic reasoning) than appeals to the creator's intentions. In defending one's own judgement in a particular case, one is also defending one's *style* of judgement, one's way of ordering the data of experience to give some kinds precedence. The attempt to convince others is not only an attempt to make them agree with one's own

98 *Ibid.* at 9.

99 *Ibid.* at 9, n.30.

100 This is a delicate issue, for as Morawetz notes, "the publicly shared understanding of what moves are comprehensible ways of proceeding is what makes the practice possible" (*ibid.* at 9–10).

101 *Ibid.* at 10.

> conclusions but also to bring them around to deploying reasons in the same way.[102]

So Morawetz depicts the deliberative practice itself evolving over time, as the collection of strategies mutually recognized by participants changes (and not just by becoming more inclusive—some strategies will fall out of favour as the "epistemic gain" to be enjoyed by endorsing one strategy over another becomes apparent in the course of the exchange).

It follows that the legitimacy of what could be theorized as intercommunal norms understood within this paradigm of deliberative practices flows not just, as Webber would have it, from "participation in a common discourse through time," but from the fact that both the conventions of what constitute valid argumentative strategies and the standards of judgement themselves are open to transformation in the process of moral conversation.

Conclusion

Taking account of diversity, as identity politics demands, entails at the very least the problematization of universal claims to validity of moral and political judgements. What this preliminary survey has gestured at is a universal*izable* approach to taking account of diverse standpoints in the service of finding a way to justify moral and political judgements that are and are seen to be legitimate.

We have seen that in his theory of judgement, Kant is describing not *how* we judge deliberately and designedly, but *that* we judge socially. And Arendt develops this point in order to demonstrate the connection between judgement, its sociality, and the retrospective and performative nature of human meaning. In the idea of a publicly shared world and the justificatory notion of communicability/publicness that both Kant and Arendt treat, lie the roots of an answer to the dilemma of how we might go about judging deliberately, in order to change our judgements to make them more inclusive, and thus more justifiable—more broadly applicable, with a claim of agreement upon members of more and more communities of judgement. And here, the directive to enlarged thinking that originates in Kant and is so perceptively celebrated and developed by Arendt comes into its own. Contemporary Arendtian theorists reveal that "enlarging our thinking" is not just a *description* of what we do in fact do when our communities of judgement are homogeneous and the topic of judgement at stake is an easy case, but what we *ought* to do, when the communities of judgement are multiple, fragmented, and competing, and the judgement at stake concerns a hard case.

Despite the limitations of the incomplete theory of judgement suggested by Hannah Arendt, her work offers some powerful hints at the shape that a viable theory of judgement capable of legitimating or expanding international legal norms grounding coercive intervention might take. Nedelsky develops the Arendtian theoretical foundation for linking the limits of validity of a judgement

102 *Ibid.* at 9–10.

to the purview of a particular community of judgement, while acknowledging the complex difficulties that remain in defining the limits and nature of such communities. Young offers a cogent analysis of the Arendtian insight that only *relative* impartiality is achievable as a consequence of the situatedness of others. Arendt herself makes it apparent that in the end, moral and political judgements are always our own, grounded in our particular, enlargeable but inescapable standpoints and not always legitimizable to others.

3 Human security and Hannah Arendt's "right to have rights"

The term "human security" was coined in deliberate contrast to the traditional international relations concept of *national security*. This transformation of scale in the shift from the institutional and collective to the human and personal has the immediate effect of challenging the dominant realist paradigm concerning the purpose and conduct of states. It focuses our attention on threats to the well-being of individual persons, rather than the perceived interests of states, and in so doing fits with the human rights agenda; it supports an analysis that sees existential threats to human flourishing as rooted in the unrealizability in practice of the human rights of individual persons.

The vision of a responsibility to protect presented by the International Commission on Human Security (ICISS) assigned an integral role to the idea of human security. As previous chapters have outlined, the concept was intended to gesture at a theoretical basis for both the existence of the responsibility to protect and the way in which the responsibility should be implemented. Despite its ambivalent reception by the international community, the concept of human security adds an important dimension to the debate over the parameters of the responsibility to protect. It helps to clarify the underlying assumptions about human flourishing that justify extending the burden of the responsibility to protect beyond state boundaries and states. In the ICISS reading, human security also grounds the context-specific calculus to determine which measures are the appropriate ones to employ when a situation arises that triggers exercise of the responsibility. The hard choices about when coercive action to fulfil the responsibility is justified can be coherently and consistently anchored in the concept of human security.

Over the past two decades, the concept of human security has gained the support of a determined minority of international legal theorists and policy-makers. They see its potential to serve as a tool for mitigating suffering by drawing attention to the necessary conditions for human flourishing. In the broad and contentious human security discourse, the concept is generally agreed to refer, at a minimum, to the physical safety of individuals, with broader definitions encompassing economic and social well-being as well. These two dimensions of human security captured in the minimalist and maximalist readings are described as "freedom from fear" (physical safety) and "freedom from want" (economic and social security).

More than half a century ago, the forms of human suffering that are addressed today by "human security" policies were the subject of the political philosophy and activism of Hannah Arendt. Arendt's work on human security reflects her lifelong preoccupation with the conditions that give rise to totalitarianism, and her own experience of statelessness during and after WWII. Her most influential contributions in this field appear in *The Origins of Totalitarianism*, where Arendt develops an historical analysis of the emergence of modern statelessness, writing with a piercing clarity about the vulnerability of those who find themselves in legal and existential limbo outside the realm of membership in a state. It is in this work that Arendt proposes the recognition of a universal "right to have rights" as a means of eliminating the denuded form of existence of those who find themselves outside the pale of the law.

The endorsement of the concept of human security by some governments and INGOs today can be seen as a contemporary attempt, in a dramatically altered international legal and political climate, to achieve the same end that Arendt hoped to accomplish by introducing the idea of a right to have rights. This chapter argues that although human security has been quietly downplayed in recent years, Arendt's notion of a right to have rights offers a powerful source of guidance to those who wish to develop this unsettled concept in a way that primarily serves humanitarian, rather than strategic, goals.

Hannah Arendt and statelessness

In *The Origins of Totalitarianism*, Arendt surveys the historical circumstances that gave rise to the calamity of statelessness in the first half of the twentieth century. She observes that the condition of statelessness—of existing outside the protective/punitive legal and political auspices of a home state—was an anomaly during the opening centuries of the modern European state system, and was long dealt with by sovereign states as an exceptional circumstance through the right of asylum or the process of naturalization. However, with the post-WWI Minority Treaties and the waves of postwar refugees from Russia, Armenia, Hungary, Germany, and Spain, followed by the millions who were housed in displaced persons camps, internment camps, and concentration camps during WWII, it became impossible to continue to use these legal techniques to cope with the growing legion of *de jure* and *de facto* stateless persons. Their sheer numbers, as well as the increasingly complete juridification of the geography of the planet (by both national and global legal orders) militated against this traditional response. As a consequence, despite differences in their particular circumstances, what all of these individuals had in common was their estrangement from any body politic.

In this exigent condition of unbelonging, Arendt notes, human rights—theoretically independent of any institutionalized source of authority, and universal in application—become unavailable in practice to those who have no state to make good upon them. The stateless are stranded, Arendt maintains: thrust into an extra-legal lacuna that is antithetical to the pursuit of both predictability, and of the political action that disrupts predictability. With the loss of the legal and political status that entitles individuals to government protection, stateless persons find themselves unable to make use of their human rights. The conclusion Arendt draws from this situation is that once an individual is prevented from participating in any political community (whether, I would suggest, through the withdrawal of her citizenship rights or the dissolution of the polity in a failing state), she is in effect expelled from the category of humanity, her existence relegated to what Seyla Benhabib describes as "a murky zone between morality and the law."[1]

As Arendt explains,

> The calamity of the rightless is not that they are deprived of life, liberty, and the pursuit of happiness, or of equality before the law and freedom of opinion—formulas which were designed to solve problems *within* given communities—but that they no longer belong to any community whatsoever. Their plight is not that they are not equal before the law, but that no law exists for them; not that they are oppressed but that nobody wants even to oppress them.[2]

Human rights are thus revealed to be civic rights, dependent upon a political community for their actualization. Arendt concludes that "[n]ot the loss of specific rights, then, but the loss of a community willing and able to guarantee any rights whatsoever," is the most damaging outcome of statelessness.[3]

But why is this outcome—the loss of a community—so destructive to the flourishing of individuals? This question can be formulated as follows: since the inborn and inalienable Rights of Man proclaimed by the American and French Revolutions were fashioned to address precisely the situation of human beings who had lost political status and could no longer rely upon states to provide a context of law-governedness, how is it that when the stateless faced these same circumstances, human rights proved unenforceable? Arendt refers to this as one of the "perplexities" of human rights. She argues that human rights originally developed as a means of defending individuals against the social uncertainty resulting from the rising power of the modern state and the new forms of economic organization that appeared in the late eighteenth century. Prior to this period, Arendt suggests, "what we must call a 'human right' today would have been thought of as a general characteristic of the human condition which no tyrant could take away."[4] With the advent of the American and French Revolutions, the "regulative idea" of humanity replaced the transcendent normative sources of the past, and the standards of interpersonal conduct and mutual concern that had once been guaranteed by tightly-woven social networks outside the realm of politics, eventually came to be underwritten only by humanity itself.[5]

1 Seyla Benhabib, "Kantian Questions, Arendtian Answers: Statelessness, Cosmopolitanism, and the Right to Have Rights" in Seyla Benhabib and Nancy Fraser, eds., *Pragmatism, Critique, Judgement: Essays for Richard J. Bernstein* (Cambridge, MA: Massachusetts Institute of Technology Press, 2004), 171 at 183.

2 Hannah Arendt, *The Origins of Totalitarianism* (San Diego, CA: Harcourt, 1968) at 295–296.

3 *Ibid.* at 297.

4 *Ibid.*

5 *Ibid.* at 298.

But precisely because human rights were grounded in a universal human nature, no authority or institution was accountable for their enforcement. Consequently, it was only through their instantiation in the laws of particular states that human rights became a source of meaningful protection for individual citizens. With the historical linkage between the universal and ahistorical Rights of Man ascribed to an abstract and disembedded subject, and the self-determination of peoples achieved through popular sovereignty, this "paradox of democratic legitimacy"[6] emerged. Ever since, the exceptionless inclusivity implied by the notion of human rights has been contradicted by the (seemingly) necessary boundedness and exclusivity of political communities that take the form of nation-states.[7]

The significance of statelessness

For Arendt the greatest significance of statelessness does not lie in the fact that it is a condition of insecurity, but in the fact that statelessness makes it impossible to *become* secure. As Arendt puts it, the plight of the stateless "is not that they are not equal before the law [in the sense that their human rights are not respected], but that no law exists for them."[8] The stateless are, in effect, the rightless. Cut off from a law-governed condition, Arendt argues, individuals become "human being[s] in general," defined only by the "abstract nakedness of being nothing but human," "thrown back … on their natural givenness."[9] Prevented from participating in political community, they cannot come together to engage in the activities of promise-making and norm affirmation that are the indispensable bases for the *exercise* of human rights.

This lack of meaningful legal personhood bars the stateless from partnership in those moral conversations about our common well-being that Arendt regards as a necessary feature of a good human life. One of the pragmatic reasons why such conversations are so central to our flourishing is that they are the forum in which the norms that safeguard our daily lives are re-appropriated and made our own. The political community in the form of the state accomplishes this by providing an institutional apparatus and public sphere in which the legal norms agreed upon by citizens act—not to guarantee, but to *promote* a context of legality. In this context, the internalization of those norms—the sense among citizens of their rightness—fosters predictability: a certainty of expectations regarding the distinction between the legal and the illegal. The means that most effectively promotes this predictability in modern states is the recognition of human rights.

6 Seyla Benhabib, "The Philosophical Foundations of Cosmopolitan Norms" in Robert Post, ed., *Another Cosmopolitanism* (Oxford: Oxford University Press, 2006), 13 at 32.

7 Jürgen Habermas argues that the new forms of democratic citizenship arising in the EU in the early 2000s appeared to revolve around a cosmopolitan solidarity based upon shared allegiance to human rights. This example demonstrates that the question that faces us today is whether the achievement of public autonomy through democratic constitutionalism is inextricably tied to the territorial boundedness of modern nation-states, or whether new forms of political agency made possible by the contemporary disaggregation of citizenship can create alternative forms of public autonomy and accountability (Habermas, *The Divided West* (Cambridge: Polity Press, 2006)).

8 Arendt, *Origins of Totalitarianism*, at 295–296.

9 *Ibid.* at 300, 297, 302.

The right to have rights

The remedy that Arendt proposes for the condition of human *in*security—*de facto* or *de jure* statelessness—is the recognition of what she calls "a right to have rights." Arendt expresses the need for such a right as follows:

> The concept of human rights can only be meaningful if they are [sic] redefined as a right to the human condition itself, which depends upon belonging to some human community, the right never to be dependent on some inborn human dignity which *de facto*, aside from its guarantee by fellow-men, not only does not exist but is the last and most arrogant myth we have invented in all our long history.[10]

Arendt's right to have rights is an attempt to fulfil this prescription, amounting simply to the right of every individual to belong to a political community, and thus, to humanity.

The first "right"

However, Arendt's redefinition of human rights takes a form that can at first appear puzzlingly recursive. What does it mean to speak of a right to *have* rights? Isn't the "right to have" itself one of those "rights" at issue? Several commentators suggest that the key to making sense of Arendt's concept lies in the dual sense of right she employs. Both Frank I. Michelman and Seyla Benhabib hold, roughly, that the first *right* in Arendt's phrase can be construed as appealing to the injunction contained in Immanuel Kant's second formulation of the categorical imperative, which directs us to "[a]ct in such a way that you treat humanity—whether in your own person or in the person of another, always at the same time as an end and never simply as a means."[11] On this reading, it is humanity in the person of each of us that is both the addressee and the principal of Arendt's reimagined right to have rights. And yet, if this first right is an ideal entitlement attributed *to* each of us in our universality (and is at the same time a demand for recognition *from* each of us), that appeals to this universality for its peremptory force, how does this differ from, as Arendt says, "be[ing] dependent on some inborn human dignity which *de facto*, aside from its guarantee by fellow-men, not only does not exist but is the last and most arrogant myth we have invented"?

An alternative interpretation of the addressee of the first *right* in Arendt's expression is suggested by James Bohman's account of the "right to nondomination," a concept that is closely analogous in its purpose to Arendt's right to have rights. (Bohman follows Philip Pettit in conceiving of nondomination as "the capability to create and to be a full member" of a scheme of social cooperation.[12]) Bohman begins from the republican conviction that "human rights are not basic liberties or

10 *Ibid.* at 631–632.

11 Immanuel Kant, *Grounding for the Metaphysics of Morals*, 3rd edn. (Indianapolis, IN: Hackett, 1981), at 36.

12 James Bohman, "Republican Cosmopolitanism" (2004) 12 *Journal of Political Philosophy* 336 at 341.

immunities from interference but rights of *membership*" [emphasis added].[13] For Bohman, rights claims can only make sense if they are addressed to political communities that are the sites of rights construction in the first place. The proper addressee of the right to nondomination is, then, the community of humanity.

Arendt's self-consciously historical understanding of rights seems to fit neatly within the mould described by Bohman. While, Arendt says, for the eighteenth century "humanity ... was no more than a regulative idea," she asserts that by the mid-twentieth century, humanity had "become an inescapable fact."[14] This new situation, in which "humanity ... has in effect assumed the role formerly ascribed to nature or history, would mean in this context that the right to have rights, or the rights of every individual to belong to humanity, should be guaranteed by humanity itself."[15]

For Arendt, *humanity*—understood not in metaphysical terms, but as the empirical incarnation of the eighteenth century ideal—has become the addressee, and consequently the guarantor, of the right to have rights. A community of real individuals, comprised of those with whom I have face-to-face relationships as well as those whose standpoints are familiar to me primarily through acts of imagination, is therefore the addressee of the first part of a claim to a right to have rights.

In her interpretation of Kant's writings on aesthetic judgment, Arendt champions enlarged thinking, a process in which I "visit" in thought the standpoints of others, in order to gain a more general or comprehensive grasp of our common situation. By exposing ourselves to those who are differently situated, and then engaging in the mental exercise of trying to imaginatively grasp what those others see and experience from their different standpoints, Arendt suggests that we will be able to arrive at judgments with a "general" validity. (Such judgments cannot be *universally* valid according to Arendt because they are not transcendental in character as a judgment based upon an inherent human characteristic (such as dignity) alone would be; instead the judgments Arendt is concerned with are dependent on context and the particular situation of the judging subject.) The development of transportation and communications technologies in the twentieth and twenty-first centuries have made it increasingly possible for us to enlarge our thinking in this way. As a result, the overlapping local communities in which each of us participates are beginning to comprise a community of humanity in fact.[16]

13 *Ibid.* at 344.

14 Arendt, *Origins of Totalitarianism*, at 298.

15 *Ibid.*

16 This claim is developed in Chapter 6, below. Onora O'Neill develops a complementary argument regarding the nature of our obligations to distant strangers. O'Neill's "practical approach" to determining the proper scope of our moral concern for those far away requires us to investigate "what assumptions we are already building into our action, habits, practices and institutions." O'Neill concludes that in numerous prosaic activities—those of banks, importers, and broadcasters, for example—we treat "distant others as if they have the abilities to act and respond"; in other words, we unreflectively treat far away strangers as if they were agents and subjects. And she asserts that, on pain of inconsistency, "what we assume in acting, we cannot selectively revoke in reaching ethical judgments" (*Bounds of Justice* (Cambridge: Cambridge University Press, 2000), 192).

This tendency already existed and was noted by Arendt when she wrote *The Origins of Totalitarianism*. The result of this historical movement has been and continues to be the halting and imperfect development of a sense of solidarity with others that goes far beyond the borders of the states we inhabit. Just as has long been the case for national political communities, our communities of comity or business or shared political commitment do not individually encompass the whole (of the inhabitants of a state, of the human race), but they do overlap with other local and specific communities to a degree that generates the sense that the whole is imaginable in a much more fine-grained way than has ever been possible before. Such a solidarity is based upon our appreciation of the vulnerability to suffering we share with others, rooted in imagined or real experiences of "the damaged life" rather than a vision of the good life;[17] consequently, it might best be described as a negative solidarity, rather than a positive one. But negative solidarity is also a consequence of the extent to which our "world"—the public sphere of action and speech—depends upon plurality.

Much of Arendt's philosophical writing builds upon the phenomenological claim that our sense of the reality of our selves and the world is intersubjectively constituted. Indeed, plurality is one of the defining features of the human condition for her. When we are prevented from appearing in public space as political actors by the existence of tyranny or "mass society" or exclusion from membership, we are "deprived of reality which, humanly speaking, is the same as appearance." Our sense of reality is derived, Arendt says, from our common, or sixth sense, which fits us into the world. Statelessness cuts off our access to this common sense, and throws us back on our *sensus privatus*, diminishing our experience of reality, and draining it of meaning.[18] For Arendt, the concept of common sense captures the ontological insight that to live is "to be in the company of men," an observation so fundamental that, as she points out, the verb "to live" was synonymous with the phrase *inter homines esse*—to be among men—for the ancient Romans.[19]

Our world-creating participation together as human beings in public space(s) gives rise to our common or collective responsibility for recognizing the right to have rights. As Arendt explains,

> [t]his vicarious responsibility for things we have not done, this taking upon ourselves the consequences for things we are entirely innocent of, is the price we pay for the fact that we live our lives not by ourselves but among our fellow men, and that the faculty of action, which, after all, is the political

17 Jürgen Habermas, *Moral Consciousness and Communicative Action*, trans. by Christian Lenhardt and Shierry Weber Nicholsen (Cambridge, MA: Massachusetts Institute of Technology Press, 1990), at 205, cited in J. Donald Moon, "Practical Discourse and Communicative Ethics" in Stephen K. White, ed., *The Cambridge Companion to Habermas* (Cambridge: Cambridge University Press, 1995), 143 at 152.

18 Hannah Arendt, *Lectures on Kant's Political Philosophy*, ed. by Ronald Beiner (Chicago, IL: University of Chicago Press, 1982), at 70.

19 Hannah Arendt, *Between Past and Future* (New York: Penguin Books, 1968), at 73.

> faculty par excellence, can be actualized only in one of the many and manifold forms of human community.[20]

Arendt is grimly aware that relying upon the sense of common responsibility—the nascent, imperfect, and informal community of humanity—for the protection and realization of a right to have rights amounts to an act of faith. She herself cautions that "[i]t is by no means certain whether this is possible," and yet subsequent events have proven that the act of faith that Arendt endorses through the idea of a right to have rights is in large measure, justified. The sense of solidarity invoked in her notion of common responsibility has had tangible consequences: with the human rights movement and the remarkable post-war evolution of international law, the recognition that each of us belongs to such a community has undeniably grown; "the rights [sic] of every individual to belong to humanity" *have*, increasingly, been guaranteed in practice by our fellow-human beings.

That guarantee is not always a reliable one, as evinced by the recent histories of Rwanda, Srebreniça, Guantanamo Bay, South Sudan, Iraq and Syria; but as events in South Africa, Namibia, Cypress, Kosovo, and the Mediterranean have shown, it has sometimes made the difference between life and death. Arendt's sensitivity to the risk inherent in such a guarantee is highlighted by Michelman, who suggests that the likely purpose of Arendt's invocation of humanity as guarantor is to "point … to an irreparable groundlessness of rights, affirming our own precarious, existential, collective self-care when it comes to creating and maintaining in this world the conditions of civility and humanity for any or for all."[21] This reading allows us to attribute a consistent caution to Arendt regarding metaphysically grandiose assumptions about human nature. At the same time, it leaves space for acknowledgement of the aspirational and open-ended character of her conception of a right to have rights.

The having of rights

The second usage of *rights* in Arendt's "right to have rights" can similarly be interpreted in a republican vein. The terminal part of the expression draws our attention to the *conditions under which* the having of rights becomes possible. "[W]e become equal as members of a group on the strength of our decision to guarantee ourselves mutually equal rights."[22] Rousseau was the first modern philosopher to observe that the normatively binding quality of the decisions of a political (rather than an ethical) community rests upon our ability to regard ourselves as the authors of those decisions. We cannot understand ourselves as the authors of the laws and political choices of our community without enjoying legal membership—the substance of which

20 Hannah Arendt, *Responsibility and Judgment*, ed. by Jerome Kohn (New York: Schocken Books, 2003), at 158.

21 Frank Michelman, "Parsing a 'Right to Have Rights'" (1996) 3 *Constellations* 200 at 207.

22 Arendt, *Responsibility and Judgement*, at 43.

consists in the mutual rights we bestow upon one another ("there is no associate over whom [each member of the social compact] does not acquire the same right that he would grant others over himself"[23]).

This second part of Arendt's concept underscores the fact that we each attribute and enjoy rights in our particularity as members of specific law-governed, rights-bestowing political communities, in other words, insofar as we are recognized legal persons within identifiable states. Therefore, the addressees of this second rights claim are just those political communities that are (currently) competent to recognize such claims—those that have the institutional form of territorial states.

For Arendt, of course, our membership in political communities is not only a practical necessity in the preceding sense, but an ontological one, as well. Arendt subscribes to the Aristotelian and, subsequently, republican idea that belonging to a political community opens up a set of possibilities for self-realization through participation. Only as a recognized member of a political community can one participate in those fundamentally political conversations about our common good, about "what is beneficial or harmful, and hence what is just or unjust" for *us*, that Aristotle believed make possible an existence that is more than "bare life."[24] Indeed, for Aristotle the capacity to have such conversations is what makes us "political animals."[25] Consequently, in Arendt's view, human rights are seen as flowing from our *membership* in a political entity, rather than as prepolitical in character.

These rights together generate what Bohman has described as "the capacity for effective action" which makes it possible to participate in the necessarily communal task of pursuing predictable life conditions (which comprises one dimension of freedom). This ontological claim is separable from the practical arguments adduced by Arendt in favour of a right to have rights, but important to acknowledge when seeking an interculturally persuasive interpretation of Arendt's concept.

Why "rights"?

Arendt's right to have rights raises a further, often-overlooked question. Why did Arendt choose a *rights claim* as the best means of fighting the suffering of those forsaken by the governments of their home states?

As Bonnie Honig points out, the right to have rights is a polemical concept that serves as both a demand that everyone should belong to some rights-bestowing and -creating polity, and at the same time, a criticism of all existing political communities, insofar as we only *require* rights "because we cannot trust the

23 Jean-Jacques Rousseau, *On the Social Contract*, trans. by Donald A. Cress (Indianapolis, IN: Hackett, 1987), at 148.

24 Giorgio Agamben, *Homo Sacer: Sovereign Power and Bare Life*, trans. by Daniel Heller-Roazen (Stanford, CA: Stanford University Press, 1998). Agamben famously employs Aristotle's distinction between *zoē* [bare life] and *bios* [life constituted in a political community] in developing Arendt's conception of statelessness so as to highlight the disposable character of life unshielded from political calculation. (See Arendt, *Origins of Totalitarianism*, at 297, 300, 302.)

25 Aristotle, *Politics*, trans. by C.D.C Reeve, (Indianapolis, IN: Hackett, 1998), at 3, 4.

political communities to which we belong to treat us with dignity and respect."[26] Hauke Brunkhorst enlarges upon this deconstructive observation in discussing the process of constitutionalization: "every transformation from texts into norms … every legal instantiation of the constitution repeatedly forgets and excludes someone all over again, and never includes everyone in every legally relevant respect."[27] Arendt's promotion of the concept of rights is thus at least partially comprehensible as part of an immanent critique of the very need for rights as a means of protection against our political communities.

Ironically, however, Arendt's advocacy of rights, when considered in tandem with her passionate support for the republican political form (and that form's traditional emphasis upon boundaries as a defining feature of political communities), is frequently mistaken for principled support for a statist international legal and political order. In fact, Arendt's decision to couch her critique of the forms of human suffering engendered by statelessness in terms of a right to have rights is a pragmatic one, and is not indicative of any attachment on her part to a natural rights framework. While Arendt is often rightly interpreted as a critic of the idea of a world republic in a Kantian vein,[28] it is not at all clear that the corollary of her opposition to such a republic is that she regarded the state in its typical mid-twentieth century form as the only possible mode of mass political organization.

Like Jürgen Habermas, Arendt regards human rights as social constructs, but indispensable ones for functioning in the particular world we live in today. Arendt self-consciously invokes the language of rights only "*within* the horizon of a concrete historical form of life," as Lisa Disch observes.[29] In the still state-centric world of capitalist market economies that characterize (more or less) all variants of modernity, authors as varied as Habermas,[30] Jack Donnelly,[31] Rhoda Howard-Hassmann,[32] and Ann Elizabeth Mayer[33] have also argued that

26 Bonnie Honig, "Another Cosmopolitanism? Law and Politics in the New Europe" in Robert Post, ed., *Another Cosmopolitanism* (Oxford: Oxford University Press, 2006), at 107.

27 Hauke Brunkhorst, *Solidarity* (Cambridge, MA: Massachusetts Institute of Technology Press, 2005), at 67.

28 See, e.g., Hannah Arendt, "Karl Jaspers: Citizen of the World?" in *Men in Dark Times* (San Diego, CA: Harcourt Brace & Company, 1968), at 94.

29 Lisa Disch, "'Please Sit Down, but Don't Make Yourself at Home': Arendtian 'Visiting' and the Prefigurative Politics of Consciousness-Reading" in Craig J. Calhoun and John McGowan, eds., *Hannah Arendt & the Meaning of Politics* (Minneapolis, MN: University of Minnesota Press, 1997), 132 at 154.

30 Jürgen Habermas, *Truth and Justification*, ed. and trans. by Barbara Fultner (Cambridge, MA: Massachusetts Institute of Technology Press, 2003); Jürgen Habermas, "Remarks on Legitimation through Human Rights" in *The Postnational Constellation* (Cambridge, MA: Massachusetts Institute of Technology Press, 2001), at 113.

31 Jack Donnelly, *Universal Human Rights in Theory and Practice* (Ithaca, NY: Cornell University Press, 2003).

32 Rhoda E. Howard, *Human Rights in Commonwealth Africa* (Totowa, NJ: Rowman & Littlefield, 1986).

33 Ann Elizabeth Mayer, *Islam and Human Rights: Tradition and Politics*, 2nd edn. (Boulder, CO: Westview Press, 1999).

rights provide uniquely useful tools for: 1) resisting the forms of oppression and injustice that typify modern institutional forms, and 2) securing democratic legitimacy in political communities that have grappled with the fact of competing comprehensive doctrines.

And finally, again, by using the language of rights to articulate the need to safeguard the means of pursuing human security, Arendt draws attention to the fact that states remain, as Onora O'Neill puts it, the primary agents of justice[34] as we approach the middle decades of the twenty-first century.

* * *

In sum, Arendt regards membership in a politico-legal community as of fundamental importance to human flourishing, for both practical and ontological reasons. For Arendt, membership in such a community is the necessary prerequisite to participation in ethical and "jurisgenerative" conversations. For Arendt, participation in these conversations is an integral aspect of a fully realized human existence, and concomitantly, it serves as the only means of working to establish conditions of human security. The right to have rights is simply a tool to ensure that individuals have access to the still-dominant institutionalized form of such membership in a politico-legal community—that is, citizenship in a state.

.In recent decades, Arendt's right to have rights has been taken up and developed by political philosophers as diverse as Jacques Derrida, Seyla Benhabib, Giorgio Agamben, Joshua Cohen, Bonnie Honig, Serena Parekh, and James Bohman. But the treatment of the right to have rights that has done the most to change the existential condition of vulnerability that Arendt sought to remedy has arguably been the work of a network of civil servants, politicians, activists, and international relations specialists who have advanced the idea of human security. These proponents of human security include the staff-members of the UN Development Program and the UN Human Security Unit; members of the Human Security Division of Canada's Department of Foreign Affairs & International Trade (most notably, former Director Don Hubert) and their counterparts in the Norwegian and Japanese governments; Commissioners Amartya Sen and Sadako Ogata, along with other participants in the UN Commission on Human Security; Gareth Evans (former Australian Prime Minister), Lloyd Axworthy (former Canadian Minister of Foreign Affairs), and others involved in the International Commission on Intervention and State Sovereignty (ICISS); former Japanese Prime Minister Keizo Obuchi; former UN Secretary-General Kofi Annan; and participants in the Human Security Network, as well as the World Federalists and numerous other INGOs. Although most of these individuals and groups would not recognize Arendt's right to have rights as the progenitor of the idea of human security, the debate over cosmopolitan norms that has culminated in the legal and policy concept of human security began with Arendt's work on the right to have rights. I will argue below that the connection between Arendt's concept and human security should not be allowed to remain solely one of historical provenance. Arendt's idea of a right to have rights offers a valuable

34 O'Neill, "Agents of Justice" (2001) 32 *Metaphilosophy* 180.

source of guidance in fleshing out the content of the still-unsettled concept of human security.

The transformation of international law

In 1951, Arendt wrote that the idea of humanity "transcends the present sphere of international law which still operates in terms of reciprocal agreements and treaties between sovereign states, and, *for the time being*, a sphere that is above nations does not exist" [emphasis added].[35] But since the end of WWII, a new space in which the idea of humanity could function as the guarantor of human rights has emerged, a transnational *inter est*—an in-between that connects and separates us, which we experience as members of a common world. This sphere has been created largely as a consequence of technological developments in communications and transportation, and subsequent increases in the speed and frequency of international economic, cultural, and political interactions; it has been nourished by, and has in turn encouraged, the rapid development of international law and a global human rights culture.

Key elements in the expansion of international law to encompass human protection concerns include the Charter of the United Nations (1945), the Universal Declaration of Human Rights (1948), the International Covenants on Civil and Political Rights and on Economic, Social, and Cultural Rights (1966), and the regional human rights conventions that have been established in Africa, the Americas, and Europe.[36] United Nations (UN) human rights conventions on the subjects of genocide, refugees, migrant workers, racial and gender-based discrimination, human trafficking, torture, and children's rights have been widely endorsed. In addition, a variety of international instruments designed to limit the harm caused to individuals by sources as diverse as land mines, small arms, and the market in conflict (blood) diamonds have enjoyed broad support. Finally, following the creation of ad hoc International Criminal Tribunals to prosecute crimes that occurred during intra-state conflicts in the former Yugoslavia and Rwanda, as well as a series of collaborative and ad hoc Special Courts (i.e., Sierra Leone, East Timor, Lebanon, Cambodia), the work of the International Law Commission culminated in the establishment of an International Criminal Court charged with prosecuting genocide, war crimes, crimes against humanity, and the crime of aggression.

35 Arendt, *Origins of Totalitarianism*, at 298.

36 These regional human rights instruments include the American Declaration of the Rights and Duties of Man (1948), the European Convention on the Protection of Human Rights and Fundamental Freedoms (1953), the American Convention on Human Rights (1978), and the African Charter on Human and Peoples' Rights (1986). In addition, the Organization of American States, EU, and African Union have all established institutions to implement and monitor these agreements, such as, for example, the African Court on Human and Peoples' Rights and the Inter-American Commission on Human Rights. Nonbinding declarations have also been adopted by other regional groups, for example, The Cairo Declaration on Human Rights in Islam (1990), adopted by the Organization of the Islamic Conference (now the Organization of Islamic Cooperation).

However, despite this remarkable evidence of the existence of a form of solidarity that makes humanity an imaginable reality (if not a functioning political community), it is apparent that we now face a "paradox of humanitarianism drowned in human disaster."[37] Widespread human rights abuses, including ethnic cleansing and genocide, have continued to occur throughout the period in which international human rights instruments have proliferated, and have never garnered greater attention than in the post-Cold War period. As the preceding list makes evident, ample international legal means now exist to address these destructive and destabilizing acts (which are regularly the causes or consequences of statelessness). However, the political will to enforce the human rights necessary to protect human beings in stateless or analogous circumstances from extreme vulnerability has been slower to develop. In addition, the UN's ability to fulfil its universalist and cosmopolitan commitment to protecting the human rights of all human beings has been impeded by the nature of the UN's collective (national) security structure, which is premised upon acceptance of the particularity of states' internal political, social, and economic arrangements.

Human security is a concept that was envisioned as a means of resolving the tension between these contradictory commitments of the UN; and in the context of the responsibility to protect, of galvanizing the political will that has sometimes been lacking when the well-being of distant populations is under threat.

Human security

The idea of human security initially enjoyed a meteoric rise to prominence in the realms of both international policy-making and international law. Its nearest historical rivals in this regard are human rights and development—two concepts which, on certain readings, it encompasses. Human security became linked with both of these ideas when it entered the lexicon of international policymaking through the 1994 UN *Human Development Report*, which defined it as comprising economic, food, health, environmental, personal, community, and political security.[38] These forms of security fall into two general categories, as the *Report*'s authors point out: those that aim at shielding individuals from chronic threats (both natural and human-made), and those that seek to protect people "from sudden and hurtful disruptions in the patterns of daily life—whether in homes, in jobs, or in communities."[39] The concept was taken up enthusiastically by members of the international community, with two distinct, but not antithetical interpretations of its content prevailing.

The Japanese government of Keizo Obuchi endorsed an ambitious definition of human security focusing on "freedom from want," which followed the United

37 Costas Douzinas, "Postmodern Just Wars and the New World Order" (2006) 5 *Journal of Human Rights* 355 at 355.

38 New Dimensions of Human Security (1994), online at http://hdr.undp.org/en/reports/global/hdr1994/, at 24–25.

39 *Ibid.* at 23.

Nations Development Program's lead in underscoring the role of development in generating the conditions for broadly-conceived human flourishing.

> Japan emphasizes "Human Security" from the perspective of strengthening efforts to cope with threats to human lives, livelihoods and dignity as poverty, environmental degradation, illicit drugs, transnational organized crime, infectious diseases such as HIV/AIDS, the outflow of refugees and anti-personnel land mines, and has taken various initiatives in this context. To ensure "Human freedom and potential," a range of issues needs to be addressed from the perspective of "Human Security" focused on the individual, requiring cooperation among the various actors in the international community, including governments, international organizations and civil society.[40]

The Canadian and Norwegian governments in turn elaborated a more modest vision of human security as "freedom from fear"; this view focused on the task of removing immediate threats to bodily security.[41]

> In our increasingly interconnected world, the insecurity of others—sooner or later—becomes a matter of our own insecurity. Protecting people in our global community, and building a sustainable foundation for peace, is a clear and pressing priority. For Canada, human security is an approach to foreign policy that puts people—their rights, their safety and their lives—first. Our objective is to build a world where universal humanitarian standards and the rule of law protect all people; where those who violate these standards are held accountable; and where our international institutions are equipped to defend and enforce those standards. In short, a world where people can live in freedom from fear.[42]

Much of the human security community has since adopted some form of dual commitment to both the freedom from fear and freedom from want approaches exemplified by the preceding statements.[43]

40 Diplomatic Bluebook (1999), Ministry of Foreign Affairs of Japan, online at www.mofa.go.jp.

41 Foreign Policy, Foreign Affairs and International Trade Canada, online at http://geo.international.gc.ca/cip-pic/cip-pic/aboutthegbp-en.aspx. (With changes of government, Canada's foreign policy commitment to human security has undergone significant alterations. In May 2008, the Human Security Program, once the centrepiece of Canada's foreign policy, was renamed, and all references to the concept of human security were removed from government webpages regarding the program.)

42 Human Security Program Policy Statement (2005), Government of Canada, online at www.humansecurity.gc.ca/psh-en.asp.

43 A typical example of such a definition:

> Human security means … protecting people from critical and pervasive threats and situations, building on their strengths and aspirations. It also means creating systems that give people the building blocks of survival, dignity and livelihood. Human security connects different types of freedoms—freedom from want, freedom from

Plainly, the view of human security that accords most closely with Arendt's understanding of the right to have rights is the minimalist one captured by the freedom from fear interpretation. Once the basic needs of survival have been met, Arendt regards the achievement of freedom from want as a goal that must depend upon a prior consensus among members of the political community about the *content* of human flourishing. For Arendt, the right to have rights is a means to the "enabling rights"[44] that allow us to build such a consensus within our local communities (and could, someday, provide the means to pursuing such an agreement among a global citizenry). When individuals are formally or systematically unable to participate in shaping political decisions, and this situation is not regarded by the organized political community as extraordinary, the right to have rights is denied and human insecurity is the result.

Human security has been employed to serve three dominant agendas in international politics. In a penetrating analysis of the relationship between the liberal peace project and human security, Susan Willett describes these as the agendas associated with the "emancipatory model" of liberal peace, emphasizing social justice concerns; the "orthodox or institutional model," focusing on freedom from fear issues; and the "conservative model" of the liberal peace, which "supports the theory that a global hegemon is a stabilizing force for the world."[45] Willett regards the hegemonic approach to international law and politics as antithetical to human security. However, it is evident that the language of human security, insofar as it is coupled with humanitarian intervention doctrines like the responsibility to protect, can be made to serve this third model of the liberal peace project as well. The account of human security that will eventually prevail, and the agenda that that account will (primarily) serve, has yet to be determined. But the most prominent of the current interpretations of human security is the one associated with the responsibility to protect; as will be apparent, the agenda that the human security concept will most effectively further will be a function of the role that the developing principle of the responsibility to protect comes to play in international

fear and freedom to take action on one's own behalf. To do this, it offers two general strategies: *protection* and *empowerment*. Protection shields people from dangers. It requires concerted effort to develop norms, processes and institutions that systematically address insecurities. Empowerment enables people to develop their potential and become full participants in decision-making. Protection and empowerment are mutually reinforcing, and both are required in most situations (Commission on Human Security (1 May 2003), online at www.humansecurity-chs.org/finalreport/index.html).

The Government of Japan defines human security as *both* freedom from want and freedom from fear (see Human Security (19 November 2007), Ministry of Foreign Affairs of Japan, online at www.mofa.go.jp/policy/oda/sector/security/action.html). For coupling of the two concepts as early as 2000 see Kofi Annan, "Secretary-general salutes international workshop on human security in Mongolia" (Address delivered at a two-day session in Ulaanbaatar, May 2000), online at www.un.org/News/Press/docs/2000/200000508.sgsm7382.doc.html

44 Henry Shue, *Basic Rights* (Princeton, NJ: Princeton University Press, 1980).

45 Susan Willett, "Insecurity, Conflict and the New Global Disorder" (2009) 32 *IDS Bulletin* 1 at 1, 2, 5.

law and politics, which will in turn be determined by how the parameters of the concept's core and penumbral meanings are negotiated in the coming years.

The responsibility to protect

The responsibility to protect is regarded by many as a dramatic innovation in international law.[46] Advocates of this principle generally present it as a natural, if rapid, outgrowth of two related phenomena—the emergence of cosmopolitan constitutionalism (see below), and the evolution of sovereignty. In order to fulfil the universal commitment to respect and promote human rights contained in the first Article of the UN Charter,[47] those who support the responsibility to protect argue that a doctrine that provides for intervention across state boundaries for human protection purposes is necessary. As has been described in earlier chapters, this doctrine was first set out in the report of the International Commission on Intervention and State Sovereignty (ICISS). The Commission was established after the 1999 NATO bombing campaign in Kosovo, to examine the state of international law regarding such "humanitarian" actions. Its report identifies the responsibility to protect as an emerging international legal principle, grounded upon a universal commitment to human security.[48]

ICISS's account describes the norm as having two core elements: 1) states bear primary responsibility for the protection of their inhabitants; and 2) when human security crises are threatened because the "home" state abdicates, or is unable to fulfil, this responsibility, the residual responsibility to protect is borne by state members of the international community and requires them to take protective action.

These uncomplicated premises foreground the needs of individual persons and in so doing, effect a paradigm shift. The operative principle in responding to human-made humanitarian crises is shown to be the responsibility to protect, rather than a politically-contentious right to intervene, and the issue of the inviolability of state sovereignty is reframed.[49] The key to accomplishing this diminution of what many, until recently, regarded as a cornerstone of the international legal order, lies in the Commission's claim that sovereignty itself has been redefined in practice; the report purports simply to be acknowledging an already-established shift in the reality of sovereignty, and drawing the logical inferences it entails.

46 This view is not universally endorsed. Some authors interpret the responsibility to protect as simply a re-packaging of the well-established practice of military intervention in the service of the imperial interests of great powers. Stephen Krasner regards the hegemonic international law that such a re-presentation serves as the regnant mode of international legal evolution; Gerry Simpson sees hegemonic dominance by great powers as a dominant trend in that evolutionary process (Krasner, *Sovereignty* (Princeton: Princeton University Press, 1999); Simpson, *Great Powers and Outlaw States* (Cambridge: Cambridge University Press, 2004); see also Danilo Zolo, *Invoking Humanity* (London: Continuum International, 2002) for supporting evidence).

47 *Charter of the United Nations*, 26 June 1945, Can. TS 1945 No. 7, Article 1(3).

48 ICISS, *The Responsibility to Protect* (Ottawa: International Development Research Centre, 2001), at 15.

49 *Charter of the United Nations*, Article 2(4), 2(7).

As the authors explain, with the spread of democratic governance around the globe, sovereignty has come to be seen, not as vesting exclusively (or even primarily) in states, but as identified with the people who inhabit those states.[50] The inference suggested by this new definition of sovereignty is that states are *for* ensuring the human security of their inhabitants. And this is by no means a novel inference to draw—it dates back at least to the advent of popular sovereignty with the French and American Revolutions of the eighteenth century, and indeed, has its roots in Aristotle's assertion that the political community "comes to be for the sake of living, but ... remains in existence for the sake of living well,"[51] where "living well" is understood in the sense of living a good human life, a life in which specifically human flourishing is possible.

This claim that the provision of human security is the defining function of a state underpins the ICISS report's argument for the existence of a responsibility to protect in the following way. First, the report's authors present the concept of a responsibility to protect as a by-product of an effort to enshrine this new understanding of the state's defining function in law. Second, the report goes on to claim that states are not only legally responsible for ensuring the human security of their own citizens, but that they are also, in both a moral and legal sense, responsible for ensuring the human security of *other* states' citizens. Setting aside the question of why this should be so, the following implications present themselves.

1) When the government of state A fails to protect the human security of its inhabitants, the governments of states B, C, ... Z become responsible for fulfilling state A's mandate.

2) In acting to fulfil the defining function of state A, states B–Z may employ coercive methods up to and including military intervention without violating the UN Charter's proscription against interfering in the domestic affairs of other states. No explicit rationale is provided by the ICISS report's authors for this claim. However, one logical inference is that, in virtue of its failure to perform its defining function, the sovereignty of state A falls into "abeyance." The concept of sovereignty in abeyance, or suspended sovereignty, has an established lineage in international law, originating in four twentieth century cases involving extraordinary circumstances in which the sovereignty of a state came into question (International Committee of Jurists report on the Åland Islands (1920), and advisory opinions by the International Court of Justice in *South-West Africa* (1950), *Namibia* (1971), and *Western Sahara* (1971)).[52]

Although suspended sovereignty is not explicitly cited in the *The Responsibility to Protect*, it provides an obvious means of lending coherence to the report's efforts to

50 ICISS, *Responsibility to Protect*, at 13.

51 Aristotle, *The Politics*, ed. and trans. by Ernest Barker (Oxford: Oxford University Press, 1946), at bk. I, chap. ii. Aristotle refers here specifically to the ancient Greek *polis*, the most comprehensive form of *koinonia*, or community, that then existed. Its closest analogue today is generally agreed to be the state.

52 See Nathaniel Berman's excellent discussion of the history of this concept in "Sovereignty in Abeyance: Self-determination and International Law," in Robert McCorquodale, ed., *Self-determination in International Law* (Aldershot, UK: Dartmouth, 2000), 51.

reconcile the UN Charter's proscription against interfering in "matters which are essentially within the domestic jurisdiction of any state"[53] with the need both to conserve international peace and security, and to work toward the realization of the human rights guaranteed by the Universal Declaration of Human Rights. By implying that the very sovereignty of a state that fails to fulfil its responsibility to protect its inhabitants' human security is suspended as a consequence of that failure, the report suggests that the crossing of territorial boundaries by states B–Z no longer amounts to an incursion against the sovereignty of state A. Because the sovereignty of state A is in abeyance, it becomes impossible for states B–Z to interfere in its domestic affairs—state A cannot be regarded as *having* domestic jurisdiction in such a situation. Again, this radical reconceptualization of sovereignty is not fully spelled out by ICISS, but the report implicitly relies upon an argument of just this shape and size when it claims both legal and moral justification for asserting a responsibility to protect. And this argument in turn rests upon the assumption that the goal of human security is an uncontroversially universal one.

The enthusiastic embrace of both human security and the responsibility to protect by many western members of the international community failed to dispel these impressions. The responsibility to protect doctrine has been cited in an impressive array of international texts, including the 2004 report of the UN's High-Level Panel on Threats, Challenges and Change, former UN Secretary-General Annan's 2005 *In Larger Freedom* report on the future of UN reform, the final statement of the UN's 2005 World Summit, and Security Council Resolution 1674 (affirming the World Summit statement regarding the responsibility to protect). The principle also became the *raison d'être* for the creation of an advisory position to the Secretary-General during Ban-Ki Moon's tenure,[54] and received widespread discussion in the wake of the devastation inflicted on Burma/Myanmar by Cyclone Nargis as a possible justification for forcible delivery of emergency aid in May 2008. The concept of human security has been endorsed not only in conjunction with the responsibility to protect in these documents, but also on its own. In addition to the early advocacy of the UN Development Program, human security has been promoted by the establishment of a UN Trust Fund for Human Security and a UN Human Security Unit, as well as by the Commission on Human Security, and the multilateral Human Security Network. Human security has been cited at the Security Council level during open debates on Women, Democracy and Security (2005) and Children and Armed Conflict (2006), and in official correspondence between the Council's President and the Secretary-General.[55] It has been the subject of General Assembly Thematic Debates in 2009 and 2018.[56] Numerous INGOs and

53 *Charter of the United Nations*, Article 2(7).

54 Edward Luck was appointed Special Adviser to the Secretary-General on the Responsibility to Protect on 28 February 2008.

55 *Letter dated 28 November 2007 from the Secretary-General addressed to the President of the Security Council*, UNSC, UN Doc. S/2007/753 (21 December 2007), online at http://undocs.org/S/2007/753.

56 Summaries of UN General Assembly Debates and Interactive Dialogues on R2P, Global Centre for the Responsibility to Protect, online at www.globalr2p.org/resources/897

national government programs and institutes, including, for example, the multiregional Friends of Human Security, the Japan International Cooperation Agency, the African Human Security Initiative, the Canadian Consortium on Human Security, and the World Federalists have also taken this principle as their inspiration. But like other contentious international legal concepts such as terrorism and the right of self-determination, the concept of human security has been left almost completely undefined in the conventional documents and resolutions that cite it.

This artful ambiguity accommodates the temptation to understand the responsibility to protect as the apotheosis of a linear evolution of international law toward the juridification of cosmopolitan norms. As long as a suitable definition of human security is adopted, the responsibility to protect can easily be interpreted as a legalized version of Arendt's notion of collective responsibility—the answer, in fact, to her frustrated lament regarding the impossibility of an international criminal tribunal,[57] just as human security can be viewed as the counterpart of Arendt's right to have rights. But while it is easy to imagine Arendt as an active supporter of some readings of human security, her record of critically scrutinizing the motives and beneficiaries of developments in international law suggests that it is unlikely that she would have countenanced a simplistic celebration of international law's moralization.

Arendtian observations on human security

The remarkable and rapid developments in international law outlined above are often interpreted as evidence for the spread of a common international ethics, associated with what Habermas terms "cosmopolitan constitutionalism." Cosmopolitan constitutionalism denotes a transnational rule of law in which solidarity is generated by allegiance to cosmopolitan norms—most notably, human rights standards—and global citizenship is realized through the institutionalized influence of varied processes of "democratic opinion- and will-formation" upon the development of transnational legal regimes and global policy outcomes.[58] At the moment, it is generally agreed by its exponents, this process is in the early stages of development; a "weak public sphere" that limits global citizens to "the politics of the appeal" is all that has been achieved so far.[59] However, authors such as Habermas, Hauke Brunkhorst, and Seyla Benhabib regard the goal of this struggle as "the completion of the constitutional project of 1789, which consists in the revolutionary correction of a blind constitutional evolution through the self-constitutionalization of democratic solidarity."[60]

This millenarian vision of linear progress, premised upon an unproblematic acceptance of the prevailing western vision of the rule of law, human rights, and democracy,[61]

57 Hannah Arendt, *Eichmann in Jerusalem*, 2nd edn. (New York: Penguin Books, 1965), at 298.

58 Habermas, *The Divided West*, 115–193; Brunkhorst, *Solidarity*, at 55–77, 113–162.

59 Brunkhorst, *Solidarity*, at 156.

60 *Ibid.* at 162.

61 For early critical analysis of this vision, see for example, Danilo Zolo, *Invoking Humanity* (London: Continuum International, 2002) at chap. 2–3 and Susan Marks, *The Riddle of All Constitutions* (Oxford: Oxford University Press, 2000).

is a narrative into which the concept of human security (and that of the responsibility to protect) can, on the prevailing reading, be seamlessly incorporated. However, Arendt's political conception of the right to have rights, and her critical analysis of its origins in late nineteenth and early twentieth century colonialism, demand a more austere and discriminating evaluation of the evolution of international legal protections for individuals in general, and the stateless in particular.

Bonnie Honig's reflections on Arendt's hypothetical response to claims that the establishment of the International Criminal Court in 2002 represented a "new normative and juridical universalism" are instructive in this regard.[62] Honig suggests that Arendt's original musings on such a court, which appeared in her discussion of Adolf Eichmann's 1960 trial on charges including war crimes, crimes against humanity, and crimes against the Jewish people in *Eichmann in Jerusalem*, were informed by two questions: 1) "what can we accomplish through law on behalf of human rights?" and 2) "what new political formations are being advantaged and legitimated thereby?"[63] These two questions also epitomize the spirit in which Arendt formulated the right to have rights. By asking these same questions about the emerging concept of human security, we can follow Arendt in performing a Derridean "double gesture" both affirming the desirability of the explicit goals of human security policies, and drawing attention to the political purposes that various versions of the human security concept might serve.[64]

In its ICISS reading, of course, human security is linked to the doctrine of the responsibility to protect as a new justification for the use of force in international affairs.[65] Human security is invoked in that context as the end whose achievement justifies both the violation of international law (in the event that Security Council agreement on the need for an intervention cannot be reached), and the deaths of innocents that will be an inevitable by-product of military action for humanitarian purposes. Arendt provides us with a precedent for understanding both the responsibility to protect, and the concept of human security that underpins it, in two registers simultaneously: both as evidence of the evolution of cosmopolitan norms, and as powerful examples of the moralization of international law in line with liberal values that serves the hegemonic strategies of western great powers and the interests of global capital.

Arendt's work on the right to have rights offers a corrective to the dominant construals of human security in a further, and more profound, sense. Human security advocates are, of course, primarily concerned with preventing widespread

62 Honig, *Another Cosmopolitanism*, at 103.

63 *Ibid.* at 104.

64 Jacques Derrida, "The Principle of Reason" (1983) 13 *Diacritics* 3 at 9.

65 In what follows, I will focus my remarks on the ICISS definition of human security because of its close connection to the influential responsibility to protect principle, and of the intercultural consultation process that gave rise to this relatively austere account (which encompasses elements of both the freedom from fear and the freedom from want agendas): "Human security means the security of people—their physical safety, their economic and social well-being, respect for their dignity and worth as human beings, and the protection of their human rights and fundamental freedoms" (ICISS, *Responsibility to Protect*, at 15).

human rights violations. It is often forgotten that the portrayal of such violations as a *security* issue is a political choice. The concept of human security de-normalizes the violations of human rights associated with civil disorder; the apocalyptic and urgent language of security replaces the familiar terminology of human rights and development, and in so doing transforms the import of these violations, and the response they elicit from us. Writing about HIV/AIDS, Stefan Elbe observes that the process of securitization "remove[s] an issue from routine democratic considerations and push[es] it into the higher echelons of the state's inner circles of power, where there is less political transparency and hence also less democratic scrutiny of issues."[66]

The upshot of this linguistic reassignment has been to remove human security from the public realm of the political, the space of democratic opinion- and will-formation. This repositioning occurs within the domestic polities of industrialized western states whose governments see themselves as the deliverers of human security to foreign populations, and also shapes expectations regarding the manner in which human security issues ought to be dealt with in countries regarded as the presumptive subjects of human security policies and interventions.

Arendt would likely have understood the securitization of human rights as part of a trend she attributed to the rise of the social sciences in the nineteenth and twentieth centuries. This was the tendency

> for government ... [to be] considered to be the appointed protector not so much of freedom as of the life process, the interests of society and its individuals. Security remain[s]... the decisive criterion ... a security which should permit an undisturbed development of the life process of society as a whole.[67]

The recent drift toward juridification of human security as a "right," is emblematic of this same process, and is indicative of what Arendt regarded as a deep confusion over what the having of rights means.

For Arendt, human security is not something that can be regarded as a right; instead, it is the proper subject matter of, and one of the most fundamental matters of concern for, politics. The state is today the preeminent venue of mutual recognition in which the constitutional norms agreed upon by citizens act, not to guarantee, but to *promote* a context of legality in which the internalization of those norms—the shared sense among citizens of their rightness—fosters an environment of predictability. Human security is thus understood by Arendt as an aspiration to be pursued through political action, rather than a right to be claimed.

For Arendt, "[p]romises are the uniquely human way of ordering the future, making it predictable and reliable to the extent that this is *humanly*

66 Stefan Elbe, "Should HIV/AIDS be Securitized?" (2006) 50 *International Studies Quarterly* 119 at 127.

67 Hannah Arendt, "What is Freedom?" in *The Portable Hannah Arendt*, ed. by Peter Baehr (New York: Penguin, 2000), at 443.

possible."[68] Again, promises, rather than rights, accomplish this task for us. The frailty and dependability of the promises that are made in public space are the frailty and dependability of human life itself. To attempt to transmute our reliance upon others—the essence of the human condition—into a rights claim we make against others grievously misconstrues the creative, risk-filled, and hopeful nature of political action.

Conclusion

The meaning of the widely-advocated, yet poorly-understood legal and policy concept of human security is not yet fixed. I have argued in this chapter that advocates of human security can find a rich source of guidance for developing this concept in Hannah Arendt's idea of a right to have rights. Arendt's notion, a philosophical ancestor of human security, shares key elements of the agenda of human security. Arendt's right to have rights emphasizes the importance of each individual's formal membership in a political community and her participation in political decision-making as prerequisites of the common pursuit of social predictability. Most human security approaches draw attention to the central role played by functioning political communities governed by the rule of law and respect for human rights in assuring that their citizens live lives free of violence.

Arendt's conception of a right to have rights assumes both the indispensability of political community and its fallibility. By drawing attention to paradoxical elements in the human condition, Arendt's analytic framework acknowledges that the instruments of law can always be deployed both in ways that further human flourishing and in ways that further projects of domination. It therefore helps to sensitize us to the variety of sometimes antithetical political projects that the discourse of human security can be made to serve, ranging from support from grassroots food security initiatives, through the imposition of low intensity democracy in the service of hegemonic international law.

Arendt's work also alerts us to the disconnect between the original interpretation of human security—that associated with the ICISS report advocating a responsibility to protect—which offers a traditional state-centric vision of the existing and future international legal order, and the innovative person-centric justification it provides for endorsing that vision. In so doing, it raises questions about the justifiability of the assumptions that states are the primary agents responsible for delivering human security, and that a state-centric international order is the framework that can best further the pursuit of human security.

Finally, Arendt's right to have rights cautions us against interpreting human security as a condition of predictability that can be guaranteed through the technical apparatus of law. Like the ancient Greeks, Arendt sees human life as defined by its very unpredictability and vulnerability. For Arendt, it is quintessentially a *political* matter to grapple with "the elementary problems of human living-

68 Hannah Arendt, "Civil Disobedience" in *Crises of the Republic* (San Diego, CA: Harcourt Brace and Company, 1972), at 92–93.

together" that human security seeks to address.[69] Her right to have rights seeks only to provide us with access to the public spaces in which promise-making and promise-keeping—the means that we use to craft always-evolving and temporary solutions to these problems—take place. Arendt's approach to the problem of human protection can thus be understood by proponents of human security as a call to *re*politicize the domain of politics. By valorizing public conversations about what "lies at the interstices of the instrumental and the moral,"[70] Arendt reminds us that the subject matter of human security must remain open to context-specific reinterpretation, that the relevant context may not be restricted to the political community of the state, and that if some are excluded from these political conversations, we all share a common responsibility to ensure their right to participate—their right to have rights.

69 Hannah Arendt, "Total Domination" in *Portable Hannah Arendt*, at 141.

70 Christian Reus-Smit, "The Strange Death of Liberal International Theory" (2001) 12 *European Journal of International Law* 573 at 585.

4 The scope of the "responsibility to prevent" atrocity crimes

A remit for intervention?

We find ourselves today in the midst of a paradigm shift in international law. INGO activists, international lawyers, politicians, and participants in the proliferating realm of transnational law are seeking a language for describing the role law is playing, and for conceptualizing the role law *should* play, in a globalizing and newly multipolar world.

For a quarter-century, many of these players were swept up by a wave of enthusiasm for the idea that international law was undergoing an inevitable evolution toward some form of cosmopolitan constitutionalism, a conviction that was fuelled by the rise in international human rights activism following the end of the Cold War. But a cascade of global events following the US-led invasion of Iraq in 2003, and the international community's muted response—including to instances of ethnic cleansing (Darfur, Myanmar/Burma), the suppression of democracy movements (Zimbabwe, Thailand, Hong Kong), invasions (South Ossetia, Georgia, Ukraine, the South China Sea), non-international armed conflicts (Syria, Ukraine, Democratic Republic of the Congo, Yemen), the protracted agonies of the global refugee crises, transnational interference in democratic elections and referenda (USA, UK, Kenya), and a deliberate assault on the World Trade Organization's ability to function[1]—have since stalled this wave, and left observers of international law and politics grasping for a conceptual framework to make sense of these developments.[2]

This moment shares important similarities and differences with the late-nineteenth century juncture when the old language of *jus gentium* was decisively displaced by a universal international law. At that time, the newly emerging positivist international legal order was grounded on familiar assumptions: that states are the sole subjects of international law, and that in the absence of any higher authority, they are bound only by their own consent—assumptions that are no longer tenable. This order was also, less explicitly, premised upon the existence of two classes of states: the civilized and the non-civilized. The "non-civilized"—generally non-European—states were excluded

1 Under President Donald Trump, the US government blocked the appointment of judges to the World Trade Organization's appeal body and threatened to withdraw from the Organization, considered a cornerstone of the global governance regime established in the post-World War II era.

2 This is, of course, a very partial list of examples of this phenomenon.

from membership in the Family of Nations that was entitled to the status of full legal subjects in modern international law.[3]

This latter postulate was reinvigorated in the post-Cold War period as a new, old way of thematizing the division between two contemporary groups of states captured the attention of international policy-makers and theorists. The groups are comprised of: 1) European states arising from the Peace of Westphalia and their settler-state heirs, and 2) former colonies and current satellites of the first group.[4] This more recent division bears ominous and unmistakable similarities to the earlier hierarchy. This account of the differences between western European-descended political communities and the "others" focuses on democratic governance, human rights, and human security—and asserts the existence of a schism between states that possess these attributes and those that do not. In the wake of the Cold War, a consensus developed among liberal democratic governments that the states which lack these features require them, not only for the good of their own citizens, but for the safety of the global community.[5] Qualms about the justice of imposing this vision of the conditions of human flourishing upon recalcitrant states that lack great power status (whether via United Nations (UN) assistance programs, the World Bank, the International Monetary Fund (IMF), or, if need be, military intervention) were soothed by the fact that this classificatory scheme implies a *de facto* moral hierarchy. Once it is accepted that the institutional structures associated with democratic governance, human rights, and human security are universal goods, it follows seamlessly that those states which support these goals ought to be regarded as good international citizens, "civilized" in the nomenclature of old. States that advocate political and social arrangements deemed to be at odds with these goals must, then, be viewed as bad international citizens, uncivilized and—as some respected academics have argued—unfit to be parties to the law of peoples.

This chapter takes a closer look at the agenda associated with this narrative of disjuncture. It does so by exploring the way that the policy goal of building human

3 Antony Anghie provides a penetrating overview of this transition in his *Imperialism, Sovereignty, and the Making of International Law* (Cambridge: Cambridge University Press, 2005); see also Marti Koskenniemi, *The Gentle Civilizer of Nations* (Cambridge: Cambridge University Press, 2001) for a slightly different but complementary periodization; and Nicholas Onuf, "'Tainted by Contingency': Retelling the Story of International Law" in Richard A. Falk et al., eds., *Reframing the International* (New York: Routledge, 2002), 26, who provides a useful survey of competing stories of international law's evolution.

4 BRICS countries (Brazil, Russia, India, China, and South Africa) and the Asian Tigers (Hong Kong, Singapore, South Korea, and Taiwan) don't fit this conceptual scheme, and for most purposes are awkwardly tacked onto the first group. In the 2010s, as the two most powerful BRICS countries, Russia and China, have re-emerged as systemic rivals to the US, they have been more explicitly associated with the second group.

5 This consensus has ebbed in the lingering wake of the security and economic crises of the 2000s and the systemic rivalries among China, a resurgent Russia, and the US that subsequently gathered force. The operative definitions of democratic governance, human rights, and human security have certainly become "thinner" as a consequence of these developments. However, as outlined in the following section, the consensus serves as the subject of this chapter because of the way it shaped dominant interpretations of the responsibility to protect.

protection capacity has been associated with the promotion of democratic governance, human rights, and human security, through various interpretations of the responsibility to protect principle. In particular, it examines assumptions built into the "responsibility to prevent" component of the principle as interpreted by the International Commission on Intervention and State Sovereignty (ICISS), and suggests that those assumptions may continue to impact the way in which "Pillar Two" of the UN's framing of the responsibility to protect is operationalized and implemented. The chapter's aim, therefore, is twofold: 1) to assess the merit of the template account of the responsibility to protect, and 2) to provide insight into the moral and empirical assumptions informing the larger project of democracy promotion which influential formulations of the responsibility to protect could be made to serve.

The responsibility to protect

As has been described in previous chapters, the 2001 ICISS report sought to address the issue of avoidable humanitarian crises by attempting to establish the moral and legal existence of states' responsibility to protect their inhabitants. On the Commission's interpretation, under certain circumstances this responsibility extends to include the inhabitants of other states who face serious human security threats.[6] As a result, the report contributes to the debate over humanitarian intervention, while trying to change the very terms in which that discourse is constructed.

ICISS's *The Responsibility to Protect* (*R2P*) weaves together both corrective and innovative elements in order to accomplish this. First, it emphasizes that military intervention should be regarded as the least desirable alternative among a range of possible international actions to address emerging human security crises that includes political and economic options. Second, the report focuses on the task of preventing humanitarian crises in order to minimize the need for considering any form of coercive intervention. Third, because it relies in part on a moral appeal, the *R2P* is able to hint at the possibility of morally justified unilateral or multilateral intervention for human protection purposes in the absence of Security Council authorization, under extraordinary circumstances.[7] Finally, the report reconceptualizes and defuses the challenge posed to state sovereignty by cross-border intervention in an original and persuasive manner.

In performing its reinterpretation of the concept of sovereignty as responsibility, ICISS relies upon the argument that the legal and political concept of sovereignty has undergone a significant transformation, and that the exclusivity and sanctity traditionally associated with it are legal fictions.[8] What are the moral and legal implications of this

6 International Commission on Intervention and State Security, *The Responsibility to Protect* (Ottawa: International Development Research Centre, 2001).

7 ICISS, *Responsibility to Protect*, at 55. As I will argue in Chapter 5, there are also plausible legal grounds emerging for such intervention, as well.

8 See, e.g., Nicholas Onuf, "Intervention for the Common Good," and Friedrich Kratochwil, "Sovereignty as Dominium," both in Gene M. Lyons and Michael Mastanduno, eds., *Beyond Westphalia?* (Baltimore, MD: Johns Hopkins University Press, 1995), at 43 and 21; W. Michael Reisman, "Sovereignty and Human Rights in Contemporary International Law," (1990) 84 *American Journal of International Law*

reconceptualization of sovereignty that underpins the assertion of a responsibility to protect? More specifically, what are the assumptions about morality that inform such a reconceptualization, and what are the implications of the *R2P*'s specific recommendations for the enterprise of international law?

The primary foundation for the responsibility to protect lies in "obligations inherent in the concept of sovereignty," according to the report's authors. These obligations are said to flow from the generally, or perhaps universally-recognized significance the authors impute to the need to assure "human security."[9] In making this claim, the authors of the ICISS report blur the distinction between moral obligations and legal ones in their attempt to redefine our understanding of the basis of sovereignty. Jürgen Habermas has observed that in contrast to our potentially unlimited moral community, "a legal community, which has a spatio-temporal location, protects the integrity of its members only insofar as they acquire the artificial status of bearers of individual rights."[10] The Commission's redefinition of sovereignty attempts to encompass those outside our political communities but within our moral universe, and then to legalize our moral obligations to them. How is this possible? The Commission provides no explicit theoretical basis for this feat of intellectual athleticism. However, in light of the traditional reliance of international relations theory upon a Hobbesian worldview, one obvious possibility is to infer that the *R2P*'s authors are implicitly depending upon a reworking of the classic Hobbesian social contract story.

Traditionally, this story justifies obligation on the part of the sovereign's subjects *internally*, and (less robustly) justifies both recognition and non-intervention by other sovereign states *externally*. If the sovereign can bring about an end to the state of nature by establishing order and thus protecting individuals from a war of all against all, it has fulfilled its (social) contractual obligation and in exchange, "deserves" to command the obedience of those within its borders; by commanding such obedience it wins the recognition of external sovereigns.[11]

(AJIL) 866 at 867–868; Susan Strange, *The Retreat of the State* (Cambridge: Cambridge University Press, 1996); Saskia Sassen, "The State and the New Geography of Power" in Saskia Sassen, ed., *Losing Control?: Sovereignty in an Age of Globalization* (New York: Columbia University Press, 1996), 1; Anne-Marie Slaughter, "International Law in a World of Liberal States," (1995) 6 *European Journal of International Law (EJIL)* 503.

9 ICISS, *Responsibility to Protect*, at 14–18.

10 Jürgen Habermas, "Remarks on Legitimation through Human Rights," in Max Pensky, ed., *The Postnational Constellation* (Cambridge, MA: Massachusetts Institute of Technology Press, 2001), at 114.

11 Of course, Hobbes does not present the obligation to obey the sovereign in quite these terms. Individuals undertake a covenant with one another to generate the sovereign in his version of the social contract. The sovereign's only obligation consists solely in refraining from killing the individual contractor on the occasion of the initial compact. However, there is a recurring sense throughout Hobbes' argument that the legitimacy of the sovereign is not fully accounted for by this contractual act, and that there is an element of "desert" to its authority to command the obedience of its subjects that that initial act of refraining is insufficient to explain.

The notion of a responsibility to protect could conceivably be interpreted as a logical extension of this narrative. First, it broadens the concept of protection to encompass more than just the negative benefit of ending systemic violence.

It mandates the more comprehensive and temporally extended good of human security, arguably including certain aspects of what is commonly referred to as "positive liberty"—the provision of which is now seen as an explicit responsibility of the state. If the government loses the ability to ensure the human security of its members, it would no longer routinely command their obedience, and would consequently lose the claim to external recognition. This part of the hypothetical rewriting of Hobbes' social contract theory seems not to constitute too great a conceptual stretch. The second part of the *R2P*'s hypothetical attribution is much more problematic. For if state A fails to execute its redefined responsibility to protect, the consequence is not simply that the populace has a legitimate right of revolution, as (arguably) in Hobbes,[12] and that state A loses to some extent its justification to claim recognition by other states, but that those other states actually become residual bearers of the responsibility to protect the citizens of state A. How can this be so? On what moral and legal bases do the members of states B, C, and D become responsible for the human security of citizens of state A in an international legal system (hypothetical and Hobbesian, but not so very distant from our own) in which only states have recognized legal personality? And finally, are these theoretical puzzles associated with the responsibility to protect too intractable to justify its endorsement? Alternatives to the classic positivist theory of international law, discussed below, might help to dissolve this conceptual logjam.

In fact, the legal machinery to establish a link between individual suffering and state responsibility is already in place, however inadequate the philosophical underpinnings of that apparatus may be. Read with a willing cast of mind, the Charter of the United Nations, the three elements of the international bill of rights, and the Convention on the Prevention of Genocide together provide as adequate a legal basis for *reactive* intervention as a widely-accepted norm of responsibility to protect could, when coupled with the same broad reading of "threats to international peace and security" proposed by the *R2P*'s authors and others before them.[13]

12 Hobbes is not generally interpreted as advocating a right of revolution. And yet, he says "[t]he obligation of subjects to the sovereign is understood to last as long, and no longer, than the power lasteth, by which he is able to protect them.... The end of obedience is protection" (Thomas Hobbes, *Leviathan: or, the Matter, Forme and Power of a Commonwealth*, ed. by Michael Oakeshott (New York: Macmillan, 1962), chap. 21). On the basis of such assertions, Alan Ryan concludes that Hobbes' theory, "built on rationalist and individualist foundations, must, in spite of its author's intentions, leave room not only for individual resistance but also *in extremis*, for fully fledged revolution" ("Hobbes' Political Philosophy," in Tom Sorell, ed., *The Cambridge Companion to Hobbes* (Cambridge: Cambridge University Press, 1996), at 241).

13 The triggering conditions for reactive intervention would almost certainly remain somewhat more stringent, however. ICISS provides a conceptual basis for broadening the definition of interventionary situations, and also suggests that intervention in the absence of Security Council authorization—ideally multilateral intervention mandated legally by the General Assembly under a "Uniting for Peace" resolution, and even perhaps (?) multilateral or unilateral action undertaken in accordance with the *R2P*

The ICISS account of the responsibility to protect relies upon a reinterpretation by the Security Council of the concept of threats to international peace and security under Chapter VII as a means of making violations of a responsibility to protect subject to legal amelioration through forms of intervention up to and including military intervention.[14] But nearly the same end could have been accomplished by updating the concept of threats to international peace and security without recognizing a responsibility to protect. In fact, as Vesselin Popovski showed in a study of post-Cold War Security Council resolutions, an interpretive revision of threats to international peace and security has been underway for some time.[15] One of the early examples of this process was SC Res. 688, in which the Security Council determined that the oppression of the Kurdish minority by the Iraqi government constituted a threat to international peace and security. This ground-breaking resolution was only the first in a series of Security Council resolutions that broadened the definition of threats to international peace and security to include serious human rights violations.[16]

criteria, but without UN authorization—could be regarded as at least morally legitimate, if highly contested, under the terms of the responsibility to protect. While I have grave concerns shared by many about action in the absence of multilateral agreement, I take ICISS's point about the need to circumvent the immobilizing requirement for Security Council agreement in exigent situations where the veto of a permanent Security Council member-state is an impediment.

The International Law Commission's (ILC's) *Draft Articles on Responsibility of States for Internationally Wrongful Acts*, is an alternative source of authority for a reconceptualization of sovereignty that accords with ICISS's vision, although it is a much more speculative and distant prospect for supporting legal actualization of a responsibility to protect (*Draft Articles on Responsibility of States for Internationally Wrongful Acts, with Commentaries (2001)*, online at http://legal.un.org/ilc/texts/instruments/english/commentaries/9_6_2001.pdf). There is some possibility that "humanitarian" intervention could eventually fall under the compass of "countermeasures of general interest," a category of acts notable for its absence from the ILC's final draft, but which nevertheless conditions the content of the draft Articles in significant measure (Denis Alland, "Countermeasures of General Interest," (2002) 13 *EJIL* 1221). As a necessary first step, violations of a state's responsibility to protect would have to be recognized as serious breaches of a peremptory norm of international law. (See generally, Pierre Klein, "Responsibility for Serious Breaches of Obligations Deriving from Peremptory Norms of International Law and United Nations Law," (2002) 13 *EJIL* 1241; Iain Scobbie, "The Invocation of Responsibility for the Breach of Obligations under Peremptory Norms of General International Law" (2002) 13 *EJIL* 1201; Christian J. Tams, "Do Serious Breaches Give Rise to Any Specific Obligations of the Responsible State?" (2002) 13 *EJIL* 1161.)

14 Martti Koskenniemi assails the legitimacy of such an interpretive move in his discussion of the history of institutional evolution at the United Nations in his "The Police in the Temple: Order, Justice and the UN," (1995) 6 *EJIL* 325.

15 Vesselin Popovski, "Development of the Ethical Principles of Intervention through UN Security Council Resolutions" (paper presented at the Ethics of Intervention workshop, Griffiths Key Centre, Brisbane, Australia, December 2004) [unpublished].

16 Many of these resolutions implicitly and explicitly rely for their justification on recognition of the "spillover" pattern that has typified intra-state conflicts in the post-Cold War era, beginning with Bosnia, Congo, and Rwanda, in which large-scale violence often spreads to neighbouring states with ethnic and economic ties to the origin state of the conflict (*ibid.* at 4). See ICISS, *Responsibility to Protect*, supp. vol. at chap. 5 for

In addition, legal means already exist to deal with the awkward question of the status of sovereignty during crises that trigger *reactive* intervention. The concept of "sovereignty in abeyance," or "suspended sovereignty" is an established device for dealing with acute situations in which internal sovereignty no longer exists for practical purposes.[17] This concept, elaborated most notably in the International Committee of Jurists' report on the Åland Islands (1920), and the *South-West Africa* (1950), *Namibia* (1971), and *Western Sahara* advisory opinions of the ICJ,[18] has recently come to scholarly attention once again as a consequence of the revival in interest in the international law of foreign occupation initially inspired by NATO's intervention in Kosovo. Suspended sovereignty has obvious application to situations of foreign occupation, international agreements that place states under some degree of international administration, and a potential revival of the UN trusteeship system, all circumstances which could arise in connection with "humanitarian" intervention.

There is, however, at least one contribution to international legal normativity made by the concept of a responsibility to protect that cannot be duplicated via existing legal mechanisms or theoretical orthodoxy. This contribution flows from what is described in the ICISS report as a state's "responsibility to *prevent*" human security crises, a constituent aspect of the umbrella concept of the responsibility to protect.

The responsibility to prevent

The ICISS report's authors describe the responsibility to protect as encompassing three component parts: the responsibility to prevent humanitarian catastrophes, the responsibility to react to such events when they occur, and the responsibility to rebuild after intervention. The responsibility to protect lies primarily with the individual state whose population is at risk, and residually with state-members of the international community when the state at issue fails to fulfil its obligation to ensure its population's human security. The state can fail in its obligations through incapacity, inaction, or as the perpetrator of policies that are the cause of a humanitarian crisis.

The *R2P* in turn identifies three types of preventive activity: early warning and analysis, direct prevention, and root cause prevention. Very briefly, with respect to *early warning*, it prescribes better analysis of data that is already available concerning brewing crises, and more effective "translation into policy prescription" of that data through a galvanizing of political will. The report argues that *direct*

a concise discussion of this characteristic of conflicts in Rwanda, Eastern Zaire, the former Yugoslavia, and East Timor, among others.

17 Alexandros Yannis, "The Concept of Suspended Sovereignty in International Law," (2002) 13 *EJIL* 1037.

18 Report of the International Committee of Jurists, League of Nations Official Journal, Special Supplement no. 3, October 1920; *International Status of South-West Africa*, Advisory Opinion (1950) ICJ Rep. 128; *Legal Consequences for States of the Continued Presence of South Africa in Namibia (South West Africa) notwithstanding Security Council Resolution 276 (1970)*, Advisory Opinion (1971) ICJ Rep. 16; *Western Sahara*, Advisory Opinion (1975) ICJ Rep. 12.

prevention measures must include political and diplomatic activities, economic measures (including both sanctions and inducements), and legal sanctions, including those made available by the creation of the International Criminal Court and the evolution of universal jurisdiction.[19] The *R2P*'s authors prescribe that these non-military direct prevention techniques should be supplemented by military means such as "stand-off reconnaissance" or a mutually-agreed preventive deployment of troops in order to make it absolutely unnecessary to employ directly coercive measures against the state.[20]

The most original aspect of the responsibility to prevent is the mandate it provides for interpreting *root cause prevention* as a key feature of the responsibility to protect. ICISS takes its inspiration for the discussion of this form of prevention from Article 55 of the Charter, which recognizes that "the creation of conditions of stability and well-being which are necessary for peaceful and friendly relations among nations" requires solutions to international economic, social, and health problems, cooperation in cultural and educational affairs, and universal respect for human rights. By adopting a broad definition of peace and security based on this Article, ICISS implies that a legal basis for Security Council intervention could be developed under Chapter VII, on *preventive* as well as on reactive grounds. ICISS downplays the possibility of non-cooperative root cause intervention, emphasizing the importance of cultural sensitivity ("it is important that developed countries be aware of the cultural barriers that may inhibit the interpretation of information … and that they … examine closely their own policies for evidence of their potential negative impact on developing countries"[21]) and the desirability of "maximum possible cooperation between helpers and those helped."[22] The report provides a general list of political, economic, legal, and military reforms that could fall under the rubric of root cause prevention. It prescribes support by external states for measures that "broadly fit within the human security framework," including the rule of law, press freedom, and democratic institutions, the evolution of civil society, and the delivery of more generous development assistance. It emphasizes that poverty, political repression, and uneven distribution of resources are predisposing factors that are widely recognized as contributing to the likelihood of armed conflict.

Of the three component forms of responsibility outlined in the *R2P*, it is the specific modes of root cause intervention justified by the responsibility to prevent that are most dependent upon the conceptual innovations associated with the responsibility to protect. For despite the fact that extensive social, economic, and political interventions have occurred and continue to occur in countries of the economic south—most notoriously under the aegis of the structural adjustment programs implemented at the behest of the IMF and World Bank[23]—little effort has been made to date to

19 ICISS, *Responsibility to Protect*, at 23.
20 *Ibid.* at 23, 25.
21 *Ibid.* at 23.
22 *Ibid.*
23 For analysis of the ideological impulse behind such programs, often dubbed the Washington Consensus, see Boaventura de Sousa Santos, "Beyond Neoliberal Governance" in Boaventura de Sousa Santos and César A. Rodriguez-Garavito, eds., *Law*

develop a legal-theoretical basis for those programs that could be interculturally legitimizable.[24]

However, the human security concept introduced in the 1994 UN *Human Development Report*, and adopted as the basis for the responsibility to protect, provides a rare credible candidate.[25] This concept aims to draw attention to the basic needs of individuals, and can on some readings imply "an ethical responsibility to reorient security around the individual in a redistributive sense."[26] Defined broadly, human security can be viewed as encompassing transnational economic issues such as global poverty, and as implying the necessity of a transformation of the existing socio-economic order. Its adoption by the UN was envisioned as a means of reforming the measures of development, until that time conceived primarily in terms of domestic GNP.[27]

This "developmentalization" of human rights was part of a larger transformation of human rights discourse that followed the Proclamation of Teheran.[28] In that document, human rights' unique international legitimacy was harnessed to an analysis of global

and Globalization from Below: Towards a Cosmopolitan Legality (Cambridge: Cambridge University Press, 2005), at 34.

24 Most of the efforts that have been made to link human rights to development have combined a push for liberal economic, as well as liberal political, reforms. However, more direct attempts have been made to harness the legitimating quality of human rights in connection with economic policies. Petersmann's proposals for an off-loading of international responsibility for the promotion and protection of human rights to the World Trade Organization constitute a particularly interesting example of this phenomenon. See Ernst-Ulrich Petersmann, "Time for a United Nations 'Global Compact' for Integrating Human Rights into the Law of Worldwide Organizations," (2002) 13 *EJIL* 621; Philip Alston, "Resisting the Merger and Acquisition of Human Rights by Trade Law: A Reply to Petersmann," (2002) 13 *EJIL* 815.

25 *Human Development Report 1994* (New York: Oxford University Press, 1994), online at http://hdr.undp.org/reports/global/ 1994/en/ at 22–46.

26 Edna Keeble, "Canadians and Global Beneficence" in Susan Sherwin and Peter K. Schotch, eds., *Engaged Philosophy: Essays in Honor of David Braybrooke* (Toronto: University of Toronto Press, 2007), 112, online at http://philosophy.dal.ca/Files/ Engaged1.pdf.

27 In the 1970s, a loose network of academics and activists began to recognize that deprivation is a result of factors beyond inadequate income, and that the once-standard utilitarian approach to measuring and determining the goals of development was unable to capture those factors. These critics argued that an approach to development that assigned primary importance to the GNP of a given state was simply defining the standard of living of that state's citizens in terms of the amount of purchased goods consumed by them, and was more accurately regarded as a measure of what Amartya Sen calls "opulence." The human security view builds on this critique, which sought to replace a preoccupation with opulence with a focus on quality of life; similarly, the human security view at the heart of the responsibility to protect aims to valorize the quality life of individuals, rather than the security of the state.

28 United Nations, *Human Rights: A Compilation of International Instruments* (United Nations Publications, 1993), 51–54; cited in Theo van Boven, "Human Rights and the Rights of Peoples," (1995) 6 *EJIL* 464. For an insightful analysis of the phenomenon of developmentalization, see also Balakrishnan Rajagopal, *International Law from Below: Development, Social Movements, and Third World Resistance* (Cambridge: Cambridge University Press, 2003), at 171–231.

concerns of particular importance to developing countries. The framing of human security as an aspect of the development agenda constituted a further step in the same direction, a kind of thematization of human rights in terms of their contribution to the goals of development and "democratic governance." The 1994 Report explains the link between human security and human development as follows: "Progress in one area enhances progress in the other.... [B]ut failure in one area also heightens the risk of failure in the other."[29] It is this understanding of human security that lies at the heart of the ICISS report.

Despite the centrality of this concept to the *R2P*, most of the interventionary activity endorsed by the ICISS report is justifiable via already-existing international legal instruments, as outlined above. Only the suggested modes of intervention that fall under the heading of the responsibility to prevent exceed those mandates. As envisioned in the *R2P*, the responsibility to prevent could conceivably be used as a *legal* basis for the extensive economic, political, cultural, and social engineering alluded to in the report. Consequently, I turn now to a closer examination of this key aspect of the responsibility to protect.[30]

The compass of root cause prevention

ICISS's international consultations revealed that even the states that asserted the most determined opposition to the idea of legalizing a right to humanitarian intervention endorsed interventionary action in certain extreme situations. ICISS set out to define, with as much precision as possible, the limits of these exceptional circumstances in which the responsibility to react is relatively undisputed. The report's authors outline six criteria for military intervention based loosely on the tradition of just war doctrine: right authority, just cause, right intention, last resort, proportional means, and reasonable prospects. The purpose of these guidelines is to provide a starting-point for developing broad-based international agreement about the kinds of situations in which intervention is necessary and appropriate, and to limit the potential for abuse of a prospective intercultural legal norm authorizing coercive intervention for human protection purposes. But although the authors take care to identify preventive responsibility as the foundational aspect of the responsibility to protect, they fail to define the parameters of acceptable *pre*-crisis intervention with similar precision.

The explanation for this omission may lie in the differential consequences of cultural relativism with regard to the problems of reactive intervention and preventive intervention. The task of summarizing the in principle agreement that already exists around the authorization of coercive intervention in exigent, "conscience-shocking" situations is challenging but feasible, largely because culturally

29 *Human Development Report 1994*, at 23.

30 Many of the criticisms surveyed in the next section will also have some application to the responsibility to rebuild; however, as the responsibility to rebuild plays a limited role in the World Summit-endorsed version of the responsibility to protect, length considerations preclude development of that argument in the present work.

relative values are not at issue. The kinds of threats to human security, and thus, international peace and security that are classified as sufficient causes of coercive intervention by ICISS are so extreme that the Commission's consultations revealed no significant opposition to them. However, the more amorphous root cause threats to human security identified by the Commission *do* involve fundamental issues of culturally relative standards of value, both with respect to the particular classes of situations that should be regarded as requiring intervention and with respect to the limits on intervention itself.

Triggering conditions for exercise of the responsibility to prevent

The state-centrism inherent in the ICISS report rests in part upon an empirical inaccuracy. The report's characterization of the capacity of states to perform the human protection function assigned to them by the responsibility to protect generally, and the responsibility to prevent in particular, is flawed. In its discussion of the responsibility to protect, the report relies upon a vision of sovereignty that assumes that states possess an unqualified ability to shape the life circumstances of their inhabitants. Much current research on transnational governance suggests that this vision is unrealistic.

Several decades' worth of social scientific observation and legal and political theory suggest that as a matter of empirical fact, many states simply do not possess the degree of autonomy and control over their populations' life conditions that would allow them to assure the human security of those populations as required by a responsibility to prevent. Saskia Sassen, Susan Marks, and Anne-Marie Slaughter have written extensively on the "disaggregation" of sovereignty that has occurred as an integral aspect of globalization. This is a phenomenon that Sassen says (with reference in particular to the virtualization of economic activity) "may be contributing to a crisis in control that transcends the capacities of both the state and the institutional apparatus of the economy."[31] While there is controversy over the import of this disaggregation for the future of states as actors in international society, there is little doubt that the proliferation of transnational and transgovernmental contacts (especially in the industrialized world of the economic north) is changing the balance of powers and functions traditionally exercised by sovereign states.[32]

As sovereignty becomes increasingly disaggregated in this way, the power to exercise authority over important economic, legal, and political decisions has become "unbundled." Sassen has demonstrated that this practical incapacity to achieve the requirements of a responsibility to prevent is characteristic not just

31 Sassen, "New Geography of Power," at 6.

32 For an early divergent assessment of the effect that globalization is having upon the constitution of traditional state sovereignty, see Christopher Schreuer, "The Waning of the Sovereign State: Towards a New Paradigm for International Law?" (1993) 4 *EJIL* 4, 447; and see also Philip Alston, "The Myopia of the Handmaidens," (1997) 8 *EJIL* 435.

of underdeveloped states suffering obvious economic or geographical disadvantages, but of highly developed and relatively advantaged ones as well.[33]

So as a matter of brute fact, partly as a consequence of the process of globalization itself, many states cannot perform the root cause (structural) preventive functions that a legalized responsibility to prevent would require. However, the ICISS report defines sovereignty in such a way that states under scrutiny—inevitably those of the economic south—will fail to carry out these open-ended preventive functions set out by the responsibility to prevent. And, because the report holds that a state's claim to sovereignty is partly constituted by its success in fulfilling the responsibility to protect (which encompasses the responsibility to prevent), the governments of such states could face challenges to their sovereign status if the *R2P*'s line of reasoning were followed to its logical conclusion. It is, in part, concerns about this conditional account of sovereignty that have constrained states of the Non-Aligned Movement from becoming supporters of the responsibility to protect, and consequently inspired UN efforts to reframe root cause prevention (see Chapter 6).

The danger here lies in the Commission's suggestion that the Security Council might expand the definition of "threats to peace and security" in Chapter VII *beyond* the list of circumstances justifying reactive intervention in the *R2P*, to include the existence of conditions—such as widespread poverty and a lack of periodic elections that meet international standards—that presumptively contribute to the emergence of threats to human security in a broad sense. The worry is that with little fanfare or explicit critical attention, the ICISS report's authors have provided a rationale for authorizing the Security Council to use coercive measures up to and including military force to intervene in states for the purpose of transforming political, economic, social, and cultural

33 Sassen's observations contribute to the discrediting of what Thomas Pogge refers to as the "purely domestic poverty thesis" (PDPT), a popular view which infuses discussions of states' failures to ensure domestic human security with a moralistic quality. Briefly, the PDPT holds that "the causes of national poverty and international inequality are purely domestic" (Pogge, "The Incoherence Between Rawls' Theories of Justice," (2004) 72 *Fordham Law Review* 1753). An exemplar of this thesis cited by Pogge occurs in the work of John Rawls, who holds that when societies do not thrive "the problem is commonly the nature of the public political culture and the religious and philosophical traditions that underlie its institutions. The great social evils in poorer societies are likely to be oppressive government and corrupt elites" (John Rawls, "The Law of Peoples" in *John Rawls: Collected Papers,* ed. by Samuel Richard Freedman (Cambridge: Harvard University Press, 1999), at 559). Both Pogge and Stephen Macedo make notably concise efforts to debunk the fallacious line of reasoning involved in the PDPT, in Macedo's case by relying upon Jeffrey Sachs' research concerning the signal contribution of geographical circumstances to persistent poverty (Jeffrey D. Sachs, "Institutions Don't Rule: Direct Effects of Geography on Per Capita Income," National Bureau of Economic Research, NBER Working Paper No. 9490 (2003), online at www.nber.org/papers/w9490), and by averring to the significance of states' particular histories of colonial exploitation and domination as well as the role played by international trade and economic policies "that allow rich countries and their corporations to exploit their advantages by making unfair rules of trade" (Macedo, "The Law of Peoples: What Self-Governing Peoples Owe to One Another," (2004) 72 *Fordham Law Review* 1728, and especially at 1726–1728).

conditions, simply because it is deemed that those conditions *could* give rise to future threats to human security. Given the recurring great power zest for intervention with the aim of "regime change," it seems conceivable that if the responsibility to protect were sanctioned in its unadulterated ICISS form as a guiding principle of international law, its constituent responsibility to prevent *could be* employed under the procedure outlined above as a mandate for undertaking sweeping legal, political, social, and cultural transformations of non-liberal states. By establishing the fulfilment of legal responsibilities that are impracticable for many states as a condition of continuing sovereignty, the responsibility to prevent could be invoked as a license for economic and political engineering in countries that lack liberal democratic political structures.

The liberal peace and the responsibility to prevent

The prescriptions associated with the responsibility to prevent rest upon a set of prevailing assumptions about the conditions that give rise to immediate threats to human security. The ICISS report's discussion of root cause prevention opens by citing Kofi Annan's assertion that "every step taken towards reducing poverty and achieving broad-based economic growth ... is a step toward conflict prevention." The former Secretary-General is further quoted as stating that preventive action must aim "to promote human rights, to protect minority rights and to institute political arrangements in which all groups are represented."[34] A useful first step in attempting to work out the implications of the responsibility to prevent is to identify the chain of assumptions and inferences implicit in the account of root cause prevention prefaced by these two statements.

Premise A1: It falls under the UN's competence (and that of ICISS) to devise strategies that will pre-emptively alter the conditions that give rise to deadly conflicts and to act upon those preventive interventionary strategies.
Premise A2: "Altering the conditions that give rise to deadly conflicts" is equivalent to fostering conditions that give rise to peaceful relations among states.
Premise B1: We know what conditions give rise to peaceful relations among states.
Premise B2: Those conditions possess economic and political dimensions.
Premise A3 and Conclusion B: If we reproduce the appropriate economic and political conditions everywhere in the world, peaceful relations will likely prevail.
Conclusion A: The UN should work to reproduce those economic and political conditions.

By unpacking the most problematic of these assumptions and inferences, it should be possible to develop a clearer picture of the possible consequences of widespread endorsement of the responsibility to prevent.

34 UN Secretary-General Kofi Annan, *We the Peoples: The Role of the United Nations in the 21st Century* (United Nations Publications, 2000); cited in ICISS, *Responsibility to Protect*, at 22–23.

Premise A1

The assumption that it falls within the legal mandate of the Security Council to employ its powers of enforcement under Chapter VII in order to pursue objectives of international justice is not itself uncontroversial. Martti Koskenniemi invokes the words of Sir Gerald Fitzmaurice (in his dissenting ICJ opinion in the *Namibia* case) to remind us of the historical limits to the purview of Security Council activity: "It was to keep the peace, not to change the world order, that the Security Council was set up."[35] This purview can of course be altered by the Council itself, insofar as it is empowered to establish the limits of its own jurisdiction.[36] The question of whether it should be is addressed below.

Premise B1

The next crucial assumption—that we know what political and economic conditions give rise to peaceful relations among states—is both popular and highly contested. Empirical claims concerning the existence and nature of a "liberal peace" forwarded by political scientists (most notably, Michael Doyle) have played a crucial role in lending credibility to this assumption. And in turn, influential scholars such as John Rawls, Fernando Téson, Francis Fukuyama, Robert Kagan, and Anne-Marie Slaughter have based their descriptive and normative work in the field of international law and international theory during the past two decades at least partly on their acceptance of these claims.[37]

The thesis of the liberal or democratic peace is based in large part on the findings of the Correlates of War Project (COW), an ongoing study that seeks to identify the factors associated with the outbreak of war and militarized disputes.[38] Doyle's original reading of the findings of COW was that "constitutionally secure" liberal democratic states have not gone to war against one another since 1816.[39] As an increasing number of states have acquired constitutional commitments to:

35 *Namibia* case, diss. op. Judge Fitzmaurice, 294, cited in Koskenniemi, "The Police in the Temple," 341.

36 The authority of the Security Council and other UN organs to establish these limits is dealt with in the *Certain Expenses of the United Nations*, (1962), ICJ Rep.151 at 168; cited in Koskenniemi, *ibid.*, n.70. See also Thomas Franck's brief but illuminating discussion of the origins of this self-interpretive power of the principal UN organs, at Franck, "Legality and Legitimacy in Humanitarian Intervention," paper presented at the American Political Science Association, Boston, MA, 2002 [unpublished], at 5.

37 See José E. Alvarez, "Do Liberal States Behave Better?" (2001) 12 *EJIL* 186. I follow Alvarez in preferring the term "liberal peace" to the more commonly-used "democratic peace" because of the superior precision of the former term.

38 See Susumu Suzuki, Volker Krause and J. David Singer, "The Correlates of War Project: A Bibliographic History of the Scientific Study of War and Peace, 1964–2000," (2002) 19 *Conflict Management and Peace Studies* 67.

39 Supporters of the liberal peace thesis often invoke Immanuel Kant's argument in *Toward Perpetual Peace* in support of their interpretation of COW data. Kant's teleological argument is frequently interpreted as predicting the inevitable development of peaceful relations among (roughly speaking) liberal states. See Michael W. Doyle,

1) the protection of basic civil rights, especially including juridical equality, 2) representative legislatures with authority bestowed by the consent of the citizenry, 3) private property rights, and 4) free market economies, Doyle suggests that a "zone of peace" encompassing these states has grown.[40] He explains this exceptional pacificity (which is limited to liberal states' relations with other liberal states) as a result of "conventions of mutual respect" that "have formed a cooperative foundation for relations among liberal democracies of a remarkably effective kind"; such relations mark such states as "fundamentally different" from those with non-liberal democratic forms of political organization.[41]

John Rawls is one among a number of authors who attributes the development of conventions of mutual respect to the internationalization of liberal institutions and principles. Rawls makes prominent use of Doyle's conclusions in his proposal for a theory of international justice that would apply to the relations among self-governing peoples, which he terms "the law of peoples."[42] Based in part upon the liberal peace thesis, as well as principles of political legitimacy, Rawls rejects the idea that all states should he recognized as formally legitimate as long as they possess an effective government. He introduces a tripartite distinction among states based on these criteria, distinguishing between liberal, hierarchical, and tyrannical regimes. The public conception of justice in liberal societies flows from a shared liberal understanding of persons as free, equal, rational, and reasonable moral agents; in hierarchical societies, the public conception of justice flows from the assumption that individuals enjoy rights only in virtue of their membership in social groups, and their political morality derives from that assumption. Both of these ideal-type societies are stipulated by Rawls to be "decent" and "well-ordered." "Decent" peoples are self-governing, pacific, and prepared to cooperate with other decent peoples. "Well-ordered" societies are "effectively regulated by a public political conception of justice."[43] In sum, "[d]ecent and well-ordered societies

"Kant, Liberal Legacies and Foreign Affairs," (1983) 12 *Philosophy and Public Affairs* 205, 323.

40 *Ibid.* at 207–208.

41 *Ibid.* at 235.

42 See John Rawls, *The Law of Peoples with The Idea of Public Reason Revisited* (Cambridge, MA: Harvard University Press, 2001) for Rawls' most developed account of the law of peoples. For incisive commentary on Rawls' international theory, see Fernando Téson, *A Philosophy of International Law* (Boulder, CO: Westview Press, 1998), 105–126; and the special issue of the *Fordham Law Review* devoted to a symposium on "Rawls and the Law" (vol. 72, 2004).

43 John Rawls, *Political Liberalism*, 2nd edn. (New York: Columbia University Press, 1996), 35. Rawls is seeking to use these terms of art to develop an idealized example of a non-liberal Muslim society ("Kazanistan"), and to that end, suggests that a non-liberal society might deny full equality to members of religious minorities or to women but still meet the criteria of decency. While such societies may place religious restrictions on eligibility for high government office, they respect basic human rights as outlined in Articles 3–18 of the UDHR. Rawls employs these definitions in an effort to reconcile the impulse to respect cultural diversity with the conviction that such respect should not serve as a carte blanche for the oppression of non-liberal others.

are not fully just by liberal lights but they meet extensive criteria of inclusion, voice, and responsiveness."[44]

Consequently, both of these kinds of states are "sovereign" according to the international ethics Rawls is proposing, and are shielded from coercion legally and morally by the law of peoples. But tyrannical regimes, which do not meet the criteria of decency and well-orderedness, enjoy no such protection. They are termed "outlaw states," "benevolent absolutisms" or "burdened societies" by Rawls. As they fail to meet the standards of sovereignty, they are not party to the law of peoples, and thus are not protected from intervention (*in extremis*) by moral or legal norms. The impact of prospective interventions on the individuals who are unfortunate enough to be born citizens of outlaw states is not considered in this moral theory of international relations.

Fernando Téson, in his influential 1998 book, *A Philosophy of International Law*, reaches similar conclusions to those of Rawls. On his view there is a division between tyrannical societies and politically legitimate (democratic) societies which distinguishes states capable of peaceful cooperation from those that are not. In practical terms, Téson's Kantian theory of international legitimacy causes him to recommend a range of exclusionary measures that include the restriction of membership in international organizations such as the United Nations to liberal democratic states; Téson further supports unilateral humanitarian intervention in certain exigent cases.[45] Building on a closely-related argument that also draws upon Kant's prescriptions for perpetual peace[46] and empirical data on the liberal peace thesis, Francis Fukuyama argues in several much-discussed works written following the disintegration of the Soviet Union that Kant's call for a "pacific federation" of republics (roughly, liberal democratic states) must be taken seriously.[47] He proposes that liberal democracies should self-consciously work together, both for collective self-defence and in order to "promot[e] ... the cause of democracy in countries where it does not now exist"; such a course of action would be, Fukuyama argues, "both morally satisfying *and* politically prudent."[48] Like Téson, Fukuyama suggests that it is the unique character of democratic political legitimacy that is responsible for the record of peaceful relations among liberal democratic states, and he, too, holds that this record can be maintained and extended only through restrictions on membership in international organizations based on a state's form of domestic political organization. In a more defensive vein, this view has been taken up more recently by Robert Kagan, who argues that "[t]he world's democracies are either supporting autocracy, through aid, recognition, amicable diplomatic

44 Macedo, "The Law of Peoples," at 1733.

45 For a detailed justification of humanitarian intervention, see Téson, *A Philosophy of International Law*, 44ff.

46 Immanuel Kant, "Toward Perpetual Peace" in *Toward Perpetual Peace and Other Writings on Politics, Peace, and History*, ed. by Pauline Kleingeld (Binghamton, NY: Vail-Ballou Press, 2006).

47 Francis Fukuyama, "The End of History?" *The National Interest* 16, (1989) 3, and Fukuyama, *The End of History and the Last Man* (New York: Macmillan, 1992).

48 *The End of History*, at 278.

relations, and regular economic intercourse, or they are using their manifold influence in varying degrees to push for democratic reform."[49]

Anne-Marie Slaughter reaches conclusions with similar implications in her important paper, "International Law in a World of Liberal States," based, again, on an endorsement of the liberal peace thesis.[50] Slaughter's project in that paper was to combine a descriptive account of a hypothetical world of liberal states with a variant of the liberal international relations theory of Andrew Moravcsik[51] in order to generate a model of how international law functions both among liberal states and between liberal and non-liberal states. (Slaughter has since changed the focus of her work significantly to take account of criticisms generated by the paper discussed here; more recently she examines the potential of government networks to promote states' compliance with transnational norms "in ways that facilitate the movement of people, goods, and money across borders," while simultaneously leaving space for what she describes as "informed divergence," or deliberately idiosyncratic normative choices on national grounds;[52] however, the impact of the classic paper discussed here endures, and continues to shape the democracy promotion project.)

For Slaughter, the operative distinction is once again between liberal and non-liberal states. Slaughter develops her positive analytical framework as a liberal alternative to realism in international law and political science. Her starting point is evidence pointing to "the distinctive quality of relations among liberal democracies … collected in an effort to explain the documented empirical phenomenon that liberal democracies very rarely go to war with one another" which she employs to identify behavioural distinctions between liberal and non-liberal states.[53] Her project is to "re-imagine international law based on an acceptance of this distinction and an extrapolation of its potential implications."[54]

This re-imagining takes a form familiar to readers acquainted with Rawls' law of peoples. Slaughter prefaces her conclusion with the observation that "the principles and postulates of classical international law have long been subject to numerous exceptions and modifications that reflect departures from the

49 Robert Kagan, *The Return of History and the End of Dreams* (New York: Knopf, 2008).

50 Slaughter, "International Law," at 510–14. Slaughter's definition of "liberalism" is distinct from Rawls', while sharing a number of common features with it. She describes liberal states as possessing a list of six correlative attributes that includes: peace, liberal democratic government, market economies, a dense network of transnational relations among social and economic actors, informal transnational and transgovernmental channels of communication and action that coexist with formal inter-state contacts, and a blurring of the distinction and hierarchy between foreign and domestic issues. Slaughter believes that this list of factors correlative with the liberal peace "can be translated into assumptions about political and economic relations among liberal States" (*ibid.* at 505).

51 Andrew M. Moravcsik, "Liberalism and International Relations Theory" (PhD diss., Harvard University, 1992).

52 Anne-Marie Slaughter, *A New World Order* (Princeton, NJ: Princeton University Press, 2004), at 213.

53 Slaughter, "International Law," at 505.

54 *Ibid.* at 538.

underlying positive assumptions of unitary and functionally identical States."[55] Her work simply attends to these exceptions, reconceptualizing the international system in a fashion that identifies and systematizes the regularities in what had historically been regarded as ad hoc and peripheral activities and relationships. As Slaughter observes in the same passage, imagining a world of liberal states is indeed more than "a purely hypothetical exercise." Slaughter's provocative and original observations concerning the processes of international and transnational governance, guided in part by the thesis of the liberal peace, lead her to conclude that a fundamental rethinking of the substance of the rules that define and serve international order is required. In this vein, Slaughter cites with approval Thomas Franck's argument that there exists a right of "democratic governance" in international law, the violation of which could serve as the basis for "an explicit [international legal] distinction among States based on domestic regime-type" and as a justification for coercive intervention in non-liberal democratic states.[56]

So once again, based on the liberal peace thesis, the claim is advanced that coercive intervention is not legally or morally proscribed when non-liberal states are its target. The arguments of Rawls and Slaughter—derived from premises not markedly different from those sketched by the authors of the idea of a responsibility to prevent—suggest the dangers that lie in a conflation of the activities of description and prescription.

But the true import of the liberal peace thesis' influence cannot be assessed without acknowledging the existence of arguments that question the very fact of a liberal peace. In protest of the seemingly axiomatic status that the liberal peace thesis assumed in international policy-making circles from the mid-1990s, there

55 Slaughter, *A New World Order* at, 213.

56 *Ibid.* See Thomas Franck's "The Emerging Right to Democratic Governance," in Robert McCorquodale, ed., *Self-Determination in International Law* (Aldershot: Ashgate, 2000), at 5. José Alvarez points out that Slaughter's support for coercive intervention in the service of liberalization predates the 1995 paper that has been the focus of this discussion of her views. Alvarez observes that Slaughter's conclusions in the 1995 article are consistent with those reached in a 1992 paper Slaughter authored (as Anne-Marie Burley), in which she claims that only liberal states can be regarded as operating within a "zone of law" (Alvarez, "Liberal States," at 184). Consequently, Slaughter (Burley) argued, the act of state doctrine ought to be used as a means of "nudg[ing] non-liberal states toward the liberal side of the divide" through the repudiation of the law of non-liberal states via the "alienage" classification (Anne-Marie Burley, "Law among Liberal States: Liberal Internationalism and the Act of State Doctrine," (1992) 92 *Columbia Law Review* 1907 at 1912).

On the problematic assumptions concerning "democratic governance" that can underlie arguments in favour of intervention in non-liberal regimes and the classification of governments as non-liberal in the first place, see e.g. Susan Marks, "The End of History?: Reflections on Some International Legal Theses," (1997) 8 *EJIL* 449; Susan Marks, *The Riddle of All Constitutions: International Law, Democracy, and the Critique of Ideology* (Oxford: Oxford University Press, 2000), at 50–75; James Crawford, "Democracy and the Body of International Law" in Gregory H. Fox and Brad R. Roth, eds., *Democratic Governance and International Law* (Cambridge: Cambridge University Press, 2000).

exists a veritable sub-genre of international theory devoted to debunking it. Critics of the thesis have assembled a case that convincingly demonstrates that while the inference that liberal states are less likely to go to war with one another is not conclusively false, it is at least assailable on numerous counts.[57]

Most notably, authors including José Alvarez, John M. Owen, David E. Spiro, Ido Oren, and Martti Koskenniemi cite methodological problems with the definitions of democracy and war used in the COW study.[58] Some critics raise questions about the statistical significance of the finding that zero cases of war between liberal states have occurred over the past 200 years, given the number and geographical situation of such states.[59] And other commentators flag the absence of a persuasive explanatory theory of the alleged phenomenon of a liberal peace.[60] In separate arguments, Koskenniemi and Alvarez each suggests that the absence of war between liberal democratic states is in fact best explained by its externalization to proxies in third party states. Consequently, the causal link that they regard the empirical data associated with the liberal peace thesis as identifying is not a link between democracy and peace, but rather between imperialism, development, and peace.[61] Like other prominent critics,[62] Alvarez applies this sceptical perspective not just to the liberal peace thesis itself, but to the arguments it has been made to serve. In considering Slaughter's use of the thesis as an explanatory factor in her analyses of states' compliance with international law, Alvarez concludes that, contrary to what proponents of the liberal peace thesis would lead us to expect, the empirical evidence suggests that "compliance with all forms of international legal

57 Criticism is not confined to Alvarez's comprehensive discussion (Alvarez, "Liberal States," at 184). See also Kenneth Waltz, "America as a Model for the World?: A Foreign Policy Perspective," (1991) 24 *PS: Political Science & Politics* 667; Marks, *The Riddle of All Constitutions*; Christian Reus-Smit, "The Strange Death of Liberal International Theory," (2001) 12 *EJIL* 573, and Martti Koskenniemi, "'Intolerant Democracies': A Reaction," (1996) 37 *Harvard International Law Journal* 231. A range of critical perspectives are collected in Michael Edward Brown, Sean M. Lynn-Jones and Steven E. Miller, eds., *Debating the Democratic Peace*, (Cambridge, MA: Massachusetts Institute of Technology Press, 1996); these include most notably, David E. Spiro, "The Insignificance of the Liberal Peace"; Christopher Layne, "Kant or Cant: The Myth of the Democratic Peace"; and Ido Oren, "The Subjectivity of the 'Democratic' Peace."

58 Koskenniemi, *ibid.* at 234–235; For a detailed discussion of terminological problems with the COW Project, see Spiro, *ibid.* and Oren, *ibid.* Oren focuses in particular on the value-laden definition of democracy that is employed in most analyses of the liberal peace data: "In all studies America receives virtually perfect scores on the democracy scale. America is the norm against which other polities are measured.... [T]he selection of the empirical criteria by which this abstract concept is described–primarily fair electoral processes and executive responsibility—is consistent with the dominant image of democracy in current American culture" (*ibid* at 266).

59 See Spiro's detailed analysis of the statistical significance of Doyle's findings (Spiro, *ibid.*); and also John J. Mearsheimer, "Back to the Future," (1990) 15 *International Security* 50–51.

60 See especially Layne, "Kant or Cant."

61 Koskenniemi, "'Intolerant Democracies,'" at 234; see also Alvarez, "Liberal States," at 243–246.

62 See, e.g., Marks, "The End of History?"; Koskenniemi, *ibid.*

obligations may not fall along 'liberal'/ 'non-liberal' lines" at all. With specific regard to a wide range of treaty regimes, Alvarez states that "the evidence that exists … does not support a liberal/non-liberal distinction with respect to the decision to be bound, the level of compliance after ratification, or the likelihood of resort to peaceful dispute resolution when treaty disputes arise."[63]

If we take these concerns seriously, we can only conclude that there are significant uncertainties and perhaps errors in the empirical claims underpinning the prescriptions advanced by Téson, Fukuyama, Rawls, and Slaughter that have led these influential theorists of international society to posit or recommend a legal distinction between the status of claims to sovereignty asserted by liberal and non-liberal states. These same empirical claims have served as an inspiration for the ICISS report's assertions concerning the necessity, normative appropriateness, and legality of wide-ranging transformations of the social, economic, and cultural institutions of non-liberal states.

Premise A3 and Conclusion B

Even if it were the case that a liberal peace existed, would it follow that reproducing certain features of liberal democracy in non-liberal states would prevent wars?

One problem with this line of reasoning is identified effectively by Amy Eckert in her analysis of the debate over the nature of the "right to democracy" or to "democratic governance" in international law. She deconstructs the arguments of two advocates of military intervention in support of such a right—W. Michael Reisman and Thomas Franck—and in so doing, reveals an important elision made by many members of the right to democracy camp.[64] Franck bases his claim that there is an emerging right to democracy on the synergy among pre-existing human rights. He regards the most important among these as the right of self-determination, understood as the right of a people "to determine its collective political destiny in a democratic fashion."[65] Reisman grounds his claim for the existence of a right to democracy in the argument that the sovereignty of the people has replaced the sovereignty of the sovereign, and holds that the exercise of a right to democracy is the only means by which popular sovereignty can be actualized.[66] Both agree generally that when the right of a population to democracy—understood as consisting in procedural liberal democracy—is violated, military intervention to restore that right is justified.[67] Eckert argues that in drawing this conclusion, both authors confuse the right of a people to freely determine their political status with one particular *outcome* of that process of self-determination: procedural liberal democracy.

63 Alvarez, "Liberal States," at 209.
64 Amy E. Eckert, "Free Determination or the Determination to be Free?" (1999) 4 *UCLA Journal of International Law & Foreign Affairs* 55.
65 Franck, "The Emerging Right to Democratic Governance," at 515.
66 Reisman, "Sovereignty and Human Rights," at 867– 868.
67 Although there are important points of disagreement in their views as to how such intervention might be undertaken legitimately.

The existence of liberal democratic procedures in previously non-liberal states is in itself no guarantee of political outcomes that would qualify those states for inclusion in the category of "liberal" states, and thus, hypothetically, as participants in a liberal peace. As Koskenniemi pointedly notes,

> it is not only, as J.S. Mill famously argued, that democracy and liberalism cannot be created by force (though that seems plausible enough) but that we simply do not know what "democracy" would mean for a Russian, Somali. Chinese, Algerian or other non-Western, non-liberal society.[68]

The assumption that liberal democracy is exportable ignores complex and unresolved questions about the extent to which it is a product of the specific cultures and histories that gave rise to its existing variants.[69] The idea that the substance of typical liberal democratic outcomes will be reproduced if the form of liberal democratic procedures is adopted imputes a universal and teleological status to one version of liberal democracy. And once procedural liberal democracy is assumed to be the universal norm, questions about the desirability of such an export and the neo-colonial agenda it may seem to serve come to seem irrelevant.

The prescription of liberal democracy as a preventive cure for war suffers from a serious logical weakness as well. For liberal peace proponents, the difficulty with moving from observations regarding the history of liberal states to prescriptions about how to avoid future wars lies in the negative character of the observations on which the inference of the existence of a liberal peace depends. The absence of wars between liberal states in the past cannot in itself serve as a persuasive basis for inductively concluding that liberal characteristics will insure states against involvement in wars in the future. Given the small sample size of states that meet the criteria of liberal democracy, the short timeline under consideration, and the lack of a broadly-accepted theory to explain the retrospective inference that grounds it,[70] such an induction cannot serve as an adequate basis for the prescription of procedural liberal democracy.

68 Koskenniemi, "Police in the Temple," at 343.

69 Hans Agné canvasses some of the methodological and epistemological issues involved in undertaking an analysis of such questions in his "Is Successful Democracy Promotion Possible? The Conceptual Problem," (2014) 21 *Democratization* 49.

70 The fact that no single theory is generally-accepted does not, of course, mean that such theories do not exist. Notable attempts to account for the liberal peace have been made by Bruce Russett, *Grasping the Democratic Peace* (Princeton, New Jersey: Princeton University Press, 1993); John M. Owen, "How Liberalism Produces Democratic Peace" in *Debating the Democratic Peace*; Doyle, "Kant, Liberal Legacies and Foreign Affairs"; see also Michael W. Doyle, "Kant and Liberal Internationalism" in *Toward Perpetual Peace and Other Writings on Politics, Peace, and History* ed. by Pauline Kleingeld (Binghamton, NY: Vail-Ballou Press, 2006).

Conclusion A

Even if the inductive move described above could be justified—regardless of our degree of certainty about the political and economic conditions that foster peace—Koskenniemi asserts that "it does not … follow that the [Security] Council should be empowered to make every state a democratic one." His comments on the evolution of the Security Council's self-defined mandate speak directly to the normative agenda of the ICISS report and its offshoots: "the extent to which a given policy or situation, national or international, might contribute to 'security' is merely one, and not self-evidently the most important, criterion whereby it may be evaluated."[71] Koskenniemi's point here is an often, if inexplicably, overlooked one: assessments regarding security and peace are inherently political rather than technical in character.

It follows that the shift from a traditional definition of international security, deriving from a "thin" notion of international order to the substantive one assumed by the *R2P* constitutes, at the very least, a failure to face a profound moral challenge by re-packaging an authentically political and ethical question as a merely technical and administrative one. At worst, this move could be construed as a Machiavellian stratagem for imposing an agenda for "democratic governance" on non-liberal states. Such an agenda aims to further the goals of trade liberalization and development, the imposition of which could erode the local legitimacy of those ends.

General conclusions

Whether the hierarchical categorization of states is based on their degree of adherence to a particular model of civilization or to a procedural vision of liberal democracy, these classificatory devices lend themselves to use as "weapon[s] to civilize the other."[72] Pratap Mehta observes that the enforcement of a legal distinction between liberal and non-liberal states would result in two classes of international sovereigns. A favoured category of states "that more or less approximate the ideals of democracy and human rights … would enjoy all the privileges and characteristics of sovereignty and the immunities it entails." The second category of "non-democracies" would be *de facto* candidates for intervention at the discretion of the members of the first group:

> Even those who have no doubt about the moral desirability of democracy and human rights balk at the prospect of giving a small group of states, usually ex-colonial powers, the moral authority to create a society of states in their own image, one in which non-liberal peoples have subordinate or no standing. On this view, while human rights and democracy may be good things, to use them as sufficient warrant to interfere in the affairs of other states would be not only to risk peace, concentrate power and authority in a few states, it would also be to arrogate to a group of states

71 Koskenniemi, "Police in the Temple," at 343– 344.
72 Alvarez, "Liberal States," at 245.

the moral authority that could not possibly be justified to participants in the international community.[73]

This vision of a two-tiered international legal order is an implicit, seemingly unintended, but unavoidable aspect of the ICISS report's discussion of the possible legalization of a responsibility to prevent. And as we have seen, it is one which disregards the reasoned doubts about the liberal peace thesis on which much of the argumentation in favour of such a division rests. As Alvarez insists, "the liberals have not yet made the case for abandoning the traditional presumption that, *at least in law*, states should not be judged by the color of their politics."[74]

Contra Mehta, I do not conclude from this analysis that genuinely *humanitarian* intervention—as might have occurred in the cases of Rwanda, Srebreniça, or Burma—should be relegated to an inchoate realm of "illegal but legitimate" activity because of the potential for abuse that its legalization might unleash.[75] Instead, I follow Jutta Brunnée and Stephen Toope in regarding international law as fundamentally aspirational. Their account of an interactional theory of international law draws inspiration from the neo-Aristotelian tenor of legal theorist Lon L. Fuller's writings. On their reading, Fuller regards law as an incomplete enterprise, a creative work in progress that exists by degrees along a continuum of normative legitimacy. This orientation leads Fuller to highlight the role played by the acceptance of the governed in constituting law and legitimacy. It results, for Brunnée and Toope, in a legal theory that emphasizes the latent persuasive power of international law, and leaves space for the theorization of its "persistently horizontal structure" as well as the nonstate-centred international legal relations that are problematic for positivist theories of international law.[76] This way of thinking about legal normativity allows us to conceptualize social justice activities coherently as an attempt to persuade in order to alter the dominant international legal and political semantics so that, for example, an alternative set of norms for conceptualizing and acting in the situations we describe now as *genocides* or *widespread, gross violations of human rights* are generated and "thickly" accepted.

There is of course, a risk in pushing the moral norm of aiding those at grave risk along what Fuller described as the "continuum of legitimacy"[77] toward its legal pole. Many commentators, notably Fuller himself, have noted the pitfalls inherent

73 Pratap Bhanu Mehta, "From State Sovereignty to Human Security (via Institutions?)" in Terry Nardin and Melissa S. Williams, eds., *Humanitarian Intervention* (New York: New York University Press, 2006), at 7.

74 Alvarez, "Liberal States," at 241.

75 Thomas Franck has argued in favour of the same conclusion regarding the desirability of an "illegal but legitimate" classification of "humanitarian" interventions, from a very different starting point ("Legality and Legitimacy").

76 Jutta Brunnée and Stephen J. Toope, "International Law and Constructivism: Elements of an Interactional Theory of International Law," (2000) 39 *Columbia Journal of Transnational Law* 22–23.

77 *Ibid.* at 69–71.

in efforts to legalize non-justiciable norms.[78] And yet, as Kenneth Winston points out, law itself cannot be defined unless we acknowledge that it is partly oriented toward ideals;[79] the moral commitment it calls forth on the part of its addressees flows largely from that aspirational quality. The success of the international human rights movement over the past five decades is often cited as a testament to the power such guiding norms can exercise on the behaviour of states and individuals.

Because interventions inevitably do occur,[80] international law can serve as a valuable tool in limiting the actions of the most powerful by shaping expectations about the criteria of legitimate intervention. By bringing intervention into the realm of law, we can build a framework for persuasion regarding these criteria. Such a framework would allow interveners to better demonstrate the felt rightness of an interventionary act, and those opposing intervention to appeal to explicit intercommunal norms that strictly circumscribe the conditions under which legitimate interventions may occur. The legalization strategy relies for its effectiveness on the ubiquitous impulse to seek acceptance of the rightness of one's actions, which lies at the root of the elaborate justificatory edifices that individuals and states develop following an action whose lawfulness is in doubt.[81] (Examples of this phenomenon include US statements regarding the prospects for freedom of Iraqi citizens under US occupation, Russian pronouncements regarding the self-determination of South Ossetians under Russian "peacekeepers'" authority, and Chinese assertions regarding the wellbeing of Uyghurs undergoing "re-education" by Chinese security forces.) The desire to normalize expectations and thus to bind and limit the actions of the most powerful, to provide a framework for justificatory

78 See for example, Lon L. Fuller, *The Morality of Law*, 2nd edn. (New Haven, Connecticut: Yale University Press, 1969), at 43; Wibren van der Burg, "The Morality of Aspiration: A Neglected Dimension of Law and Morality," in W.J. Witteveen and Wibren van der Burg, eds., *Rediscovering Fuller: Essays on Implicit Law and Institutional Design* (Amsterdam: Amsterdam University Press, 1999), at 170. Van der Burg develops his argument with reference to the example of treaties raised by John H. Jackson in *World Trade and the Law of GATT* (New York: Lexis-Nexis Matthew Bender, 1969). Jackson argues that if "norms of obligation" are mixed with "norms of aspiration" in the same instrument, there is a risk that states may behave as if the strict obligations established in those treaties are mere aspirations (761–762).

79 Kenneth I. Winston, "The Ideal Element in a Definition of Law," (1986) 5 *Law & Philosophy* 89.

80 See Oded Löwenheim, "'Do Ourselves Credit and Render a Lasting Service to Mankind': British Moral Prestige, Humanitarian Intervention and the Barbary Pirates," (2003) 47 *International Studies Quarterly* 23 for an illustration of the ubiquity of the language of humanitarian justification employed by military interveners during the past 150 years.

81 This drive to persuade is dealt with in divergent ways in Rousseau's discussion of the activity of the legislator who seeks to "persuade without convincing," and in Habermas' delineation of the three universal validity claims that every speech act makes, implicitly or explicitly: a claim to the truth of what is said (or assumed); a claim to the "rightness" of the linguistic utterance in the given context, or of the underlying norm; and a claim to the speaker's truthfulness. For more detailed discussion of this point, see Chapter 2.

persuasion regarding an interventionary act, to generate predictability … all of these are reasons to subscribe to and develop the legal normativity of the responsibility to protect.

However, this chapter has attempted to demonstrate some of the dangers inherent in the comprehensive vision of legal normativity proposed by ICISS by arguing that this model is susceptible to co-optation by the democracy promotion project often associated with the liberal peace thesis. The ICISS authors' version of the responsibility to protect risks further entrenching a schism in the international community whose practical consequences the responsibility to protect was intended to redress.

The question remains then, how to enlist the potential of international law for bringing about change, without risking the perversion of the intended ends of the responsibility to protect? One obvious route presents itself: develop practices of legality[82] that focus on the *responsibility to react* aspect of the responsibility to protect. Broaden the generally accepted reading of threats to peace and security under Chapter VII to include the list of parameters outlined in the *R2P* discussion of the responsibility to react, so that the standard for Security Council agreement on the legality of intervention will no longer require evidence of "genocidal intent" in cases of widespread killings and human rights abuses.[83] But by no means allow the international legal interpretation of threats to peace and security to be so inflated that the subject matter of the responsibility to *root cause* prevention (and perhaps also of the responsibility to rebuild) could be construed as falling within its compass.

This prescription will frustrate many proponents of the ICISS approach who see its insistence upon the intrinsic connection among the three responsibilities to prevent, react, and rebuild as a welcome departure from the popular tendency to focus on exigent

82 I use this term in a sense close to that of Jutta Brunnée and Stephen Toope (*Legitimacy and Legality in International Law* (Cambridge: Cambridge University Press, 2010)), and the argument that follows benefits greatly from their insights. For these authors, a "practice of legality" occurs when "a social norm, reflecting a shared understanding that meets the criteria of legality is upheld through practice that is congruent with the norm" (47). I would emphasize that such norms evolve through the practices that refer to it, and the shared understandings that initially give rise to it can also be transformed through a hermeneutic interchange. These practices can be negative as well as positive, serving to delimit the norm and distinguish its "legitimate" and "illegitimate" uses.

In terms of the autopoietic theory of law, this process entails the elaboration of secondary norms, described by Gunther Teubner as a form of norm creation "in which norms are applied to norms." When "a certain denseness and duration" is achieved in the iterative development of such secondary norms, the primary norms that they support and elaborate (as in cases of specific norms recognized as general principles under Article 38 (1)(c), such as sustainable development) might be regarded as examples of "structural coupling" between law and politics at the level of a global polity (Teubner, *Constitutional Fragments: Constitutionalism and Globalization* (Oxford: Oxford University Press, 2012), at 105).

83 ICISS, *Responsibility to Protect*, at 29–37 for a detailed discussion of the Commission's proposed criteria for reactive intervention.

situations only, with little regard for their origins or long-term consequences.[84] However, this very limited approach to legalizing intervention for human protective purpose—dubbed the MSF (for *Médécins sans frontières*) model by David Dewitt because of its exclusive focus upon crisis situations[85]—possesses several marked advantages.

A legally normative responsibility to react would still put further pressure upon the Security Council to intervene in situations that meet the *R2P*'s lowered threshold of violence, and would affirm the evolution of the concept of sovereignty as defined in part by the fulfilment of responsibilities for human protection. But in so doing, it would *not* create a legal technique for authorizing intervention for political or economic (and potentially, social or cultural) engineering purposes in countries deemed non-liberal and thus—in the greatly expanded sense allowed by ICISS—threats to international peace and security.

This solution to the dilemma posed by the ICISS interpretation regarding a responsibility to prevent attends to the common concerns raised by Mehta, Alvarez, Marks, and Reus-Smit, discussed above. A model of circumscribed intervention, instantiable through a legal technique that allowed for juridical realization of the responsibility to react via a Security Council resolution, would not create the possibility of invoking the responsibility to prevent (or the responsibility to rebuild) as a basis for invasive economic or political interventions justified in law in terms of perceived domestic legitimacy.

But would the realization of only one of the three elements of the responsibility to protect constitute a betrayal and trivialization of ICISS's efforts to bring world attention to the whole arc of predisposing conditions, violent conflict, and interventions' consequences?

The tripartite vision of international state responsibility proposed by ICISS would not necessarily be lost if the ambit of the Security Council's definition of threats to peace and security was limited to include only causes for reactive intervention.[86] Insofar as formal legality would attach only to the conditions triggering the responsibility to react, the crystallizing legal norm would depend only upon a "negative solidarity" among individual members of the world community. Such a negative solidarity would be rooted in the phenomenological experience of what Habermas terms "the damaged life," tapping into the embodied vulnerabilities particular to the human form of being, rather than a positive solidarity based on a vision of the good life.[87]

84 Although that tendency may be fading in light of the sustained public discussion of the problem of "exit strategy" following the American invasion of Iraq.

85 Personal communication (November 2004).

86 For example, the ILC's *Draft Articles on State Responsibility*, discussed above, suggest other means of pursuing legal recognition of norms of responsibility regarding post-intervention rebuilding, at least.

87 Jürgen Habermas, *Moral Consciousness and Communicative Action*, trans. by Christian Lenhardt and Shierry Weber Nicholsen (Cambridge, MA: Massachusetts Institute of Technology Press, 1990), at 200; cited in J. Donald Moon, "Practical Discourse and Communicative Ethics," in Stephen K. White, ed., *The Cambridge Companion to Habermas* (Cambridge: Cambridge University Press, 1995), at 152.

Such negative solidarity could not suffice as the basis for the moral community that would be required to ground a juridically realizable responsibility to prevent. It could, however, serve as an adequate foundation for a thin notion of human security, and for intercultural agreement on the criteria of reactive intervention.

This does not mean that we have to dismiss the ambition for developing norms of state responsibility for rebuilding and preventing altogether. The achievement of positive solidarity might be possible—but it would require that we undertake the messy and painful labour of explicitly debating our values, rather than deceiving ourselves into thinking that we can or should limit moral discussion to questions of form ("justice" in the parlance of recent political theory). Such a task will not always be successful, of course, and never enduringly so. But whether or not a positive solidarity that appeals to a common vision of the ends of human life is achievable, only a thicker definition of human security based on such agreement could suffice to legitimate actions undertaken under the rubric of a responsibility to prevent.[88]

Those involved in a debate of this sort would have to consider challenges to the prevailing wisdom regarding the nature of liberal democracy, its benefits and weaknesses. Since the prescription of liberal democratic procedures and institutions lies at the heart of both the responsibilities to prevent and rebuild, tensions between the liberal and democratic strands of liberal democracy would have to be openly acknowledged and explored in such a debate. Participants seeking an agreement on values would be challenged to acknowledge that the representation of a certain version of liberal democracy as the apogee of political development attenuates the emancipatory and critical force that richer readings of democracy might have. They would also have to consider the logical consequence of this claim: the argument that a narrow reading of liberal democracy stifles revolutionary politics, and helps to perpetuate the "structural violence" of the existing global distributionary order.[89]

If supporters of the full-blown version of the responsibility to prevent wish to make a moral and legal claim that will inspire the recognition of members

88 Brunnée and Toope's work developing Lon L. Fuller's notion of a normative continuum is germane here. If law is not viewed as "an inherently superior form of normativity," then the benefit to be gained by legalizing a responsibility to prevent becomes even less apparent (Brunnée and Toope, *Legitimacy and Legality*, at 72).

89 The concept of "structural violence" refers to the combined impact of systemic inequalities of opportunities, resources, and power, both within and among states. For further discussion see Johan Galtung, "Violence, Peace and Peace Research," (1969) 6 *Journal of Peace Research* 167; cited in Susan Marks, "The End of History," at 473.

of a world community, such an ongoing persuasive and deliberative enterprise must be undertaken openly. Never should agreement on its foregone conclusion be assumed. Such an approach would revalorize truly political discourse: deliberation and persuasion about our purposes, identities, and strategies—the subject matter that lies "at the interstices of the instrumental and the moral."[90] The import of this chapter has simply been to indicate the enormity and gravity of this task.

90 Reus-Smit, "Strange Death," at 576.

5 The international legal character of the responsibility to protect

This chapter examines the responsibility to protect's legal normativity and concludes that it has the character of a general principle of international law. This conclusion breaks with the idea that the responsibility to protect is solely a moral and political norm—a view that was widely adopted immediately following the 2005 World Summit.[1]

In order to understand the principle's developing nature as a norm of international law, the chapter canvasses a variety of interpretations of the responsibility to protect, and focuses on the common impulse among them. The normative core of all major variations of the responsibility to protect involves a commitment to halting or averting avoidable, "event-driven" human suffering that affects large populations. The justification for this commitment rests on two inferences (although the degree to which the inferences are made explicit varies among interpretations): 1) that protecting a population against suffering is a precondition of human flourishing, and 2) that providing this form of security is linked to the primary function of states. When states abdicate or fail to fulfil this responsibility, it becomes a collective responsibility borne by actors beyond the home state.

This normative impulse has its international legal origins in the colonizing projects of the nineteenth century, as does the language frequently used to describe the triggering conditions for the norm's collective dimension. So, for example, a responsibility to protect response is often said to be demanded by events that are "conscience-shocking"[2] or actions that "shock the conscience of mankind."[3] Predictably enough, these colonial roots and the record of interventions as civilizing missions (outlined in Chapter 4), have

1 United Nations Secretary-General Ban Ki-Moon, "Human Protection and the 21st Century United Nations," Cyril Foster Lecture, Oxford University (1 February 2010), online at www.un.org/sg/en/content/sg/speeches/2011-02-02/cyril-foster-lecture-oxford-university-human-protection-and-21st

2 Report of the Secretary-General, *Implementing the Responsibility to Protect*, (12 January 2009), A/63/677, at para. 9.

3 International Commission on Intervention and State Sovereignty, *The Responsibility to Protect* (International Development Research Centre: Ottawa, 2001), at xii. I employ the non-gender neutral term "mankind" throughout this article in the context of the phrase "the conscience of mankind" because this is the term that has frequently been used in the past century to refer to a common sense of juridical right and wrong in authoritative texts considered in these pages. In order to demonstrate this continuity of usage, I quote the term accurately and refrain from substituting "humankind," the

generated suspicion among the historical targets of these crusades, as well as others alive to these interventions' disastrous consequences.[4] This scepticism helps to explain the variations among existing interpretations of the responsibility to protect. The most prominent among these are the International Commission on Intervention and State Sovereignty (ICISS) and post-World Summit United Nations (UN) versions, as well as the interpretive approaches subsequently introduced by Brazil and China, and the emendations subsequently put forward by the UN, all of which are surveyed in Part I, below.

This chapter understands these variations in the interpretation of the responsibility to protect as gambits in the deliberative practice of international law. I argue that they, along with other acts of jurispersuasion, contribute to the formation of practices of legality[5] that help to define and stabilize the core and penumbral elements of the responsibility to protect, understood as a general principle of international law.

Part II summarizes a neo-formalist understanding of ways in which international legal norms come into existence. It begins with the traditional list of sources of international law provided in Article 38(1) of the Statute of the International Court of Justice (ICJ). It considers, in particular, features of general principles of international law in order to establish the criteria for identifying norms that fit into this class. Part III focuses on a sub-category of this class that includes human rights and human rights protection norms, and provides a rough overview of the uneven development of this often-overlooked type of general principle. Finally, in Part IV of the chapter, evidence that the responsibility to protect is an example of the *human rights and human rights protection* sub-category of general principles of international law is summarized.

These arguments and evidence are assembled here with two aims. The first is to show that the ambiguous arc of development of the *human rights and human rights protection* sub-category helps to explain why the responsibility to protect's legal normativity as a general principle has been largely overlooked. The second is

term's presumable referent. For ease of reading, I omit the customary "[sic]" that would draw attention to the sexist connotation of the original language.

4 See for example, Ikechi Mbeoji, *Collective Insecurity: The Liberian Crisis, Unilateralism, and the Global Order* (Vancouver: UBC Press, 2003), at 103–142; "A Commentary on 'Renewing the United Nations: A Programme for Reform,'" policy brief prepared by the South Centre at the request of the Group of 77, online at www.g77.org/doc/policy%20brief.htm#What%20role%20for%20the%20UN

5 I borrow this term from Jutta Brunnée and Stephen J. Toope to designate the practices that reflect the *sensus communis juris* with respect to particular human rights and human rights protection norms. As I outline below, the emergence of these practices forms part of the *riconoscimento giuridico di esigenze della coscienza pubblica* (RG) process that gives rise to general principles of international law of the third sub-category. This use differs from that of the original authors, who apply it primarily to describe the way in which bindingness attaches to norms of international custom and treaty law that exhibit the eight "criteria of legality" identified by Lon L. Fuller (Jutta Brunnée and Stephen J. Toope, *Legitimacy and Legality in International Law: An Interactional Account* (Cambridge: Cambridge University Press, 2010), at 47).

to illustrate that the responsibility to protect's history is not one of competing, all-or-nothing definitional skirmishes, in which one normative account is displaced by a successor. Instead, it comprises a complex dialogical exchange that forms part of a collective effort to locate core and penumbral meanings over time.

I The responsibility to protect: major variants and common themes

The ICISS report and R2P

Thus far, the ICISS version of the responsibility to protect, as the most theoretically consistent formulation of the principle, has been the focus of critical analysis in this book. This "R2P" version of the responsibility to protect identifies the norm's primary purpose as "to halt or avert human suffering."[6] All subsequent interpretations of the principle retain this commitment. As has been outlined in previous chapters, in R2P the responsibility to protect "the human needs of those seeking protection or assistance"[7] is broken down temporally into three constituent responsibilities: to prevent, to react, and to rebuild. The responsibility to protect attaches first to the home state. If human security within the state becomes so compromised that "major harm to civilians" is occurring or imminent,[8] and the state is unable or unwilling to protect those under threat, the R2P interpretation asserts that a "residual" or "fallback" responsibility devolves upon the international community of states.[9] This idea of shared responsibility for human protection against widespread, event-induced suffering is also common to all major variants of the responsibility to protect.

The circumstances in which the responsibility to protect applies *collectively* to agents beyond the home state are divided into two broad categories by the R2P account. One of these categories outlines the triggering conditions that justify coercive action up to and including military intervention under crisis conditions involving a home state's failure to protect its population. The other category refers to pre-crisis, structural circumstances, and depends upon a posited causal link between certain economic, social, and political conditions and an increased likelihood of atrocity crimes (see Chapter 4).

In the ICISS approach, the triggering conditions under circumstances of crisis are: 1) "large scale loss of life, actual or apprehended, with genocidal intent or not, which is the product either of deliberate state action, or state neglect or inability to act, or a failed state situation"; or 2) "large scale 'ethnic cleansing,' actual or apprehended, whether carried out by killing, forced expulsion, acts of terror or rape."[10] The precise *pre-crisis* structural conditions are acknowledged to be uncertain; and although such factors as unequal resource distribution, poverty, and

6 ICISS, *Responsibility to Protect*, at xii.
7 *Ibid.* at 15.
8 *Ibid.* at 16.
9 *Ibid.* at 17.
10 *Ibid.* at 32 (emphasis omitted).

political repression are mentioned in the report, the specific levels of inequality and poverty, and types and severity of political repression that would constitute root causes of human protection crises are not defined.[11]

For the ICISS authors, these first and second contexts in which the responsibility to protect applies *collectively* are woven together and given logical coherence through the human security concept (see Chapter 1). This concept and its connection to human flourishing are employed to justify and require collective involvement in both pre-crisis preventive intervention by outside actors (responsibility to prevent) and protective intervention in crisis circumstances (responsibility to react).

ICISS drew two distinct conclusions about the nature of the responsibility to protect's legal normativity. Based on its review of interventions from 1945–1999, and its consultation with an array of global actors during 2000–2001,[12] ICISS determined that the responsibility to protect was "an emerging guiding principle" of customary international law at the turn of the twentieth century.[13] It further observed that the responsibilities associated with the crystallizing norm already had independent legal grounds in existing international law (the UN Charter, the Genocide Convention, the Geneva Conventions and Additional Protocols, the Rome Statute of the International Criminal Court, and other international human rights agreements).[14]

The final conclusion reached by the Commission concerning the *implications* of the responsibility to protect's developing legal normativity is the one that has provoked the greatest controversy. It pertains to the precise nature and scope of the collective aspect of the responsibility to protect in catastrophic circumstances. When a home state is "unable or unwilling" to fulfil its responsibility to protect the human security of its inhabitants, the ICISS reading of the norm holds that the most legitimate authority to undertake fulfilment of the default, collective responsibility in the state's place is the UN Security Council.[15] However, if a situation arises in which the Security Council fails to take action to fulfil the responsibility to protect, ICISS asserted that "state practice, Security Council precedent, established norms, emerging guiding principles, and evolving customary international law" support the view that "the [UN] Charter's strong bias against military intervention is not to be regarded as absolute when decisive action

11 ICISS, *Responsibility to Protect*, at 23.

12 *The Responsibility to Protect: Research, Bibliography, Background*, supp. vol. (International Development Research Centre: Ottawa, 2001) is a supplementary volume to the ICISS report that contains the summary of research conducted by fifteen international scholars on these case studies. The consultations to identify common ground among global actors on the issues explored in the case studies primarily took the form of roundtable discussions involving more than 200 government, inter-governmental, NGO, civil society, and academic representatives in Beijing, Cairo, Geneva London, Maputo, New Delhi, New York, Ottawa Paris, St. Petersburg, Santiago, and Washington (ICISS, *Responsibility to Protect*, at ix).

13 ICISS, *ibid.*, vol. 1, at 15.

14 *Ibid.* at 16.

15 *Ibid.* at 53.

is required on human protection grounds."[16] Consequently, the report references the "Uniting for Peace" procedures as an alternative means of fulfilling the responsibility to protect through action by the General Assembly. (When dissension among the permanent five members of the Security Council causes the Council to fail to exercise its primary responsibility for addressing threats to international peace and security, these procedures provide for the General Assembly to convene in plenary session within 24 hours and proceed directly to consider the matter at issue.[17]) In fact, the Commission even allowed for the possibility that the responsibility to protect requirement could be met, under extraordinary circumstances, by actors other than the Security Council or the General Assembly through action by regional or ad hoc coalitions, or even individual states. The ICISS commissioners were at pains to underscore the dangers of these "bespoke" means of fulfilling the responsibility to protect—but suggested that by the opening of the twenty-first century there was a growing consensus that in the worst of the worst crises, the responsibility to protect human security may prevail over the traditional privileges of state sovereignty: "if the Security Council fails to discharge its responsibility in conscience-shocking situations crying out for action, then it is unrealistic to expect that concerned states will rule out other means and forms of action to meet the gravity and urgency of these situations."[18]

The UN's post-World Summit "RtoP"

The UN's post-World Summit effort to develop the responsibility to protect norm was led by Secretary-General Ban Ki-moon and the Special Adviser on the Responsibility to Protect he appointed in 2008, academic Edward Luck. With the support of the UN's Office on the Prevention of Genocide and on the Responsibility to Protect, the norm was operationalized via three "pillars" which were based on paras. 138 and 139 of the World Summit Outcome Document of 2005. This approach, dubbed "RtoP," was outlined in Secretary Ban's 2009 report to the General Assembly on implementation:

> Pillar 1) States bear the primary responsibility to protect their populations from genocide, war crimes, ethnic cleansing and crimes against humanity.
> Pillar 2) The international community is committed to providing assistance to states in building capacity to protect their populations from these four crimes and to assisting those which are under stress before crises arise.

16 *Ibid.* at 18.

17 This process was developed in 1950 in Resolution 377 (V) through an amendment to the General Assembly's rules of procedure intended to address the Security Council's failure to fulfil its Charter obligations in connection with the Korean War. Rule of Procedure No. 65 can be triggered either by a procedural vote in the Security Council or by a request made of the Secretary-General by a majority of UN member states. (See *Resolution on Uniting for Peace*, GA Res. 377, UN GAOR 5th Sess. UN Doc. A/RES/377 (V) A (3 November 1950), online at www.un.org/ga/search/view_doc.asp?symbol=A/RES/377(V); and also ICISS, *Responsibility to Protect*, at 53.)

18 ICISS, *ibid.* at 55.

Pillar 3) The international community is responsible for taking timely and decisive action to prevent and atrocity crimes when a state is manifestly failing to protect its population.[19]

The RtoP approach tackles the delineation of circumstances under which the collective aspect of the responsibility obtains in a structurally similar way to ICISS. It outlines a collective obligation to support the home state in taking preventive, capacity building actions, as well as a set of triggering conditions under which the collective responsibility to protect necessitates coercive and potentially military involvement under Pillars 2 and 3. The terminology of "atrocity crimes" is introduced as an umbrella concept to capture the four types of triggering conditions: genocide, crimes against humanity, war crimes, and ethnic cleansing. As Secretary-General Ban stressed, the UN's RtoP focus on atrocity crimes aimed to address only the most imminent threats, and offered a parsimonious account of the range of circumstances in which affronts to the traditional bounds of state sovereignty might be countenanced.[20] This atrocity crime language also emphasized that the responsibility to act flows from the *criminal* nature of the triggering circumstances, and that fulfilment of the responsibility to protect is a mandatory response to crime or threatened criminal acts.[21] In addition, the terminology also complements that of the Rome Statute of the International Criminal Court (1998), which is authorized to prosecute individuals alleged to have committed these four international crimes.[22]

The language of human security—which has become controversial in part because of the ICISS authors' redefinition of sovereignty in terms of a state's effectiveness in providing human security for its inhabitants—is relegated to a lesser role in the UN's post-World Summit reading. A free-standing account of the responsibility to protect norm that is not directly dependent upon, nor necessarily linked to, the human security concept came to be favoured by the secretariat because of the prevailing political winds.[23] The burden of providing theoretical

19 *Report of the Secretary-General, Implementing the Responsibility to Protect* UNGAOR, 63d Sess. UN Doc. A/63/677 (12 January 2009), online at www.undocs.org/ A/ 63/677, at 8–9.

20 UN Secretary-General Ban, "Human Protection and the 21st Century UN"; and also his "Off the Cuff" press conference, (23 February 2011), online at www.un.org/apps/ sg/offthecuff.asp?nid=1733

21 For development of this point see Don Hubert and Ariela Blätter, "The Responsibility to Protect as International Crimes Prevention" (2012) 4 *Global Responsibility to Protect* 33. At the same time, the threshold for triggering the responsibility to consider military forms of coercive intervention is raised from "unable or unwilling" in ICISS's interpretation to a state's "manifestly failing" to fulfil its responsibility to protect, in accordance with the World Summit Outcome Document (GA Res. 60/1, UN GAOR, 60th Sess., UN Doc. A/RES/60/1 (24 October 2005), online at www.who.int/hiv/universalaccess2010/worldsummit.pdf at para. 139).

22 UN General Assembly, *Rome Statute of the International Criminal Court* (last amended 2010), 17 July 1998, online at www.refworld.org/docid/3ae6b3a84.html

23 Aidan Hehir, "From Human Security to the Responsibility to Protect: The Co-option of Dissent," (2015) 23 *Michigan State International Law Review* 675.

continuity that explains why the responsibility to protect applies collectively to outside actors in *both* catastrophic and pre-catastrophic conditions was instead assigned to the concept of human protection, described by Secretary-General Ban as "a subset of the more encompassing concept of human security" that "addresses more immediate threats to the survival of individuals and groups."[24] This is a conceptually shakier solution for justifying a collective responsibility to respond to pre-catastrophic conditions, but it served to solidify the support of a cross-section of states for Pillar 3 intervention in catastrophic circumstances of atrocity crime.[25]

Perhaps the most significant post-World Summit innovation in the UN's approach to the responsibility to protect was the secretariat's decision to de-emphasize, and even explicitly deny any claim that the norm possessed an inherent international legal character. Thus, in the 2009 Thematic Debate on the Responsibility to Protect, Special Adviser Edward Luck asserted that it was a "tired canard" that the responsibility to protect possesses legal normativity, and that the principle is "a political, not legal, concept."[26] And in the same period Secretary-General Ban's deliberate description of the principle as a "moral and political responsibility to protect populations" implicitly endorsed this tactical retreat by omitting any mention of the responsibility to protect's legal character.[27]

The RtoP approach is thus best understood as an attempt to fulfil the mandate provided by the political compromise reflected in the World Summit Outcome Document. It develops certain less-controversial features of the responsibility to protect, but does not define the concept's limits. During its continuing evolution, the UN's framing of the responsibility to protect has shifted in emphasis as the secretariat has sought to operationalize and implement the norm in practice. These discursive and pragmatic shifts have reflected the impact of perspectives on the norm introduced by Brazil and more recently, China, as well as UN personnel's experiences of attempting to operationalize the norm in a turbulent global environment.

Brazil's RwP interpretation

Although the World Summit endorsed the responsibility to protect by consensus, the principle's implementation in practice has been criticized and at times opposed by roughly 20 states in subsequent UN General Assembly and Security Council votes and thematic debates.[28] As noted above, concerns were voiced more

24 Ban, "Human Protection and the 21st Century UN," at 1.

25 Marcos Tourinho, Oliver Stuenkel and Sarah Brockmeier, "'Responsibility while Protecting': Reforming R2P Implementation," (2016) 30 *Global Society* 144.

26 Special Adviser to the Secretary-General Edward Luck, *Remarks to the General Assembly on the Responsibility to Protect: Thematic Debate on the Responsibility to Protect* (23 July 2009), online at www.un.org/ga/president/63/interactive/protect/luck.pdf, at 3.

27 Ban, "Human Protection and the 21st Century UN," at 2.

28 Jennifer Welsh, Patrick Quinton-Brown and Victor MacDiarmid, "Brazil's 'Responsibility While Protecting' Proposal: A Canadian Perspective," *Canadian Consortium on the R2P* (12 July 2013), at 2.

forcefully following the Libyan intervention in 2011 and the opening years of the Syrian conflict that followed the Arab Spring.

And yet, many of these same states have endorsed elements of an interpretive strategy proposed by the Brazilian government in late 2011 under the label "responsibility while protecting" (RwP).[29] As a BRICS member, a country that has suffered mass atrocities, and a past public critic of the RtoP model, Brazil's contributions to the evolving discussion of the responsibility to protect have commanded widespread attention. The crux of the country's RwP proposal was to affirm the importance of the responsibility to protect while re-thematizing the concepts of prevention and prudence that had been so central a part of the original ICISS approach. In order to accomplish this, Brazil introduced a clarifying distinction between collective responsibility and collective security, with significant consequences.[30] It envisaged that in pre-catastrophic situations, the collective responsibility to prevent atrocity crimes could be fulfilled by a range of nonstate actors including international organizations, civil society, NGOs, and others, as well as by states acting alone or in collaboration. The RwP vision reiterates the ICISS and RtoP insistence on early warning capacity, and underscores the need to develop trusted, neutral mechanisms for creating reliable assessments, and for bringing them to the attention of decision-makers working within the UN's collective security architecture.

In Brazil's RwP approach, while in the pre-catastrophic phase the responsibility to protect can be borne by a range of state and nonstate actors, in the catastrophic phase the responsibility can apply only to the agents empowered within the UN Charter system to address threats to international peace and security. This means that under the RwP reading, only the *preferred* two options outlined in the ICISS version are contemplated as acceptable authorizing mechanisms for extreme forms of coercive action (such as universal sanctions or military action): the Security Council, or the General Assembly through the Uniting for Peace procedures.[31] This push for clarity around authorization is closely connected to a broad emphasis on accountability.[32] There is thus a stress upon the importance of developing clear criteria prior to the authorization of any coercive intervention (building on the very preliminary and theoretical ICISS discussion of criteria for

29 The Brazilian proposal was introduced by President Dilma Rousseff during an open General Assembly debate on the subject of "protection of civilians in armed conflicts" and further formalized in a subsequent letter ("Letter Dated 9 November 2011 from the Permanent Representative of Brazil to the United Nations Addressed to the Secretary-General" (9 November 2011), A/66/551–S/2011/701, online at www.securitycouncilreport.org/atf/cf/%7B65BFCF9B-6D27-4E9C-8CD3-CF6E4FF96FF9%7D/POC%20S2011%20701.pdf

30 Welsh et al., "Brazil's 'RwP' Proposal," at 2.

31 "Permanent Representative of Brazil to the UN," at l.c. (note 2), para. 8.

32 See Thorsten Benner, "Brazil as a Norm Entrepeneur: the 'Responsibility while Protecting' Initiative," GPPi working paper (March 2013), online at www.gppi.net/fileadmin/user_upload/media/pub/2013/Benner_2013_Working-Paper_Brazil-RWP.pdf

military intervention[33]), chronological sequencing and political oversight,[34] and close monitoring of any interventionary action.[35]

Although the RwP was not further elaborated by Brazil after 2012, it did succeed in drawing attention to important areas of weakness in the responsibility to protect's implementation, which impacted further development of the principle by the UN.[36] It also succeeded in reigniting constructive engagement with the responsibility to protect and helped to broaden the geographical range of states actively participating in the interpretive community around the norm.[37]

China's RP approach

Notable among the states that took up Brazil's invitation to re-examine the responsibility to protect was the People's Republic of China. China was not a natural supporter of the ICISS interpretation of the norm because of the country's historical commitment to a Westphalian model of state sovereignty, which its fraught relationships with the Republic of China (Taiwan), Tibet, and the Xinjiang Uyghur Autonomous Region have served to reaffirm. Nevertheless, in 2011 China chose not to exercise its veto during a Security Council vote on Resolution 1973—the resolution that authorized intervention for human protection purposes in Libya on responsibility to protect grounds. Subsequently, when the NATO-led intervention overstepped its mandate and eventually effected regime change to remove the Qaddafi government, China reacted by vetoing (along with Russia) a series of draft Security Council resolutions that aimed to impose sanctions on the Syrian government in connection with evidence of atrocity crimes committed against its population beginning in 2011. It was in this highly contentious context that the Brazilian RwP proposal was launched.

RwP's impact on the Chinese government's position on the responsibility to protect made itself felt very quickly. The concept of "Responsible Protection"

33 "Permanent Representative of Brazil to the UN," at para. 7, and compare with ICISS, *Responsibility to Protect*, at chap. 6.
34 "Permanent Representative of Brazil to the UN," at paras. 6, 7.
35 *Ibid.* at para. 11.
36 Welsh, et al., "Brazil's 'RwP' Proposal," at 7.
37 Tourinho et al. observe:

> The terms of the debate as established by RwP allowed for the participation of a wide range of states and civil society actors, coming from more diverse backgrounds than just traditional R2P advocates, fellow BRICS countries (Brazil, Russia, India, China, South Africa) or the G77. In the Lima Declaration at the III Summit of the Arab and South American States, members supported RwP and argued that it should be discussed at the UN as well as within the Union of South American Nations (Union de las Naciones Suramericanas—UNASUR) and the Arab League. In January 2013, at the 7th Ministerial Encounter of the South Atlantic Peace and Cooperation Zone, participants recognized the importance of RwP and expressed the willingness to discuss the issue further. Even Venezuela, a country known for its resistance to R2P, welcomed the discussions initiated by the Brazilian proposal ("Reforming R2P Implementation," at 143; notes omitted).

(RP) was introduced in an opinion article in the *China Daily News* in March 2012 by Ruan Zongze, the vice-president of the China Institute for International Studies, and then later presented in more expansive form in a second semi-official publication by the same author.[38] It has since been discussed in the context of think tank conferences and workshops and in speeches by Chinese government officials.[39] The RP concept takes up the concerns raised by the RwP agenda regarding coercive military intervention for human protection purposes and maps out criteria for determining whether such action is justified, monitoring any action that does occur under the rubric of the responsibility to protect, and ensuring that rebuilding takes place.

RP's six elements repackage features drawn from prior interpretations of the responsibility to protect, in particular those associated with the responsibilities to react and to rebuild on the ICISS reading. Taken together, they affirm recognition of a norm of human protection that includes the possibility of military intervention, while articulating a more stringent set of threshold conditions for authorizing such action.[40]

UN-R2P

Increasingly broad and substantive participation by state members in the interpretive community of the responsibility to protect since 2011 has influenced the UN's subsequent framing of the concept.[41] This is perhaps most

38 Ruan Zongze, "Responsible Protection," China Daily News (15 March 2012), online at www.usa.chinadaily.com.cn/opinion/2012-03/15/content_14838556.htm, and "Responsible Protection: Building a Safer World," China Institute of International Studies (15 June 2012), online at www.ciis.org.cn/english/2012-06/15/content_5090912.htm

39 For example, at the Chatham House International Law Programme, global experts network meeting (April 2014), Chatham House, London, UK. See also Andrew Garwood-Gowers, "China's 'Responsible Protection' Concept," (2016) 6 *Asian Journal of International Law* 89 at 101.

40 Since the launch of the RP perspective, China has continued to participate in international fora on issues associated with the responsibility to protect, as when it introduced a resolution at the UN Human Rights Council urging "mutually beneficial cooperation" to promote human rights with the goal "of building a community of shared future for human beings" (Ryan Mitchell, "Was the UN Human Rights Council Wrong to Back China's 'Shared Future' Resolution?" EJILTalk! (10 April 2018), online at ejiltalk.org/was-the-un-human-rights-council-wrong-to-back-chinas-shared-future-resolution/). On this point see also Sonya Sceats, "Guest Post: China as a Shaper of International Norms," Opinio Juris (17 March 2015), online at http://opiniojuris.org/2015/03/17/guest-post-china-as-a-shaper-of-international-law/?utm_source=feedburner&utm_medium=email&utm_campaign=Feed%3A+opiniojurisfeed+%28Opinio+Juris%29; and Zheng Chen, "China and the Responsibility to Protect," (2016) 25 *Journal of Contemporary China* 686.

41 This engagement is exemplified by the General Assembly's decision to undertake a formal plenary meeting on the responsibility to protect on 25 June and 2 July 2018, following the topic's inclusion on the Assembly's 72nd session Formal Agenda. 113 countries supported the motion to conduct the formal thematic meeting (21 opposed),

evident in the increased emphasis placed upon accountability in official UN statements on the norm in the years following the Brazilian and Chinese contributions to its interpretive development. The August 2017 report of the Secretary-General on implementing the responsibility to protect is subtitled "Accountability for Prevention." Its executive summary opens by stating the need to close the gap between UN member states' commitment to the responsibility to protect and the lived reality of those threatened with atrocity crimes, asserting that: "[o]ne of the principal ways in which we can do so is by strengthening accountability for the implementation of the responsibility to protect and by ensuring rigorous and open scrutiny of practice, based on agreed principles."[42] The main concerns raised in both Brazil's and China's interpretations of the responsibility to protect are included in this guiding statement. In his opening remarks to the 2018 formal General Assembly debate on the principle, Secretary-General António Guterres demonstrated again that the UN's current approach to the responsibility to protect was deeply informed by the spirit common to the contributions of not just Brazil and China, but of the Non-Aligned Movement generally when he observed that: "[o]ur over-arching challenge is to uphold the principle while preventing its mis-use."[43]

This reflexive and politically sensitive approach to continuing development of the responsibility to protect norm in recent years has been pursued in a range of other ways under UN leadership, as well. Instances of this incremental evolution include the terminology used to describe this "UN-R2P" interpretation of the norm, the UN secretariat's characterization of the nature of legal obligations it entails, and the effort to transform facts on the ground in connection with the responsibility to protect's legal normativity.

Since 2017, the UN webpages devoted to the responsibility to protect have been largely divested of references to the RtoP acronym that was introduced to distinguish the post-World Summit thematization of the principle from the ICISS version.[44] This may reflect the continuing use of the R2P acronym by a number of civil society and hybrid organizations, and in particular, the use of "R2P" by the Global Centre for the Responsibility to Protect's Global

and the same number contributed statements to the interactive dialogue (Global Centre for the Responsibility to Protect, "UN General Assembly Formal Debate on R2P and Mass Atrocity Prevention," *R2P in Focus*, no. 18 (September 2018)).

42 *Report of the Secretary-General, Implementing the Responsibility to Protect: Accountability for Prevention*, UNGAOR, 71st Sess. UN Doc. A/71/1016-S/2017/556 (10 August 2017), online at www.undocs.org/A/71/1016-S/2017/556, at 1.

43 Secretary-General's Remarks to the General Assembly Debate on the Responsibility to Protect [as delivered] (25 June 2018), online at www.un.org/sg/en/content/sg/statement/2018-06-25/secretary-generals-remarks-general-assembly-debate-responsibility

44 The only discernible uses of the RtoP acronym still present in late 2018 were in the form of the short titles on two clickable links allowing visitors to the website of the Office on Genocide Prevention and the Responsibility to Protect to access further information (www.un.org/en/genocideprevention/index.html#).

Network of R2P Focal Points.[45] In fact without fanfare, some of the more recent materials produced under UN auspices have employed the R2P acronym to refer to the norm.[46] This apparent shift in nomenclature may reflect an organic understanding of the responsibility to protect's evolution that aligns with the account of core and penumbral negotiation provided in these pages.

At the same time, there have been quiet moves toward more fully acknowledging the legal bona fides of the concept. The UN's enhanced focus on accountability has been achieved in part through detailed reiteration of the multiple legal bases for the responsibility to protect, both domestic and international. *The Framework of Analysis for Atrocity Crimes* [47]—a prevention tool produced by the Office of the Special Advisers on the Prevention of Genocide and on the Responsibility to Protect—is representative of this trend. Like the 2017 Secretary-General's report on *Implementing the Responsibility to Protect,* [48] it stresses the legal nature of the obligation of states to fulfil the responsibility to protect, albeit by recounting the existing international legal prohibitions on specific atrocity crimes, rather than by focusing directly on the international legal normativity of the responsibility to protect itself.[49]

This effort to enhance attention to the legal aspect of the responsibility to protect's normativity has a domestic dimension, as well. The home state's responsibility to protect takes on a domestic legal force to the extent that international legal prohibitions enshrined in international human rights treaties have been implemented in domestic legislation. One of the consequences of encouraging states to participate in the Global Network of R2P Focal Points is increasing adherence to such treaties. The regional organizations that form part of this

45 Global Centre for the Responsibility to Protect, "Global Network of R2P Focal Points," online at www.globalr2p.org/our_work/global_network_of_r2p_focal_points. The Global Centre is not alone in preferring this usage; the Asia-Pacific Centre for the Responsibility to Protect is another prominent UN partner-organization that employs the R2P acronym.

46 See for example, UN Department of Public Information, Outreach Programme on the Rwanda Genocide and the United Nations, (March 2014), online at www.un.org/en/preventgenocide/rwanda/about/bgresponsibility.shtml

47 UN, *Framework of Analysis for Atrocity Crimes: A Tool for Prevention* (July 2014), online at www.un.org/en/genocideprevention/international-law.html, at 2–3; UN Secretary-General's report (as above), at paras. 10, 11, 15.

48 Report of the Secretary-General, *Implementing the Responsibility to Protect: Accountability for Prevention* (10 August 2017), A/71/1016-S/2017/556, at paras. 13, 16.

49 This effort to enhance attention to the legal aspect of the responsibility to protect's normativity has a domestic dimension, as well. The home state's responsibility to protect takes on a domestic legal force to the extent that international legal prohibitions enshrined in international human rights treaties have been implemented in domestic legislation. One of the consequences of encouraging states to participate in the Global Network of R2P Focal Points is increasing adherence to such treaties. The regional organizations that form part of this umbrella group of states raise awareness of domestic risk factors and support states in nationally-led resilience-building to prevent atrocity crimes.

umbrella group of states raise awareness of domestic risk factors and support states in nationally-led resilience-building to prevent atrocity crimes.

These developments in the UN's interpretation of the core elements of the responsibility to protect principle reflect the unfolding interpretive dialogue concerning the principle.

* * *

This recent history of interpretive dialogue concerning the responsibility to protect and the emergence of corresponding practices of legality is a narrative of agreement and contestation over the boundary between the core and penumbral elements of the norm. The following account of general principles of international law is meant to be situated against this backdrop as a contribution to the jurispersuasive dialogue. It aims to shed light on an unappreciated dimension of the responsibility to protect's existing international legal normativity as a general principle of international law.

II General principles

Determining the status of a principle in international law is normally accomplished by referring, implicitly or explicitly, to the framework of sources contained within Article 38(1) of the *Statute of the International Court of Justice* (ICJ).[50] Although this Article is not an exhaustive catalogue, it is widely-regarded as an efficient summary of the main sources of international law, and was included by the committees of international legal experts that produced the ICJ's Statute in order to provide guidance to the Court's judges.[51]

The language of Article 38 is almost identical with that of the *Statute of the Permanent Court of International Justice* (PCIJ), authored by the PCIJ's Advisory Committee of Jurists in 1920, as mandated by the League of Nations.[52] The sources of international law that the *ICJ* judges are directed to consider in their work are thus reflective of the conventional thinking of a century ago.[53] These sources include:

50 *Statute of the International Court of Justice*, 26 June 1945, Can. TS 1945 No. 7, online at www.icj-cij.org/documents/?p1=4&p2=2, at Art. 38, para. 1.

51 The Statute of the ICJ was the product of the deliberations of no fewer than three Allied-sponsored international committees of jurists that met between 1942–1945, as well as the representatives who participated in the 1945 San Francisco Conference that created the UN Charter (The Registrar of the ICJ, *International Court of Justice Handbook*, 5th ed., (ICJ: The Hague, Netherlands, 2004, 2013), online at www.icj-cij.org/files/publications/handbook-of-the-court-en.pdf, at 15–16).

52 League of Nations, *Statute of the Permanent Court of International Justice*, 13 December 1920, 6 LNTS 170, 379. The language contained in Art. 38(1)(c) of the *Statute of the ICJ* originally appeared in Art. 38 (3) of the Statute of the PCIJ. These two clauses have identical elements, but employ different numbering systems. For simplicity's sake, where sense allows I will refer in what follows to both of the clauses using the more recent numbering system associated with the current Statute of the ICJ.

53 The PCIJ's Advisory Committee of Jurists was composed of members from Belgium, Great Britain, the U.S.A, Japan, Italy, France, Norway, Spain, the Netherlands, and

a international conventions, whether general or particular, establishing rules expressly recognized by the contesting states;
b international custom, as evidence of a general practice accepted as law;
c the general principles of law recognized by civilized nations;
d subject to the provisions of Article 59, judicial decisions and the teachings of the most highly qualified publicists of the various nations, as subsidiary means for the determination of rules of law.[54]

It is the second of these sources, international custom, that was initially identified by ICISS as giving rise to the responsibility to protect. Although there is a case to be made for regarding the norm as emerging customary international law, its persuasiveness depends upon acceptance of a revisionist theory of sources of international law.[55] This chapter does not attempt to make that case, since its purpose is a more general one: simply to establish that the responsibility to protect demonstrates international legal normativity. It does so by showing that the responsibility to protect independently exhibits characteristics associated with another of the classic sources of international law, general principles of international law.[56]

Section (c) of Article 38(1) identifies "general principles of law recognized by civilized nations" as a source of international legal norms. Until the last decades of the twentieth century, general principles were not widely invoked in ICJ decisions, and they have formed the least-understood element of the catalogue of sources of international law included in Article 38. Nonetheless, this chapter argues that the general principles clause, interpreted as an expression of a common sense of juridical right and wrong (*sensus communis juris*), supports claims that norms based on "elementary considerations of humanity" are or could become principles of international law. Norms that fit

Brazil—a company unlikely, on its face, to represent non-western legal traditions effectively.

54 *Ibid.* Until recently, this list has been widely regarded as exhaustive. However, this view is increasingly being challenged. An early critic was Sir Gerald Fitzmaurice; more recently, Yasuaki Onuma (*A Transcivilizational Perspective on International Law* (Leiden: Brill/Nijhoff, 2010)) and the Third World Approaches to International Law (TWAIL) school have developed detailed critiques of this position.

55 Contention over variants of such a theory has recently fuelled debate concerning the International Law Commission's work on the *Identification of Customary International Law*, led by Special Rapporteur Sir Michael Wood. The ILC began work on the identification of customary international law in 2012, and received feedback and guidance from the UN General Assembly's Sixth (Legal) Committee (of state representatives) throughout the process (http://legal.un.org/ilc/summaries/1_13.shtml). Jean d'Aspremont canvasses debate over the ILC's decisions regarding the scope of its study in "Customary International Law as a Dance Floor: Part I" (EJIL:Talk! (April 2014), online at www.ejiltalk.org/customary-international-law-as-a-dance-floor-part-i/).

56 The responsibility to protect may well exhibit *parallel* forms of international legal normativity, like a number of other international legal principles, including the prohibition on the use of force (proscribed by the UN Charter, Art. 2(4) and international custom).

into this sub-category of general principles are 1) human rights, and 2) human rights protection norms, such as the precautionary principle, the principle of sustainability, and the responsibility to protect. These and other rules that flow from the requirements of public conscience are most coherently and accurately interpreted as general principles of international law, although they may *also* possess or acquire the characteristics of customary international law norms.[57]

General principles and the League of Nations' Advisory Committee of Jurists

The most influential early appearance of the idea that international legal rules could originate in a common sense of juridical right and wrong occurred in the preamble of the 1899 Hague Convention II dealing with Regulations on the Laws and Customs of War on Land[58] and was repeated in the 1907 Hague Convention IV[59] on the same subject, in a passage known as the Martens Clause.[60] The humanitarian law rules whose existence is asserted by this clause are deemed to be binding on states, although they do not find their origin in state practice or the *opinio juris* of states, but in the "laws of humanity and dictates of the public conscience" ("*droits des humanités et des éxigences de la conscience publique*").[61]

57 Antonio Cassese is a notable exception to the general interpretive trend, having taken seriously the possibility that as international law develops, such norms might also be regarded as general principles of international law ("Martens Clause," at 188).

58 *Convention (II) with Respect to the Laws and Customs of War on Land and its Annex: Regulations Concerning the Laws and Customs of War on Land*, The Hague, 29 July 1899, online at www.icrc.org/applic/ihl/ihl.nsf/Article.xsp?action=openDocument&documentId=9FE084CDAC63D10FC12563CD00515C4D

59 *Convention (IV) with Respect to the Laws and Customs of War on Land and its Annex: Regulations Concerning the Laws and Customs of War on Land*, The Hague, 18 October 1907, online at www.icrc.org/applic/ihl/ihl.nsf/0/1d1726425f6955aec125641e0038bfd6

60 These treaties affirmed that in conflict situations for which relevant laws of war had not yet been devised, "the inhabitants and the belligerents remain under the protection and the rule of the principles of the law of nations, as they result from the usages established among civilized peoples, from the laws of humanity, and the dictates of the public conscience" (this is the ICRC's unofficial English translation (*ibid.*)).

The clause containing this passage was named for the distinguished Russian international law scholar, jurist, and diplomat Fyodor Fyodorovich Martens (also known as Friedrich Fromhold Martens), who suggested its inclusion in the 1899 *Hague Convention.*

61 The original reads: "*les populations et les bélligerants restent sous la sauvegarde et sous l'empire des principes du droit des gens, tels qu'ils résultent des usages établis entre nations civilisées, des lois de l'humanité et des éxigences de la conscience publique*" (*Convention (IV) concernant les lois et coutumes de la guerre sur terre et son Annexe: Règlement concernant les lois et coutumes de la guerre sur terre*, La Haye, 18 octobre 1907, online at https://ihl-databases.icrc.org/dih-traites/INTRO/195.https://ihl-databases.icrc.org/dih-traites/INTRO/195).

In his much-cited 1953 work, *General Principles of Law as Applied by International Courts and Tribunals*, [62] Bin Cheng offers a reading of general principles of law that situates this source as part of the tradition of attributing a law-creating capacity to a common sense of juridical right and wrong. He argues that the PCIJ Advisory Committee's decision to include general principles on an equal footing with treaties and international custom among the formal sources of international law was a product of the ten members' theoretical commitments and national juristic traditions, but also a reflection of various draft schemes received for consideration by the Committee from both states and individuals[63] (influences that are often overlooked by commentators on the genesis of general principles). These draft schemes appear to have informed the suggestion of Baron Édouard Descamps, Chairman of the Advisory Committee, that in addition to conventions and customary international law, the new Court should have recourse to "*les règles de droit international telles que les reconnait la conscience juridique des peuples civilisés.*"[64] A version of Descamps' proposal was, of course, eventually agreed to by the Committee members, and the English wording settled upon to describe this source was the well-known formulation: "general principles of law recognized by civilized nations," which echoed several of those guiding draft schemes.[65]

Bin maintains that as a consequence of this genealogy, any reading of the final PCIJ language regarding general principles must be informed by an understanding of the precise denotations of two key terms that figured in the original French-language proposal presented by Descamps to the Advisory Committee. Because the proceedings of the Committee were conducted exclusively in French,[66] Committee members' use-in-practice of these terms—"*la conscience juridique*" and "*des peuples civilisés*"—must be considered in assessing the scope of general principles in Article 38 (3), and ultimately, Article 38(1)(c).[67]

62 Cambridge: Grotius Publications Ltd., 1987.

63 Bin, *General Principles*, at 6. No fewer than 15 draft plans and detailed commentaries were provided by states, organizations, and expert individuals to the Advisory Committee of Jurists to aid in their deliberations regarding the new Court. See Advisory Committee of Jurists, *Documents Presented to the Committee Relating to Existing Plans for the Establishment of a Permanent Court of International Justice, 1920*, online at www.icj-cij.org/pcij/serie_D/D_documents_to_comm_existing_plans.pdf

64 Permanent Court of International Justice: Advisory Committee of Jurists, *Procès-verbaux of the Proceedings of the Committee, June 16-July 24, 1920, with Annexes* (The Hague: Van Langenhuysen Brothers, 1920), online at https://archive.org/stream/procsverbauxof00leaguoft#page/ii/mode/2up, at 306.

65 Bin, *General Principles*, at 7.

66 The exception to this practice was the American member, Elihu Root, who spoke in English (*Procès-verbaux*, at iv).

67 Bin, *General Principles*, at 8–9.

"La Conscience Juridique"

In contrast to typical English usage, in French, the word "*conscience*" is not only applied to moral judgements regarding one's own conduct, but may refer to a variety of different realms—*conscience morale*, but also *conscience religieuse, conscience publique*, and *conscience juridique.* [68] Thus, Bin concludes that more apt English translations of Descamps' phrase "*la conscience juridique des peuples civilisés*" would be "'the sense common to all civilized peoples of what is juridically right or wrong,' or ... 'the *opinio juris communis* of civilised mankind.'"[69] (Hereinafter, I will render the first phrase in Bin's suggested translation as "the *sensus communis juris*" in the interests of both precision of usage and consistency with earlier chapters of this book.)

"Des Peuples Civilisés"

The second part of the French formulation that came to be translated as "general principles of law recognized by civilized nations" has been widely denigrated as anachronistic and racist in the decades since the Second World War. But this infamous phrase, "*des peuples civilisés,*" also calls for closer scrutiny. It had its genesis in an amendment to Descamps' proposal offered by Elihu Root, the sole Committee member who spoke and wrote in English. As Bin points out, Root employed the term "civilised nations" when apparently referring to Descamps' term, "*peuples civilisés.*" In so doing, the American was using an expression identical with that which appeared in the English translation of Descamps' phrase used by the Committee of Jurists. Moreover, the earlier *French* translation of Root's amendment by the Committee of Jurists had employed "*peuples civilisés.*" In Bin's words:

> Looked at from this angle, the word "nation" in Art. 38 I (c) should be understood not in its politico-legal sense, as it is used in "League of *Nations*," "United *Nations*" or "Inter*nation*al Law," but in its more general sense of a people, as for instance, the Scottish *nation*, the French *nation*, the Maori *nation*, etc. Some further support for this view may be found in the fact that at certain stages of the drafting of the Article, the word *nation* in clause 3 was written with a small *n*, while the same word in clause 4, in the sense of a country, was written with a capital *N.* [70]

This suggests that the inclusion of the term "nations" in Article 38 Article 38(1)(c) can be interpreted to indicate that *communities* were meant to be the locus of the juridical conscience that is the subject matter of the clause, and that these communities might

68 *Ibid.* at 8.
69 *Ibid.* at 9.
70 *Ibid.* at 9, n. 34, citing *Texte adopté en Iere Lecture*, Art. 35, at 659, *Procès-verbaux*, at 665–666.

not be organized in the form of centralized and hierarchical polities with the formal status of *states.*

The explicit language of the Article tells us, however, that in order to participate in the recognition process of a general principle, these communities must be "civilized." Without question, the term "civilized" conveyed the discriminatory Eurocentric presumption that only normative orders characteristic of centralized and hierarchically-organized political communities could be understood as having the character of "Law." This is why the polysemic "*peuples*" required the adjective "*civilisés*" in the initial formulation of the clause. However, once the drafting process resulted in the substitution of the English term "nations" for "*peuples*," the adjective "civilized" was *retained.* The significance of the continuing presence of "civilized" in the clause flows from the fact that—in this period—the recognition of a political community as having state status was closely correlated with its being considered "civilized"[71]: if states were the sole intended referent of the term "nations" in Article 38, it would have been redundant to include the adjective "civilized."

At the time of drafting, many non-European societies were classified by Europeans and their settler colonies as lacking "Law" because they did not conform to a European standard of politico-legal centralization and hierarchy. Approaching the qualifying phrase "of civilized nations" in this way suggests that its function was "to safeguard against subjectivity and possible arbitrariness on the part of the judge" as s/he seeks to interpret the content of the common sense of juridical right and wrong invoked by Article 38(1)(c) as a source of international law.[72] The functional purpose of including the phrase "of civilized nations" in Article 38 (3) was thus to interject a gatekeeping mechanism for filtering candidates for general principles of international law—one whose merits and interpretation are open to contemporary critique and revision.

Three types of general principles

Examination of the proceedings of the 1920 Advisory Committee reveal that the discussion of general principles encompassed at least three different forms of legal norm, reflecting aspects of both positive law and natural law traditions. All three of these forms have been acknowledged in subsequent jurisprudence of the ICJ and other international tribunals:

> 1) The first was that of general principles common to the domestic legal systems of "civilized nations," that could provide "elements of legal reasoning and private law analogies" to be adapted to the needs of the international legal order.[73] For this sub-category of norm, "[t]he idiosyncracies of local law

71 This point has been developed by Antony Anghie in his indispensable *Imperialism, Sovereignty and the Making of International Law* (Cambridge: Cambridge University Press, 2004), at chap. 2.

72 Bin, *General Principles*, at 25.

73 Oscar Schachter, *International Law in Theory and Practice* (Hague: Martinus Nijhoff, 1991), at 16.

are discarded" and the core of the principle is abstracted from its particular municipal expressions.[74] Examples of this form include the principles that "any breach of an engagement involves an obligation to make reparation," of estoppel,[75] and municipal law analogies concerning the rules of evidence, jurisdiction, and procedure.

2) The second sub-category was general principles of international law, described by Oscar Schachter as "abstractions from a mass of rules ... so long and so generally accepted as to be no longer directly connected with state practice,"[76] and by Bin as including "latent rules" of the sort routinely relied upon by international tribunals.[77] Examples include principles of good faith and the freedom of the seas.

3) The third was the sub-category described in the preceding paragraphs, a class of dynamic and "unformulated principles"[78] of law expressive of "elementary considerations of humanity." As will be shown, axiomatic examples are human rights and human rights protection norms. The *sensus communis juris* that identifies principles in this sub-category is "objectively validated"[79] through recognition by an appropriate interpretive community, which subsequent practice and judicial and scholarly opinion suggest is not limited to states.

The third and fourth parts of the chapter examine the types of norms that fit into this third sub-category of general principles, and the evidence that the responsibility to protect is one such norm.

III Theoretical interlude: the "how"

The "riconiscimento di esigenze della coscienza pubblica" *process*

The process by which norms belonging to the third sub-category of general principles come to be recognized as possessing a distinctively legal character was first identified clearly by Giuseppe Sperduti in his 1958 *Lezioni di dirito internazionale*, in an argument described by Antonio Cassese as both "rigorous" and "original."[80] Guided by the Martens Clause, Sperduti argues that there is an

74 Charles T. Kotuby Jr. and Luke A. Sobota, *General Principles of Law and International Due Process* (Oxford: Oxford University Press, 2017), at 20.
75 See *Chórzow Factory* (Merits), PCIJ, Ser. A, no. 17, p.29 and *Eastern Greenland* (1933), PCIJ, Ser. A/B, no. 53, at 52 62, 69.
76 Schachter, *International Law*, at 18.
77 *Ibid.* Bin's interpretation of the purpose and effect of the Committee's decision on this point is at odds with that of Antonio Cassese. See Cassese, *International Law in a Divided World* (Oxford: Clarendon Press, 1986), at 170–171, §94.
78 Bin, *General Principles*, at 23.
79 Bruno Simma and Philip Alston, "The Sources of Human Rights Law: Custom, Jus Cogens, and General Principles," (1988–1989) 12 *Australian Year Book of International Law* 82 at 102.
80 Cassese, "The Martens Clause: Half a Loaf or Simply Pie in the Sky?" (2000) 11 *EJIL* 188, at 191, n.6.

international norm-creation process similar to but distinct from the customary process, which recognizes the "*esigenze della coscienza pubblica*," or demands of public conscience, in the form of general rules of international law.[81]

Norms produced in this way, according to Sperduti, include the prohibitions of the slave trade and wars of aggression. They typically originate as moral norms, but are transformed through the recognition process; prior to their thematization in public conscience (often through their application to a particular problem or crisis commanding public attention or repugnance), "*sono non soltanto fornite di valore giuridico*," but through the process of the "*riconoscimento giuridico di esigenze della coscienza pubblica*" (RG process),"*altresì di un valore pratico di grado elevato.*"[82] Sperduti observes that this transformative recognition of the demands of public conscience often takes place through the reiteration of the norms in international conventions and declarations.[83] Although he does not explicitly identify those norms produced through the RG process with the general principles of Article 38(1)(c), his work provides an early description of the method of juridification of such norms and a provenance for it.

More recently, aspects of the same dynamic process have been recognized by authors such as Gunther Teubner and Ruti Teitel. Teubner's discussion of the phenomenon of "social positivization" highlights cases in which "scandalized norms" temporarily arouse the attention of global publics following a local crisis. Teubner posits that these norms, which originally lack an international legal character, become integrated into "global law" as secondary rules that are incorporated into the validity decisions of arbitral tribunals associated with the diverse types of regulatory bodies.[84] The rapid emergence of an international legal norm prohibiting the use of sexual violence as a weapon of war serves as an example of this progression. Following global publicity accorded to incidents of such organized violence during the 1992–1995 Bosnian War and during the 1994 Rwandan genocide,[85] an "extraordinary public

81 Giuseppe Sperduti, *Lezioni di Diritto Internazionale* (Milano: A. Giuffrè, 1958), at 70.

82 *Ibid.* at 69. ("[T]hey have no legal value by themselves" but through the process of the "legal recognition of the demands of public conscience," they gain "a high level of practical value (author's translation).")

83 *Ibid.* at 68–71.

84 Teubner adopts Andrew Hurrell's notion of a "common law constitution" to describe how "fundamental rights are positivized in transnational (public and private) regimes: an iterative decision-making process occurs between the rulings of arbitration tribunals, decisions of national courts, contracts of private actors, social standardizations, and the scandalization actions of protest movements and NGOs" (Hurrell, *On Global Order: Power, Values, and the Constitution of International Society* (Oxford: Oxford University Press, 2007), at 53; cited in Teubner, *Constitutional Fragments: Societal Constitutionalism and Globalization* (Oxford: Oxford University Press, 2012), at 130).

85 Accounts of mass rape in the Bosnian War were initially spread to a global public through diverse sources, including NGO reports such as that of Amnesty International (*Bosnia-Herzegovina: Rape and Sexual Abuse by Armed Forces* (January 1993), AI Index: EUR 63/01/93), and first-person narratives, such as those recorded in Alexandra Stiglmayer, ed., *Mass Rape: The War Against Women in Bosnia-Herzegovina*, trans. Marion Faber (Lincoln, NE: University of Nebraska Press, 1994). Much of this material was documented in the Reports of the UN Commission of Experts which directly mandated the creation of the ICTY, based on testimony provided by NGOs,

outcry"[86] was translated into Security Council resolutions, including the one establishing the International Criminal Tribunal for the Former Yugoslavia (ICTY),[87] and eventually read back into then-existing prohibitions of crimes against humanity, war crimes, and torture in the enabling statutes and jurisprudence of the International Tribunal for Rwanda and the ICTY, and later incorporated into the Rome Statute of the International Criminal Court.[88]

Ruti Teitel's work documenting the impact of a broad and deep turn toward protection of persons in international law provides further illustration of the multiplex impacts of the RG process. In *Humanity's Law*, she chronicles the rise of a "humanity-based framework" across the formerly distinct international legal fields of human rights law, criminal law, and war law, drawing on a rich array of examples from the jurisprudence and practice of international courts, tribunals, and international organizations.[89]

The RG process moves norms that express elementary considerations of humanity along the continuum of normativity. This process involves a hermeneutic interchange between the activities of relevant interpretive communities and the accretion of practices congruent with the norm in question.[90] Such practices, undertaken by a panoply of local and transnational NGOs,

private sources, states, intergovernmental organizations and UN bodies (see esp. *Second Interim Report of the Commission of Experts Established Pursuant to Security Council Resolution 780*, (6 October 1993), UN Doc. S26545).

86 Serge Brammertz and Michelle Jarvis, eds., *Prosecuting Conflict-Related Sexual Violence* (Oxford: Oxford UP, 2016), at 21. For a general overview of the international legal response to the epidemic of sexual violence in Bosnian-Herzegovina, see pp. 20–30.

87 UNSC Res. 798 (18 December 1992), UN Doc. S/RES/798; UNSC Res. 808 (22 February 1993), UN Doc. S/RES/808.

88 See *Statute of the International Criminal Tribunal for Rwanda*, UNSC Res. 955, S/RES/955(1994), 8 November 1994, Art. 3(g), available at www.un.org/ictr/statute.html, and esp. *Prosecutor v. Jean-Paul Akayesu*, Judgment, ICTR-96-4-T, Sept. 2 1998, paras. 688, 598. In the Statute of the International Criminal Tribunal for the Former Yugoslavia (25 May 1993), see esp. Art. 5(g), and in the jurisprudence of the ICTY, see esp. *Prosecutor v. Furundžija*, Judgment, IT-95–17/1-T, Dec. 10, 1998, paras. 183,185, and *Prosecutor v. Dragoljub Kunarac*, Radomir Kovac and Zoran Vukovic (Judgment), Case No. IT-96–23/1- T (Feb. 22, 2001), para. 436. Further expansion of the list of international crimes of sexual violence in the enabling statute of the ICC adds enforced prostitution, forced pregnancy, sexual slavery, enforced sterilization and other forms of sexual violence of equivalent gravity to the definitions of war crimes and crimes against humanity (*Rome Statute of the International Criminal Court*, adopted July 17, 1998, 2187 UNTS 90, 37 ILM 1002 (entered into force July 1, 2002), art. 7, 8, online at http://untreaty.un.org/cod/icc/statute/romefra.htm).

89 Ruti G. Teitel, *Humanity's Law* (Oxford & New York: Oxford University Press, 2011).

90 This part of the argument owes an intellectual debt to Jutta Brunnée and Stephen Toope's concept of "practices of legality," outlined above in the introductory chapter (*Legitimacy and Legality*, at 27–28). The term "relevant interpretive communities" employed here corresponds to the usage of "relevant communities of judgement" discussed previously in Chapter 2, using the preferred nomenclature of Hannah Arendt and Jennifer Nedelsky.

international organizations, civil society actors, domestic and international tribunals and courts, private and hybrid transnational standard-setting organizations, corporate actors, and states, elaborate and limit such emerging norms.[91] As Jutta Brunnée and Stephen Toope observe, "[a]ll that is required to begin the process of law-building in international society is a shared understanding that law is needed in a given context."[92]

The RG process is most easily appreciated if international law is conceived on the model of a deliberative practice, "a discourse with the shared purpose of forming and defending judgements," as outlined in previous chapters.[93] A deliberative practice is a type of Wittgensteinian language game in which participants form an interpretive community. Such interpretive communities engage in activities in which the articulation of reasons in order to make and defend judgements is a primary activity, such as judicial decision-making, moral reasoning, and aesthetic criticism. As shared ways of proceeding are negotiated over time, participants deploy argumentative strategies and animating norms that may not initially be recognized as valid by other interlocutors; their degree

91 These nontraditional participants in international law's evolution and ascertainment inspire questions about authority and process. Determining which nonstate actors play a role in formulating and authoritatively expressing a *sensus communis juris* around an emerging general principle is part of the challenge of engaging with a robust reading of Article 38(1)(c). "Relevant" interpretive communities that participate in the RG process include judges on international and domestic courts and tribunals, government legal advisers and diplomats, international lawyers in private practice, activists, scholars, intergovernmental organizations such as the UN and the Intergovernmental Panel on Climate Change, INGOs such as the International Committee of the Red Cross and Red Crescent and Human Rights Watch, and arguably, global web movements such as 38 Degrees and Avaaz, new hybrid organizations involving private transnational actors such as Goodweave and the Forest Stewardship Council, and what Achilles Skordas terms the "media of global reach" (Skordas, "Hegemonic Custom?" in Michael Byers, ed., *United States Hegemony and the Foundations of International Law* (West Nyack, NY: Cambridge University Press, 2003), at 322).

The appropriateness of including the organizations on the preceding list among relevant interpretive communities is premised in part on their active embrace of the "culture of accountability" on which trust in institutions is arguably founded (see Eyal Benvenisti, "Upholding Democracy Amid the Challenges of New Technology: What Role for the Law of Global Governance?" (2018) 29 *EJIL* 9 at 14). Such organizations gain their status as legitimacy-generating institutions by foregrounding democratic accountability; they achieve this by fostering bidirectional communication with members/audiences, such as random sample polling of members, and this helps to support claims of representativeness. It must be noted that real and growing concerns exist about the potential for manipulation of such actors through the combined forces of fragmentation and technological innovation, which closely parallel worries about the manipulability of traditional national election and referenda outcomes. A contextualized attention to the issue of gatekeeping is therefore a pressing priority as the general principles category receives further elaboration.

92 Brunnée and Toope, *Legitimacy and Legality*, at 354–355.

93 Thomas Morawetz, "The Epistemology of Judging," in Dennis Patterson, ed., *Wittgenstein and Legal Theory* (Boulder, CO: Westview Press, 1992), at 1.

of openness to new gambits and indeed, classes of interlocutors, may vary over time.[94]

However, part of what it is to engage in a deliberative practice consists in the construction of conversational and conceptual bridges that seek to make diverse argumentative strategies intelligible. At its most productive, the process of creating such bridges entails what Hannah Arendt called "enlarged thinking," and leads to a form of mutual understanding that can result in what she termed a *sensus communis.* The "bindingness" of law depends upon the presence in some measure of such a *sensus communis juris.*

In this way, the "core" and "penumbra" of an emerging general principle is staked out, and indeed, the boundary between the core and penumbral content of any given international legal concept can fluctuate over time as the locus of an initial overlapping consensus among members of relevant interpretive communities shifts.[95] The deliberative practice of the participating interpretive communities, through their practical and rhetorical engagement *develops and applies* the norm, contesting and refining its meaning and range of application. This practice in itself produces an iterative filtering, or gatekeeping effect accomplished through the ongoing deliberative dialogue by relevant interpretive communities (whose memberships are also subject to contestation and deliberation).

Thus, while recognition of general principles often originates in a moral recoiling from a crisis in which elementary considerations of humanity are at issue, this does not produce a wholesale transplanting of moral precepts into international law. To borrow a phrase of Jean Cohen's, the general principles that result from the RG process "are always the contextual product of struggle, *of efforts to achieve mutual recognition, political justice, legal standing, and so forth*" [emphasis added].[96]

The deliberative practice of interpretive communities is consequently not neutral. It is, as Martti Koskenniemi observes, "a process of articulating political preferences into legal claims that cannot be detached from the conditions of political contestation in which they are made."[97] In the spirit of Koskenniemi, the deliberative practice of international law is also a "hegemonic technique,"[98] undertaken as a means of securing specific outcomes in particular fields of contestation, and

94 Within the framework of his influential theory of law-ascertainment, Jean d'Aspremont refers to the activity of interpretive communities understood in similar terms as "communitarian semantics" (*Formalism and the Sources of International Law* (Oxford & New York: Oxford University Press, 2011), at 196).

95 I employ these terms of art with apologies to the memory of H.L.A. Hart for some minor violence wrought to the purposes for which he introduced the distinction between "core" and "penumbral" meanings of a legal concept (H.L.A. Hart, "Positivism and the Separation of Law and Morals," (1958) 71 *Harvard Law Review* 593). See further discussion below.

96 Jean L. Cohen, "Rethinking Human Rights, Democracy and Sovereignty in the Age of Globalization," (2008) 36 *Political Theory* 599.

97 Martti Koskenniemi, "International Law and Hegemony: A Reconfiguration," (2004) 17 *Cambridge Review of International Affairs* 198.

98 *Ibid.* at 199.

simultaneously to impose and maintain a certain interpretation of the "rules of the game" of international law *tout court.*

IV A preliminary genealogy of the third category of general principles in the Charter era

The idea that the demands of public conscience—inspired by elementary considerations of humanity—can give rise to international legal norms is developed through a handful of key judicial decisions delivered in the UN Charter era. The majority of these formulations frame these norms as general principles. In general, when the "public conscience" interpretation of general principles appears, it is typically—but as will be shown below, not necessarily—grounded in a natural law approach to international legal theory.

As the character of this third sub-category of general principles developed, elementary considerations of humanity (ECH) were sometimes invoked directly as themselves constituting a general principle of international law, as in the ICJ's influential decision in the *Corfu Channel* case,[99] the *Nicaragua* decision[100] and Judge Mohamed Shahabuddeen's dissenting opinion in the *Nuclear Weapons Advisory Opinion* case.[101] On other occasions, this sub-category of general principles is instead referred to through instances of the general class that it represents, as in Judge Kotaro Tanaka's dissenting opinion in the *South West Africa Cases.* [102]

But a review of the peripatetic development of international law in this area suggests that ECH are more precisely interpreted as giving rise to a sub-category of general principles that themselves put into practice considerations of humanity, namely, *human rights and human rights protection norms.* The uneven and sometimes-contradictory history of international jurisprudence around the concept of ECH makes it apparent that ECH are most coherently understood as jurisgenerative: a source of international law, via the dictates of public conscience.

Corfu Channel and ECH

In the first case decided by the ICJ in 1949, this third sub-category of general principles was invoked by the Court in its finding that the Albanian government was under obligation to alert those in transit through its territorial waters of the existence of a minefield:

> Such obligations are based, not on the Hague Convention of 1907, No. VIII, which is applicable in time of war, but on certain general and well-recognized

99 *Corfu Channel Case (United Kingdom v Albania)*, Merits, [1949] ICJ Rep. 4.

100 *Military and Paramilitary Activities in and against Nicaragua (Nicaragua v. United States of America)*, Merits, [1986] ICJ Rep. 39.

101 *Legality of the Threat or Use of Nuclear Weapons Case*, Advisory Opinion, [1996] ICJ Rep. 226, dissenting opinion of Judge Shahabuddeen.

102 *South West Africa Cases (Ethiopia v. South Africa; Liberia v. South Africa)*; Second Phase, [1966] ICJ Rep. 6, dissenting opinion of Judge Tanaka.

> principles, namely: elementary considerations of humanity, even more exacting in peace than in war; the principle of the freedom of maritime communication; and every State's obligation not to allow knowingly its territory to be used for acts contrary to the rights of other States.[103]

In employing language drawn from the Martens Clause and originally applied to the specific context of humanitarian law, the Court makes clear in this decision that it conceives of "elementary considerations of humanity" as "a free-standing general principle of international law."[104] This understanding of ECH played a notable role decades later in the *Nicaragua* and *Nuclear Weapons Advisory Opinion* cases (see below).

The South West Africa Cases: human rights and human rights protection norms

In his important dissenting opinion in the *South West Africa Cases*, Second Phase (1966), Judge Tanaka reaches the conclusion that human rights and human rights protection norms are general principles of international law.[105] These ICJ cases concerned South Africa's attempt to extend its colonial authority over Namibia under the League of Nations mandate system into the Charter era. The applicants—Ethiopia and Liberia—argued that the apartheid system administered by South Africa in Namibia[106] violated norms prohibiting racial discrimination and segregation that had the status of general principles of international law under Article 38(1)(c).

In his dissent, Judge Tanaka offers an evolutionary account of this clause, relying on the *procès-verbaux* of the PCIJ Advisory Committee of Jurists, Baron Descamps' original proposal regarding "*la conscience juridique reconnait des peuples civilisés*," and Bin Cheng's interpretation of the deliberations of the Committee.[107] Tanaka adopts the view that the structure of the entirety of Article 38 reflects a self-conscious intention by the Committee members to strike a compromise among purely positive and natural law elements, intended by the Committee members to acknowledge the law-generating roles of both consent-based sources and sources "deeply rooted in the conscience of mankind and of any reasonable man."[108] Judge Tanaka reasons that part (c) of the Article provides for recognition of two categories of law possessing "an international character." The first is "common elements among diverse national laws"—with attention both to statutory provisions and to their "underlying or guiding 'principles,'" but

103 *Corfu Channel*, at 22.

104 Matthew Zagor, "Elementary Considerations of Humanity," in Karine Bannelier, Theodore Christakis and Sarah Heathcote, eds., *The ICJ and the Evolution of International Law: The Enduring Impact of the Corfu Channel Case* (London, UK: Routledge), at 264; see also on this point Pierre-Marie Dupuy, "*Les 'considérations élémentaires d'humanité' dans la jurisprudence de la Cour Internationale de Justice*," in René-Jean Dupuy and L.A. Sicilianos, eds., *Mélanges en l'honneur de N. Valticos* (Paris: Pédone, 1999), at 117–130.

105 *South West Africa Cases*, diss. op. Tanaka, at 298.

106 The territory of Namibia was then known as South West Africa.

107 *Ibid.* at 295, 299.

108 *Ibid.* at 298.

also to "one and the same law [that] exists and … is valid through all kinds of human societies in relationships of hierarchy and co-ordination."[109] Principles of the second type include norms that form part of the "law of the world community"[110] and are reflective of what Bin calls "juridical truth"[111] (or, in the context of this discussion, ECH). In Judge Tanaka's view, the role of states is simply declaratory where such rules are concerned.[112]

Consequently, he reasons, "[a]s an interpretation of Article 38, paragraph 1 (c), we consider that the *concept of human rights and of their protection* is included in the general principles mentioned in that article" [emphasis added].[113] The principles of human rights and of human rights protection are therefore themselves sources of international law under the provisions of Art. 38(1)(c), in Judge Tanaka's understanding.[114] Furthermore, in a slightly different connection, Judge Tanaka observes that "the legislative imperfections in the definition of human rights and freedoms and the lack of mechanism for implementation do not constitute a reason for denying their existence and the need for their legal protection."[115] Gaps in the machinery of international human rights identification and protection as a consequence of failures of states are not, therefore, impediments to recognition of the legal character of human rights and human rights protection principles. On Judge Tanaka's view, Art. 38(1)(c) "does not require the consent of States as a condition of the recognition of the general principles. States which do not recognize this principle or even deny its validity are nevertheless subject to its rule."[116]

Thus, among its many contributions to the clarification of general principles of international law, Judge Tanaka's opinion identifies the sub-category of general principles to which the products of the RG process belong—that of human rights and human rights protection norms.

Nicaragua and ECH

In the 1986 *Nicaragua* case, the ICJ affirmed that ECH give rise to general principles. More specifically, the Court found that certain of those principles are expressed, and in some respects developed, in the humanitarian treaty law of the Geneva Conventions, and in particular in Common Article 3 of the four Geneva Conventions of 1949.[117]

109 *Ibid.* at 296, 295, 296.
110 *Ibid.* at 296.
111 Bin, *General Principles*, at 24; cited in *South West Africa Cases*, diss. op. Tanaka, at 295.
112 *Ibid.* at 297.
113 *Ibid.* at 298.
114 *Ibid.* at 300.
115 *Ibid.* at 290.
116 *Ibid.* at 298.
117 *Military and Paramilitary Activities in and against Nicaragua (Nicaragua v. United States of America)*, Merits, [1986] ICJ Rep., at 113–114.

The Nuclear Weapons Advisory Opinion and ECH

This understanding of ECH as having jurisgenerative force was memorably confirmed again a decade later in dissenting opinions delivered in the Court's *Nuclear Weapons Advisory Opinion* (1996).

In that instance, the ICJ considered a question submitted by the UN General Assembly: whether the threat or use of nuclear weapons was permitted under international law.[118] In a complex decision that drew on multiple international legal sources, the majority of the Court found that the threat or use of such weapons would generally be contrary to the rules of international law applicable in armed conflict, but that the ICJ lacked sufficient basis to reach a definitive conclusion regarding the legality of their use in a self-defensive situation where a state's survival was at risk. This decision was accompanied by several important dissents relevant to the discussion at hand, including those of Judges Mohamed Shahabuddeen and C.G. Weeramantry.

Judge Shahabuddeen's opinion turns on his view that

> [t]he circumstance that there is no "comprehensive and universal prohibition of the threat or use of nuclear weapons as such" in customary or conventional international law does not conclude the question whether the threat or use of nuclear weapons is lawful; more general principles have to be consulted.[119]

Relying upon several complementary strands of argument, he determined that ECH comprise such a source—and in so doing makes an important contribution to showing that ECH themselves constitute a general principle in the Art. 38 sense. Judge Shahabuddeen concludes that ECH do impose a prohibition on the threat or use of nuclear weapons.[120] His reasoning rests upon two main points: 1) that the use of nuclear weapons would result in multi-generational suffering on an enormous scale or even the extinction of life on earth and that such prospects would fundamentally contradict ECH; and 2) that the "dictates of public conscience" regarding these prospects can be translated "into a normative prohibition."[121] In the course of the substantial dissenting opinion he delivers, Judge Shahabuddeen at times asserts clearly that the locus of jurisgenerative authority is ECH, as when he cites Sir Gerald Fitzmaurice: "considerations of humanity give rise in *themselves* to obligations of a legal character."[122] Following the reasoning of

118 This followed a 1993 request by the World Health Organization (WHO) for an ICJ advisory opinion on the legality of the use of nuclear weapons in armed conflict; the Court found this request outside its jurisdiction on the grounds that the question did not fall within the scope of the WHO's constitutionally-mandated activities, and thus failed to fulfil the criteria for admissible advisory opinion requests by specialized agencies under UN Charter Art. 96(2).

119 *Nuclear Weapons*, diss. op. Shahabuddeen, at 377.

120 *Ibid.* at 424.

121 *Ibid.* at 409.

122 Sir Gerald Fitzmaurice, *The Law and Procedure of the International Court of Justice*, Vol. I, 1986, at17, note 4; cited in *Nuclear Weapons*, diss. op. Shahabuddeen, at 407.

the *Corfu Channel* decision, Judge Shahabuddeen holds that the Martens Clause imports principles of humanity and the demands of public conscience into international law; he adds that it is the courts' role to interpret whether these give rise to a general principle (or principles) "in the light of changing conditions."[123]

Judge Weeramantry's parallel dissent in the case highlights the "legal relevance" of global public opinion to the development of public international law.[124] It emphasizes that considerations of humanity and the dictates of public conscience have lawmaking force, and that as they have evolved under the influence of human rights culture since the creation of the UN Charter and the Universal Declaration of Human Rights, so has their impact on public international law.[125]

V Human rights and human rights protection norms

This strand of interpretation of the relationships among elementary considerations of humanity, a *sensus communis juris*, and the dictates of public conscience has persisted, and has attracted contributions from legal academics, as well as jurists. Noteworthy influences include Bruno Simma and Philip Alston's insightful 1986 paper describing the potential for interpreting and developing the general principles clause in this vein[126] and René Jean Dupuy's argument highlighting the *Corfu Channel* decision's recognition of elementary considerations of humanity as constituting a general principle of international law[127] More recently, aspects of this interpretive approach have begun to attract growing interest among scholars and judges because of their relevance in explaining the proliferating sites of legal normativity in a globalizing international society, and have inspired important work by Antonio Cassese and Matthew Zagor.[128]

Mention of two further decisions from the bench of the ICJ will be made here, because they not only provide insights into aspects of the RG process, but also offer examples of three specific human rights protection norms that have been recognized as general principles of international law. These examples of products of the RG process serve as a bridge between the preceding theoretical discussion of Article 38(1)(c) and the analysis of the legal character of the responsibility to protect principle that follows.

123 *Nuclear Weapons, ibid.*, at 406 and 405–411 generally.
124 *Ibid.* at 438–439.
125 *Ibid.* at 490.
126 Simma and Alston, "Human Rights Law."
127 Dupuy, "*Les 'considérations élémentaires d'humanité.'*"
128 Cassese, "The Martens Clause"; and Matthew Zagor, "Elementary Considerations of Humanity," in Karine Bannelier, Théodore Christakis, Sarah Heathcote, eds., *The ICJ and the Evolution of International Law: Enduring Impact of the Corfu Channel Case* (London: Routledge, 2011), at chap. 17.

Sustainable development

In his separate opinion in the *Gabčíkovo-Nagymaros Project* case (1997), Judge Weeramantry offers strong support for an inclusive account of the demands of public conscience and an expansive reading of the role of nonstate actors in developing a practice of legality in support of emerging legal norms of this type.[129]

The *Gabčíkovo-Nagymaros* dispute arose as a consequence of the *Budapest Treaty* concluded in 1977 between Hungary and Czechoslovakia (succeeded as a party in 1993 by the Slovak Republic). The treaty committed the parties to cooperate in the construction of an extensive waterworks along the Danube River, which forms the international boundary between the countries. The purposes of the project were to eliminate flooding, create a source of hydroelectric power, and improve the navigability of the river. In the early 1980s, because of economic difficulties and popular protests inspired by concerns about the environmental impact of the project, Hungary suspended its involvement, and then attempted to withdraw completely. This led Slovakia to undertake an alternative means of achieving the project's goals, which involved diverting the Danube. The two countries jointly brought their dispute to the ICJ.

In his separate opinion, Judge Weeramantry makes a wide-ranging and philosophically sophisticated case for recognizing the international legal character of the principle of sustainable development (SD). He bases this argument in part on the observation that international law has entered a new era in which it "looks beyond [the interests of individual states] and their parochial concerns to the greater interests of humanity and planetary welfare."[130] Although Judge Weeramantry's primary aim is to demonstrate the customary international legal character of the SD principle, the arguments he adduces offer direct, and perhaps equally strong, support for regarding it as a general principle of law as well (as he himself recognizes).[131] Judge Weeramantry describes SD as providing the conceptual and legal apparatus for reconciling the human rights to development and to the protection of the environment.[132] These features of SD—which makes it indispensable for the realization of two human rights—places the principle squarely in the category of human rights protection norms.[133]

Like Judge Tanaka (with whose opinion in the *South West Africa Cases* he demonstrates familiarity[134]), Judge Weeramantry emphasizes the evolutionary potential of international legal principles: "The ethical and human rights related aspects of environmental law bring it within the category of law so essential to human welfare that we cannot apply to today's problems in this field the standards of yesterday."[135] With this assertion, Judge Weeramantry affirms Judge Tanaka's

129 *Gabčíkovo-Nagymaros Project (Hungary v. Slovakia),* Judgment, [1997] ICJ Rep. 7.
130 *Ibid.* at 118.
131 *Ibid.* at 109–110.
132 *Ibid.* at 90–92.
133 *Ibid.* at 118.
134 *Ibid.* at 114.
135 *Ibid.*

observation that human rights and human rights protection standards that inform the *sensus communis juris* of humankind change over time.[136]

For Judge Weeramantry, international law recognizes both *global* legal traditions (not only the municipal laws of polities with the form of modern states[137]) and contemporary practices of legality involving nonstate actors and fora[138] as having discursive authority. As he concludes: "when the Statute of the Court described the sources of international law as including the 'general principles of law recognized by civilized nations,' it expressly opened a door to the entry of such principles into modern international law."[139]

The principle of prevention and the precautionary principle

Perhaps counter-intuitively, the growing inclusiveness (and therefore, diversity) of the interpretive community perceived as relevant to international lawmaking does not preclude the development of a *sensus communis juris* with regard to certain issues. This insight is expressed within the rubric of a natural law approach by Judge Antônio Augusto Cançado Trindade in his separate opinion in the *Pulp Mills* case (2010).[140] In this opinion, Judge Cançado Trindade argues in favour of recognizing the general principle status of two environmental law principles derived from a *sensus communis juris*. His genealogy of these general principles emphasizes both the RG process (through his discussion of the role played by a "universal juridical conscience") and the evolving nature of fundamental international legal norms generally.[141]

Judge Cançado Trindade holds that both the principle of prevention and the precautionary principle possess the status of general principles under Art. 38(1)(c).[142] The *Pulp Mills* case that provided the occasion for his analysis involved a dispute between Argentina and Uruguay over the environmental effects of wood pulp mills on the banks of the River Uruguay which had been authorized by the Uruguayan government. The river constitutes an international boundary between Uruguay and Argentina, and is the subject of the 1975 *Statute of the River Uruguay*, a treaty which establishes both procedural and substantive obligations for

136 Judge Tanaka underscores "the transformation of law inevitably produced by change in the social substratum" throughout his discussion of the international legal status of human rights and human rights protection norms (*South West Africa Cases*, at 291).

137 *Ibid.* at 93, 97, 109.

138 *Ibid.* at 93–94.

139 *Ibid.* at 109–110.

140 *Case Concerning Pulp Mills on the River Uruguay* (Argentina v. Uruguay), Judgment, [2010] ICJ Rep. 11, sep. op. Cançado Trindade.

141 A theme which Cançado Trindade takes up again in his separate opinion in the *Whaling in the Antarctic* case in a discussion of "the gradual formation of an *opinio juris communis* in the present domain of contemporary international law" (*Whaling in the Antarctic*, (Australia and New Zealand (intervening) v. Japan), Judgment [2014], sep. op. Cançado Trindade, at 358).

142 *Pulp Mills* case, sep. op. Cançado Trindade, at 157, 159.

the parties. In their preliminary submissions to the Court in the *Pulp Mills* case, both Argentina and Uruguay, had expressly referred to the principles of prevention and precaution.[143]

In Judge Cançado Trindade's view, these two general principles are, like others of the human rights and human rights protection class, "indicators of the degree of evolution of the *status conscientiae* of the international community as a whole."[144] He explains the origins of these international legal norms as follows:

> General principles of law emanate, in my perception, from human conscience, from the *universal juridical conscience*, which I regard as the ultimate material "source" of all law. A clear illustration is provided by the gradual acknowledgment, in the last decades, of the principles proper to a domain like that of International Environmental Law—such as those of prevention and precaution—as consciousness has emerged of the pressing need to secure the protection of the environment, given its vulnerability, the risks surrounding everyone, and the harmful consequences of irreparable damages caused to it. The awakening of such consciousness has accounted for the assertion of those principles [emphasis added].[145]

As Judge Cançado Trindade's argument makes clear, exemplary norms of this type are those concerned with the fragility of embodied human life on this earth, embedded as it is in rich relationships of interchange with the animate and inanimate worlds. Such principles are inspired by a "negative solidarity" and are best understood as norms of the human rights and human rights protection class identified first by Judge Tanaka in the *South West Africa Cases.* [146]

The nature of human rights and human rights protection norms

This form of solidarity is based upon our appreciation of the vulnerability to suffering we share with others, rooted in imagined or real experiences of "the damaged life" rather than a vision of the good life.[147] Consequently, it is best

143 *Ibid.* at 161, 171.

144 *Ibid.*, at 213.

145 *Ibid.* at 156; see also *Ibid.* at 159, 161–162.

146 Cançado Trindade further observes that general principles of this ilk, originating in international law (as opposed to those deriving from municipal legal orders), are distinguished by their having a substantive content (*ibid.* at 153); compare this view with observations by Judges Al-Khasawneh and Simma in their joint dissenting opinion in this case, which suggest that these kinds of international legal principles (whatever the origin of their legal character) are typically instantiated in procedural rules (*ibid.*, diss. op., Al-Khasawneh and Simma, at 108).

147 Jürgen Habermas, *Moral Consciousness and Communicative Action*, trans. by Christian Lenhardt and Shierry Weber Nicholsen (Cambridge: Massachusetts Institute of Technology Press, 1990), at 205; see also J. Donald Moon, "Practical Discourse and Communicative Ethics" in Stephen K. White, ed., *The Cambridge Companion to Habermas* (Cambridge: Cambridge University Press, 1995), at 152.

described as a negative solidarity, rather than a positive one. This negative solidarity serves as the ground for a *sensus communis juris* and can eventually give rise to a shared conviction that law is needed (the demands of public conscience).

This phenomenological reading of the basis for legal recognition of the felt need for human security offers an alternative to the standard natural law approach adopted by most advocates of a "public conscience" basis for general principles. At the same time, it does not preclude a natural law justification. It does not depend upon a presumption of universally shared values, but on a phenomenological observation of shared human vulnerability. The particular harms that become the focus of public conscience at any given moment can evolve, as widely-held notions of the defining qualities of a flourishing human life change over time, depending on which communities are included in the interpretive conversation and what the material conditions of their existence are at any given time. This reading can allow for multiple, culturally and theoretically distinct accounts of the justification for recognizing an emerging general principle's international legal normativity, leaving room for intercultural legitimation through an overlapping consensus over time.

The general principles of SD, prevention, and precaution outlined above fall into the camp of human rights and human rights protection norms classified by Judge Tanaka as a neglected aspect of general principles of international law.

The preceding discussion has asserted that human rights and human rights protection norms identified by a series of jurists and publicists in the past century can be understood as the products of a process of legal recognition of the demands of public conscience, inspired by ECH. This RG process is the means by which norms like sustainable development and the principles of prevention and precaution have been recognized as general principles of international law. These norms are examples of a neglected sub-category of the general principles source of international law acknowledged in Article 38(1)(c), which affirms that international legal normativity can find its genesis in the "demands of public conscience" inspired by ECH, when these are appropriately validated.[148]

This "public conscience" sub-category affirms the legal relevance of a community sense of the requirements of juridical right and wrong (a *sensus communis juris*). As a dimension of Article 38(1)(c), it shares with the more-commonly-cited types of general principles a "revolutionary potential," since it "allow[s] a court to bring to bear a source of law that is not entirely based on the consent of states."[149] The public conscience dimension further recognizes the jurisgenerative

148 Appropriate validation encompasses a variety of gatekeeping issues connected with the recognition of non-traditional participants (and their argumentative strategies) in the interpretive communities of international law, including criteria for determining whether the normative assertions of those actors may have been manipulated by malicious third parties.

149 David S. Berry, *Caribbean Integration Law* (Oxford: Oxford UP,), at 173. Widespread state consent to recognizing the legal status of a developing norm remains a crucial factor in ensuring adherence, as Jutta Brunnée and Stephen Toope suggest:

capability of nonstate actors, in the sense that the RG process translates a moral impulse derived from civil society and rooted in ECH into a legal norm, and accomplishes this transformation through a procedure of validation and elaboration that involves both state and nonstate agents.

VI The responsibility to protect as a general principle

The responsibility to protect is a human rights protection norm, and a general principle of international law. It is rooted in ECH that generate a sense of negative solidarity, which grounds a *sensus communis juris* that in turn can give rise to demands of public conscience. Practices of legality have been established through the RG process, and these practices have been tested through a series of attempts to apply the norm in human protection crises during the first two decades of the twenty-first century. These practices of legality, practical applications of the norm, and deployment of reasons by participants in a rich interpretive community have helped to clarify the parameters of the legal normativity of the responsibility to protect, as outlined below.

As is often the case with principles inspired by ECH, the felt need for the responsibility to protect crystallized following episodes of scandalization inspired by human-made, large scale "avoidable catastrophes" that occurred during the 1990s, just following the end of the Cold War. The most prominent among these were the 1992–1993 famine and disintegration of civil order in Somalia and the botched humanitarian aid and military interventions that followed, the ethnic cleansing and organized sexual violence of the 1992–1995 Bosnian War, the 1994 Rwandan genocide, the 1995 Srebreniçan genocide, and finally, the threatened ethnic cleansing of Albanian Kosovars in 1999. These horrific events occurred largely within the borders of individual states, and in each case included forces of the actual or aspiring government of the state among the aggressors. They led to a series of assertions from political and legal authorities of global standing, by turns grave and impassioned, about the demands of public conscience for human protection. These are echoed in UN Security Council resolutions (SC Res.) and reports of the period (e.g. SC Res. 798 (1992): "appalled by reports … strongly condemns these acts of unspeakable brutality"[150]; SC Res. 925 (1994): "strong

> Law's existence is grounded in shared understandings, buttressed by adherence to the criteria of legality in day-to-day practice. Enforcement, or its lack, is especially relevant to one of the [Fullerian] criteria of legality: the congruence of rules and international practice. When posited rules are consistently evaded or undermined without legal consequence, the rules themselves are compromised because the community of practice recognizes that the declared rule is hypocritical, or that power is being abused without response. In such cases, law itself is undermined. Enforcement matters not because force is necessary for the existence of law, but because adherence is necessary, and enforcement can support or diminish adherence (*Legitimacy and Legality*, at 355).

One of the most effective means of enforcement is, of course, the coercive action of states.

150 UN SC Res. 798, (18 December 1992), UN Doc. S/RES/798.

condemnation of the ongoing violence ... expressing its outrage"[151]; Report of the Secretary-General on the fall of Srebreniça: "shocking events" ... "'darkest pages of human history'"[152]). As outlined previously, these culminated in the call for recognition of the "crystallizing" responsibility to protect principle as a measure to prevent or address "conscience-shocking" violations of human security on a large scale.[153]

From the start, the responsibility to protect (R2P) was conceived quite explicitly as a human rights protection norm. In the ICISS report's opening pages, the principle's foundations are described as lying in "a ... transition from a culture of sovereign impunity to a culture of national and international accountability"[154] that the authors assert supports "intervention for human protection purposes, including military intervention in extreme cases."[155]

From its earliest endorsements by the UN High-Level Panel on Threats, Challenges and Change (2004), Secretary-General Annan's *In Larger Freedom* report (2005), and the World Summit Outcome Document (2005) approved by all 191 member states of the United Nations, the core elements of the responsibility to protect have been unequivocally and repeatedly affirmed—that states bear primary responsibility for protecting their inhabitants from atrocity crimes, and that there is a collective responsibility to help states fulfil this defining obligation, which in extreme circumstances requires timely and decisive action when a home-state fails to protect a threatened population. The varied confirmations of these core ideas from state and nonstate actors from northern, southern, industrialized and industrializing countries consistently depict the responsibility to protect as a norm of human rights protection expressive of a *sensus communis juris* shared by a public of global scope.

Even a very partial and impressionistic summary of the evidence of the existence of such a *sensus communis juris* must include the following:

- In 2000, the African Union's *Constitutive Act* (Article 4 (h)) asserted "the right of the Union to intervene in a member state pursuant to a decision of the Assembly in respect of grave circumstances, namely: war crimes, genocide, and crimes against humanity."[156]
- More than 70 Security Council resolutions refer to the responsibility to protect, and the Council has reaffirmed the principle at least six times. In resolutions and presidential statements addressing crisis situations around the world, the Council has pointedly reasserted the primary responsibility of state governments to protect their populations, and has mandated peace operations on

151 UN SC Res. 925, (1994), UN Doc. S/RES/925.

152 *Report of the Secretary-General Pursuant to General Assembly Resolution 53/35: The Fall of Srebreniça* (15 November 1999), UN Doc. A/54/549, at 6–7.

153 ICISS, *Responsibility to Protect*, at 55.

154 *Ibid.* at 14.

155 *Ibid.* at 16.

156 *Constitutive Act of the African Union*, 11 July 2000, online at www.africa-union.org/root/au/AboutAU/Constitutive_Act_en.htm, Art. 4(h).

two occasions to provide support to governments in fulfilling their responsibility to protect.[157]

- As of 2019, at eight informal and interactive General Assembly dialogues, and two General Assembly formal debates on the responsibility to protect conducted since 2009, more than 120 states have contributed to substantive discussions of the norm.
- The elements of the responsibility to protect are routinely described as constituting fundamental normative standards in authoritative international debates and statements. Between 2005 and 2019, the responsibility to protect was cited in over a dozen General Assembly resolutions.[158]
- The Human Rights Council has adopted more than 40 resolutions that refer to the responsibility to protect.[159]
- Action in fulfilment of the responsibility to protect is widely credited with having defused post-election violence around Kenya's elections in 2007–2008.[160]
- Following the release of the ICISS report, a thoroughgoing restructuring of the UN's organizational structure was undertaken, using a human rights lens that prioritized the protection of persons. This was further sharpened in 2013 with the Secretary-General's launch of the Human Rights up Front initiative, aimed at ensuring that "protecting human rights is at the centre of all UN action and understood to be the responsibility of all UN personnel."[161]
- Geopolitically diverse countries (including, for example, Canada, the UK, Australia, Brazil and China) have devoted resources and political capital to officially (or in the case of China, unofficially) sponsoring interpretations of the responsibility to protect principle.
- The Libyan UN mission's deputy permanent representative asked that the UN Security Council act on its responsibility to protect the Libyan people from the forces of Muammar el-Qaddafi during the 2011 Libyan revolution.[162]

157 Global Centre for the Responsibility to Protect, *About R2P*, online at www.globalr2p.org/about_r2p

158 For a list of these resolutions, see Global Centre for the Responsibility to Protect, *UN General Assembly Resolutions Referencing R2P*, online at www.globalr2p.org/resources/1133

159 UN Human Rights Council, Documents and Resolutions, online at www.ohchr.org/EN/HRBodies/HRC/Pages/Documents.aspx; cited in "#R2P: Reflections on the Responsibility to Protect at 10, Part 1: A Norm for Our Times," Protection Gateway (24 April 2018), online at https://protectiongateway.com/2015/04/22/r2p-reflections-on-the-responsibility-to-protect-at-10-part-1-a-norm-for-our-times/, at 2.

160 Roger Cohen, "How Kofi Annan Rescued Kenya," *New York Review of Books* (14 August 2008), online at www.nybooks.com/articles/2008/08/14/how-kofi-annan-rescued-kenya/

161 UN Development Programme, "Putting Human Rights Up Front" (7 August 2018), online at https://stories.undp.org/putting-human-rights-up-front

162 Ibrahim O. Dabbashi used the phrase "the principle of the right to protect" in his widely-reported plea to the Security Council. The context of his remarks makes it evident that he is referring to the responsibility to protect principle ("Libya's UN

- A proliferating group of civil society organizations from around the world has fostered and promoted scholarship on the responsibility to protect. These include not only prominent transnational entities like the International Crisis Group, the Human Protection Hub, the Asia Pacific Centre for R2P and the Global Centre for the Responsibility to Protect, the World Federalist Movement, and the International Coalition for the Responsibility to Protect, but also smaller and local organizations like the Budapest Center for Mass Atrocities Prevention, (Hungary), Justice without Frontiers (Lebanon), Semillas para la Democracia (Paraguay), West African Civil Society Forum (Nigeria).[163]
- More than 60 states have participated in the national focal point initiative on the responsibility to protect, a program led by senior national officials in each participating state who undertake to build domestic resilience against atrocity crimes through measures that include enhancing participation in and adherence to international treaties on human rights and humanitarian law, enacting domestic legislation to support the protection of at-risk groups, and participating in regional and sub-regional arrangements designed to support these activities. Among these are the Latin American Network for Genocide and Mass Atrocity Prevention, the International Conference on the Great Lakes Region, and the Global Action against Mass Atrocity Crimes initiative. The countries involved in such networks come from every region in the world.[164]

On these and further grounds, the Secretary-General concluded in his 2017 report on implementing the responsibility to protect that:

> The consensus on the purposes of the responsibility to protect spans every continent. There is no longer any question that the protection of populations from atrocity crimes is both a national and an international responsibility, which is universal and enduring.[165]

The nature of this responsibility is described in this 2017 report as *triadic*, encompassing, in the Secretary-General's words, "legal, moral and political responsibilities."[166]

* * *

This chapter's survey of significant moments in the dialogical evolution of international law regarding the responsibility to protect supports this

Diplomats Break With Qaddafi," *New York Times* (21 Feb. 2011), online at www.nytimes.com/2011/02/22/world/africa/22nations.html?_r+0).

163 For a more extensive list of local organizations, see International Coalition for the Responsibility to Protect, online at www.responsibilitytoprotect.org/index.php/about-coalition/current-members

164 UN Secretary-General, "Implementing the Responsibility to Protect: Accountability for Prevention," (10 August 2017), UN Doc. A/71/1016-S/2017/556, at 2–3.

165 *Ibid.* at 3.

166 *Ibid.* at 4.

conclusion. The chapter has identified the imperfectly-understood class of international legal norms to which the responsibility to protect belongs, and sketched the process by which the principle's core and penumbral elements are being negotiated. This dialogue has encompassed diverse interpretations of the responsibility to protect and differences regarding the proper application of the norm. Efforts to invoke or refrain from invoking the principle in contested circumstances have served to clarify the boundary between penumbral and core understandings of the responsibility to protect. Examples include France's short-lived attempt to rally support for applying the norm when the government of Myanmar refused external aid for victims of Cyclone Nargis in 2008,[167] and later the same year, the Russian Federation's roundly-rejected claim that it was fulfilling its responsibility to protect in securing the effective separation of South Ossetia from Georgia and briefly occupying parts of Georgia itself.[168] When atrocity crimes indicators developed in Darfur (beginning in 2003), Sri Lanka (2009), and Côte d'Ivoire (2010–2011) but evoked inadequate responses from the international community to prevent predictable massacres,[169] the animating ideas of the responsibility to protect framed global condemnation. Following Security Council authorization of intervention in Libya on responsibility to protect grounds in 2011, criticisms of NATO's involvement in regime change led by the BRICS countries demonstrated an important limit on the core elements of the norm.[170] The ensuing hesitancy of the Security Council to act on the responsibility to protect principle and the serial P5 failures to respond effectively in human security crises that followed (including, but not limited to, the protracted conflict in Syria and related refugee crises, the ongoing crisis in the Democratic Republic of Congo, and the humanitarian disaster in Yemen) in turn inspired a critical outcry from the General Assembly and civil society actors from around the world asserting the

167 Luck, "Responsibility to Protect," at 5.

168 See for example, Christopher J. Borgen, "The Language of Law and the Practice of Politics: Great Powers and the Rhetoric of Self-Determination in the Cases of Kosovo and South Ossetia," (2009) 10 *Chicago Journal of International Law* 1, and Erna Burai, "Parody as Norm Contestation: Russian Normative Justifications in Georgia and Ukraine and Their Implications for Global Norms," (2016) 30 *Global Society* 67.

169 United Nations Group of Experts, Report on the Situation of Human Rights in Darfur, prepared by the Group of Experts mandated by Human Rights Council resolution 4/8, (8 June 2007), UN Doc. A/HRC/5/6, online at https://digitallibrary.un.org/record/601301?ln=en; Gerrit Kurtz and Madhan Mohan Jaganathan, "Protection in Peril: Counterterrorism Discourse and International Engagement in Sri Lanka in 2009," (2016) 30 *Global Society* 94; and Marco Chown Oved, "In Côte d'Ivoire, a Model of Successful Intervention" *The Atlantic* (9 June 2011), online at www.theatlantic.com/international/archive/2011/06/in-c-te-divoire-a-model-of-successful-intervention/240164/

170 The escalation of NATO's involvement in Libya was criticized as an opportunistic abuse of the principle and an instance of overreaching that realized the very fears that had fuelled resistance to "humanitarian intervention" by many formerly-colonized states. For discussion of this point see Gerrit Kurtz and Philipp Rotmann, "The Evolution of Norms of Protection," (2016) 30 *Global Society* 13 at 13–16.

need to fulfil the responsibility to protect the security of human persons in these crises.[171] The differences in emphasis and political failures of implementation among these cases are undeniable; but the preceding analysis shows that they are best explained as examples of the working out of the boundary between the core and penumbral elements of the responsibility to protect, and not as evidence that the norm lacks international legal status.

From the theoretical perspective of this book, the meaning of these variations can therefore be appraised only if they are interpreted as part of a larger context of articulation and negotiation of the responsibility to protect principle. The argumentative gambits that offer non-mainstream readings of the norm are only intelligible in the context of the lengthy roster of state- and civil society-driven endorsements and enactments of the responsibility to protect sampled above. This dialogical web of interchange around the formation of international legal norms has been characterized in this text as a deliberative practice: a common effort by members of an interpretive community to form and defend judgements. The paradigm of international law as a deliberative practice highlights the evolutionary potential of international law, as the collection of reasoning strategies mutually recognized among participants changes.

This model of international law as a deliberative practice helps to explain how the responsibility to protect meets the criteria of a general principle of international law, and does so in part as a consequence of the international legal agency of nonstate actors. It is a product of the demands of public conscience, recognized and confirmed through the RG process identified by Giuseppe Sperduti, and reflective of a *sensus communis juris* that has been shown to be widely shared among many nonstate and state actors. In sum, the responsibility to protect is a human rights protection norm of international law, of the class first explicitly outlined by Judge Tanaka in his *South West Africa Cases* opinion.

171 See for example the comments of the representatives of Azerbaijan, Georgia, Guatemala, Malaysia, Morocco, Pakistan, South Africa, Spain, and Thailand summarized in United Nations Information Centre, "Security Council Considers Protection of Civilians in Armed Conflict and Stronger Peacekeeping Mandates," summary of Open Debate of the United Nations Security Council on Protection of Civilians in Armed Conflict (29 August 2013) online at https://un.org.au/2013/08/29/security-council-considers-protection-of-civilians-in-armed-conflict-and-stronger-peacekeeping-mandates/; and also comments of the representatives of Denmark, Rwanda, and the U.K. cited in United Nations, Meetings Coverage and Press Releases, "'Responsibility to Protect' Remains Worthy, yet Elusive, Concept in Decade after World Leaders Pledge to End Atrocities, General Assembly Hears," summary of Thematic Panel meetings, UN Doc. GA/11764, (26 February 2016), online at www.un.org/press/en/2016/ga11764.doc.htm; and the Statement on behalf of the Group of Friends of the Responsibility to Protect, delivered by Her Excellency Ambassador Alya Ahmed S. Al-Thani, Permanent Representative of the State of Qatar to the United Nations before the Open Debate of the United Nations Security Council on Women, Peace and Security: Sexual Violence in Conflict (23 April 2019), online at www.globalr2p.org/media/files/final-version-gof-r2p-statement-open-debate-unsc-sexual-violence-in-conflict.pdf

6 Distant strangers and our responsibility to protect

The emerging legal concept of a responsibility to protect, and its companion principle, human security, have been assigned contrasting roles in the seemingly incompatible stories of the evolution of global law associated with two sets of authors—on the one hand, the cosmopolitan constitutional vision of Immanuel Kant and Jürgen Habermas, and on the other, the hegemonic international legal order described by Carl Schmitt and Detlev Vagts.

Previous chapters have explored problems with the cosmopolitan narrative preferred by early proponents of the responsibility to protect and of human security. Here, I review key elements of that narrative in order to establish the existence of an often-overlooked commonality it shares with the discourses of hegemonic international law.

As outlined in Chapters 3 and 4, cosmopolitan constitutionalism is inspired by Immanuel Kant's teleological vision of the development of international society toward an eventual condition of perpetual peace. While contemporary cosmopolitan constitutionalists differ about such matters as the desirability of a league of democratic states or a world government, all endorse the methodology of legal pacifism as a means of reducing the incidence of war between states. Cosmopolitan constitutionalists point to the expansion of international law since the introduction of the Charter of the United Nations[1] in 1945 and the rapid rise of a worldwide "human rights culture" as evidence of the fundamental accuracy of Kant's vision of an eventual liberal peace. Many authors in this tradition regard instances of violations of international law, and refusals to participate in international legal institutions by great powers (most notably, of course, the USA, Russia, and China) as aberrations in a generally linear progression toward a condition of global liberal democracy and international peace.[2]

1 *Charter of the United Nations*, 26 June 1945, Can. TS 1945 No 7.

2 Some regard these "aberrations" as potentially threatening to a cosmopolitan constitutional order. Jürgen Habermas and Jean L. Cohen have been influential proponents of this view, and each has advocated a bolstering of state sovereignty—a kind of wishful legal centrism—as a means of safeguarding the future development of global constitutionalism (Habermas, *The Divided West* (Cambridge: Polity Press, 2006), at 140–141, and Cohen, "Whose Sovereignty? Empire Versus International Law," (2004) 18 *Ethics and International Affairs* 1 at 14–15). Interestingly, at the same time, both authors recommend a partial reconceptualization of sovereignty by encouraging the decoupling of authority from territoriality.

No such teleological vision animates hegemonic international law (HIL) theories. The most salient feature of the formal international order on an HIL reading is the myth of the equality of states. HIL theorists explain changes in the international legal system by identifying the patron-client relationships and interstate dynamics that come into being as a consequence of the hierarchical ordering that prevails in fact among states. This ordering is in large part a result of the logic of colonialism:

> Historians of international law have long noted how those who established the field and its rules have usually been serving powerful states' interests, and not only (or not at all) moral precepts thought to be contained in natural law. The present Euro-centric nature of international law, and … of international organizations generally, can also be explained in terms of the exercise of power. Colonial rulers exported their notions of law, national and international, onto their subjects and when IOs [international organizations] were established, their mandates, organs, procedures and delegations of authority all had to find favor with the powerful, who, as in the case of the UN [United Nations], were the original framers of IO charters.[3]

Hegemony is generally understood by contemporary HIL theorists as a matter of degree, "ranging from empire to first among equals."[4] It has multilateral as well as unilateral manifestations, and perhaps counter-intuitively, can serve as a vehicle for leadership and not only for "institutionalized supremacy"[5] or command. José Alvarez distinguishes among two main types of hegemony: unilateral, and global or collective.[6] In Gerry Simpson's work on the history of international law, the collective form of (legalized) hegemony is further broken down into two main sub-categories, which he terms "liberal pluralism" and "liberal anti-pluralism."[7] Liberal pluralism refers to a Westphalian understanding of community among states that privileges a traditional interpretation of Article 2(7) of the UN Charter ("Nothing contained in the present Charter shall authorize the United Nations to intervene in matters which are essentially within the domestic jurisdiction of any state"[8]). It therefore allows for no formal distinctions among states based on their domestic conduct, and assigns ontological priority to states. Liberal anti-pluralism, on the other hand, rejects the adage that good fences make good neighbours, and instead emphasizes the UN Charter's foundational commitment to human rights.[9]

3 José E. Alvarez, *International Organizations as Law-makers* (Oxford: Oxford University Press, 2005), at 199.
4 Detlev F. Vagts, "Hegemonic International Law," (2001) 95 *American Journal of International Law* (*AJIL*) 843 at 848.
5 José E. Alvarez, "Hegemonic International Law Revisited" (2003) 97 *AJIL* at 874.
6 Alvarez, *International Organizations*, at 200, 215–216.
7 Gerry Simpson, *Great Powers and Outlaw States* (Cambridge: Cambridge University Press, 2004) at 69–88.
8 *Charter of the United Nations*, Art. 2(7).
9 *Ibid.* at Preamble, Art. 1(3).

It insists upon making hierarchical and potentially exclusionary distinctions among states based upon their internal performance, as well as their external actions, and these distinctions rest upon an ontological prioritization of persons.[10]

In HIL terms, we now appear to be embroiled in a period of significant backlash against the strictures imposed by liberal anti-pluralist hegemony. The scrutiny of both states' domestic human rights records and of their international conduct hampers the freedom of action of great powers, as well as of those less-dominant states.[11] The renewed empire-building aspirations of China and Russia, and the pressures posed by restive domestic populations seeking economic and social opportunities in those countries, coupled with anti-colonial sentiment in Africa, the Middle East, and Latin America, and populist and nativist political trends in the USA and Europe have conspired to challenge the simplistic, ahistorical categorization of states into "outlaws," "failures," and "saviours" that typified the liberal anti-pluralist hegemony of the post-Cold War era at its height.

In sum, cosmopolitan constitutionalism is primarily a descriptive and prescriptive theory, with the explicit goal of legal pacifism—achieving peace through law. The goal of the HIL approach, in turn, is primarily explanatory in character—it provides an account of why global peace remains and must remain elusive—but with the potential for a prescriptive twist of the sort employed most notably by Carl Schmitt (his Nietzschean ontology makes his agonistic account of the history of international law necessarily hortatory).[12]

Despite the apparent contrast between cosmopolitan constitutionalist and HIL law accounts of the evolution of international law, however, both perspectives are committed to the same legal centrist methodology. Although neither perspective contends that there is a single, enduring sovereign power making and enforcing law over time at the international level (as would be the case with legal centrist accounts of municipal law generation), the law-creating *agents* that both families of theories describe are inevitably states or combinations of states, rather than other forms of collectivities, and the coercive force exercised by the dominant states is almost always directed against other states (or congeries of individuals treated as if they belonged to states, such as members of Daesh (the Islamic State), Boko Haram, and al-Qaeda and its affiliates).

10 Simpson, *Great Powers*, at 76–77.

11 Alvarez, "Hegemonic International Law Revisited," at 873. An example of organized resistance to such scrutiny is provided by the Russian Federation-led challenge that began in 2011 to the "Dublin Process"—an initiative of High Commissioner for Human Rights Navi Pillay aimed at reforming and strengthening the UN human rights treaty bodies. This resistance effort succeeded in forcing a compromise in 2014 (Christen Broecker, "Reform of the United Nations' Human Rights Treaty Bodies," *American Society of International Law Insights*, (8 August 2014), online at www.asil.org/insights/volume/18/issue/16/reform-united-nations-human-rights-treaty-bodies).

12 See for example, Carl Schmitt, *The Concept of the Political*, trans. and with an introduction by George Schwab, expanded ed. (Chicago and London: The University of Chicago Press, 1996, 2007), at 52–53, 78–79.

Both approaches agree that the only place we can look for "real" law creation and law enforcement is the state or, on rare occasions, constellations of like-minded states. In the case of law creation by aggregates such as the UN or the European Union (EU), the legitimacy of these rules is regarded as directly dependent upon: 1) the mechanisms of democratic opinion- and will-formation (in the case of cosmopolitan constitutionalist arguments),[13] and/or 2) the command of a preponderance of coercive forms of power by state-members of the collectivity in question. This reliance upon the predominance of the state sustains the very different narratives provided by cosmopolitan constitutionalist and HIL theorists because each perspective, in a distinct way, both draws upon and supports the comforting assertion that states offer institutional means for affirming law as an emanation of a deliberate will.

The ICISS account of the responsibility to protect that much of this book has focused upon is reconcilable, in theory, with both cosmopolitan constitutionalist and hegemonic international legal theory approaches because it shares the largely unacknowledged legal centrist premise common to both (as do subsequent state-backed interpretations, including RtoP, RwP, RP, and the UN's second-generation, "UN-R2P").

What is most original and most problematic in the ICISS version of the responsibility to protect is the linkage of the human security idea to the definition of sovereignty, and then in turn, the unexplained extension of the obligation posited between states and their subjects to entities beyond the state in both crisis and pre-crisis circumstances.[14] On a consistent reading of the ICISS view, two forms of legitimacy turn upon acceptance of these linkages. The legitimacy of a state's claim to sovereignty depends upon acceptance of the first, and the legitimacy of the international community's global governance regime rests on acceptance of the second. And so the case for unilateral "humanitarian" intervention that was once made solely in moral terms (whatever the multiple and underlying motivations may have been in particular instances) is presented using the vehicle of the responsibility to protect in the language of legal pacifism, and grounded upon an inferred cause-and-effect relationship between a particular set of economic, political, social, and legal circumstances and a condition of peace.

A number of problems arise as a consequence of the responsibility to protect's legal centrist assumptions and the set of double linkages that are premised upon them in the ICISS account; two of the most germane of these challenges have been discussed in previous chapters. The first is the absence of intercultural agreement on a sufficiently thick account of human flourishing to support a robust definition of human security—since only such a rich view of human security could provide an adequate basis for attributing legal normativity to a root-cause

13 Habermas, *The Divided West.*

14 In this context, "crisis" refers to a situation where atrocity crimes are occurring or are thought to be imminent on credible grounds. "Pre-crisis" refers to a situation where risk factors for atrocity crimes are present, but no imminent threat of their commission exists based on the best available information.

responsibility to prevent ("structural prevention"). The second is a susceptibility of all current mainstream versions of the responsibility to protect to "hijacking"—both by countries that do buy into the liberal cosmopolitan vision of the future that it is explicitly premised upon, and by countries that do not. (Examples of these include, respectively, the UK and USA in their *post facto* justifications of the second invasion of Iraq and the NATO-led coalition that intervened in Libya;[15] and Russia, in justifying its invasion of Georgia in 2008.[16])

But a third set of problems also flows from the understandable failure of the state-sponsored authors of dominant versions of the responsibility to protect to move beyond legal centrism in seeking to delineate and develop the responsibility to protect norm. These difficulties are a result of a persistent failure to inquire more closely into the logical links that explain the responsibility of states for the human security of their inhabitants, and of entities beyond the state for ensuring that security when the home state fails. A conditional understanding of sovereignty is but one of the difficult likely consequences of such an investigation.[17] For the logic of a fully-developed reading of the responsibility to protect requires us to look beyond the state for agents who are susceptible to bear and act upon the burden it imposes.

Justice and the place of persons

In its original form, the responsibility to protect is presented by the authors of the ICISS report as the solution to a problem of justice: the problem of ensuring human security for all. There are two dominant ways of understanding questions of justice that extend beyond the limits of individual states. As Rainer Forst observes, we can organize our thinking about such issues either by focusing on principles of *international* justice, or of *global* justice.[18] Forst argues that while

> the former view takes political communities organized into states to be the main agents of justice (i.e., who is asked to be just and who receives just treatment), the latter takes persons, regardless of their political membership, as the primary focus of justice.[19]

15 British and US rhetoric before and after the invasion falls neatly within the "liberal anti-pluralist" tradition identified by Gerry Simpson; both states labelled Iraq an outlaw state, and as such outside the purview of "normal" international legal rules (*Great Powers and Outlaw States*, at 76).

16 As I discuss below, many of the weaknesses of the ICISS version of the principle have been remedied through the targeted development by the UN of policies and procedures designed to limit such abuses. Consequently, the efforts to misapply the principle in each of these cases was ineffective.

17 Gelijn Molier, "Humanitarian Intervention and the Responsibility to Protect After 9/11," 53 (2006) *Netherlands International Law Review* 37 at 49.

18 Rainer Forst, "Towards a Critical Theory of Transnational Justice," in Thomas Pogge, ed., *Global Justice* (Oxford: Blackwell, 2001).

19 *Ibid.* at 169.

A useful way to appreciate the implications of this difference in orientation is to identify who or what each view takes as the proper *subjects of recognition* when questions of justice arise; the international justice view begins with the assumption that justice is premised upon the mutual recognition of equal, autonomous, self-governing states, while the global justice orientation's starting point is the equality of individual citizens.

However, the responsibility to protect is conceptualized by ICISS in a way that the authors claim prioritizes *both* sets of principles described by Forst, despite the deep incompatibility of the intuitions underlying them. The goal of the responsibility to protect—roughly, to protect individuals' lives against violent disruption—is guided by a principle of *global* justice, because it is essentially concerned with individuals. But the means that is promoted by ICISS to achieve that goal is conceived only within (and thus is limited by) the conceptual framework of *international* justice. States alone are designated as agents assigned the responsibility to protect on ICISS's, and all subsequent, accounts. As a consequence, there is a mismatch between the universal (moral) application of the responsibility to protect, and the state institutional machinery that currently exists to enforce it.

As noted previously, Jürgen Habermas has observed that "[t]he moral universe, which is unlimited in social space and historical time, includes all natural persons with all the complexities of their life histories. By contrast, a legal community, which has a spatio-temporal location, protects the integrity of its members only insofar as they acquire the artificial status of bearers of individual rights."[20] In Habermasian terms, what the ICISS approach seeks is an expansion of our legal communities to make them isomorphic with the ideal moral community of all persons. The ICISS report aims to distinguish itself partly in terms of its commitment to the plights and perspectives of individual persons; however, the conceptual framework it employs in order to ensure the protection of those individuals is a legal centrist one that, ironically, defines the state as the only active agent burdened by the responsibility to protect. As a result, the ICISS commissioners advocate a top-down method of expanding the pool of persons subject to mutual legal claims, via the intermediary of states.

The justification for this legal centrist approach is that ICISS presents it as part of the fundamental purpose of states that they should seek to protect the human security of their inhabitants; indeed, this task is regarded as so central to states' *raison d'être* that the report's authors argue that recognition of sovereignty itself is premised upon a state's success in this task. But the ICISS account lacks a sufficiently strong logical connection between the responsibility of one state to foster the human security of its own members, and the posited responsibility of other states to do the same for the first state's citizens. Subsequent formulations of the responsibility to protect have only exacerbated this problem by undercutting the (already-weak) logical connection between the collective responsibility of outside

20 Jürgen Habermas, "Remarks on Legitimation through Human Rights," *The Postnational Constellation*, trans. and ed. by Max Pensky (Cambridge, MA: MIT Press, 2001), at 114.

actors for the citizens of a non-fulfilling home state in pre-catastrophic conditions, and the collective responsibility that obtains in catastrophic situations.

In order for the initial move from home state responsibility to a responsibility borne by outside actors to be coherent, one of two things is required: either 1) a *realpolitik* explanation of the onus upon states to intervene to aid other states' inhabitants which would suffice to explain a solely political normativity (and neither the ICISS report nor subsequent interpretations present self-interest as a primary source of the responsibility to protect—although ICISS acknowledges that such an interest provides a necessary condition for intervening), *or* 2) some moral or legal claim borne by individual human beings must be identified, which can be translated into legally-mandated action through the membership of those individuals, as citizens, in states.[21] One approach to addressing this under-developed aspect of all major interpretations of the responsibility to protect is suggested by the work of Onora O'Neill, who outlines key features of this second type of claim in her work on the proper scope of moral concern, discussed below.[22] She points out that it is not necessary to provide a detailed account of the metaphysical foundations of an obligation of type 2 in order to furnish what is needed, in moral terms, for action of the sort mandated by the responsibility to protect. All that is required is an answer to the question "Whom must we (or I) count as an agent or subject in taking this action?"[23]

Cultural relativism

The thinness of the ICISS commissioners' justification for their two foundational claims surely originates in concern over the possibility that a thicker account of the ontological bases for moral community would open them up to charges of, at worst, cultural imperialism, and at best, cultural insularity.[24]

A clear-eyed appreciation of the reality of cultural (and ethnic, and religious) diversity inhibits and problematizes our ability to assert the universality of standards of value, including the kind of criteria that might be employed to justify the first claim, above—that our moral community should be understood to encompass all human beings. Religious and cultural beliefs, as well as philosophical arguments regarding the proper scope of our moral concern, characteristically refer to a foundational story about human nature in order to explain why certain entities

21 Chapter 5 sketches a phenomenological grounding for such a claim in negative solidarity.

22 Onora O'Neill, *Bounds of Justice* (Cambridge, Mass.: Cambridge University Press, 2000). O'Neill works within the western tradition of moral philosophy, but as outlined below, her conclusions lend themselves to intercultural legitimation within a wide variety of intellectual and spiritual traditions.

23 *Ibid.* at 193.

24 The distinction between thin and thick construals was originally made by Gilbert Ryle, but was popularized and expanded upon by Clifford Geertz ("Thick Description: Toward an Interpretive Theory of Culture," in *The Interpretation of Cultures* (New York: Basic Books, 1973), at 7).

should be included as members of our moral communities, and others should not. Some particular feature of this nature is generally identified by such accounts as qualifying those who possess it for membership in our moral communities: typical examples include dignity, a soul, or the capacity for practical reason or suffering.

The stumbling-block posed by the multiplicity of these accounts for any attempt to formulate an interculturally legitimate claim about the extent of our moral communities is obvious, and discussions of the problem have been well-rehearsed elsewhere.[25] In a short paper on the issue of global justice, however, Onora O'Neill develops an interculturally legitimizable argument for an inclusive construal of the extent of moral community. She sidesteps the challenges posed by cultural, religious, and other forms of diversity to universal claims, by refusing to ground her argument in favour of an expansive moral community on any explicit account of human nature at all. Instead, O'Neill makes her case on the basis of what we already do in our daily lives.[26]

O'Neill and distant strangers

O'Neill begins with the Christian parable of the Good Samaritan, a tale of moral guidance with analogues in many other religious and ethical traditions. The Good Samaritan was traversing the road to Jericho when he stopped and risked himself to help the stranger who had been beset by thieves. O'Neill observes that, like the Good Samaritan, most of us have no hesitation in regarding the nearby stranger as a proper subject of our moral concern and responsibility. Why then, she asks, does the distant stranger in a faraway land not merit the same consideration?

The explanation does not lie, for most of us, in a denial that the distant other possesses some defining feature of humanness or agency which is necessary for moral standing. As O'Neill observes, we routinely behave as if distant others did possess moral standing. In trying to determine the philosophically and practically defensible

25 For representative examples, see the essays collected in Martin Hollis and Steven Lukes, eds., *Rationality and Relativism* (Cambridge, MA: MIT Press, 1982), and Michael Krausz and Jack W. Meiland, eds., *Relativism: Cognitive and Moral. Relativism: Cognitive and Moral* (Notre Dame, IN: University of Notre Dame Press, 1982).

26 O'Neill's discussion of the scope of moral concern in this paper is part of a larger project aimed at sketching a "critical account" of practical reason. O'Neill's purpose in developing such a description is to meet the challenge of ethical and cultural pluralism. She holds that this critical account of practical reason that "neither permits arbitrary moves nor lacks accessible authority" (*Bounds of Justice*, at 26), "allows for the thought that what might seem a reason for me or for the insiders of some tradition, even a reason that is burnt into souls, may not be any sort of reason for others (*ibid.* at 25)." In other words, her critical account seeks to avoid a Kantian "private use of reason"; the argument she develops in order to encourage us to regard ourselves as bearing responsibility for the travails of distant others is couched in terms meant to be as widely accessible as possible, "by linking it with other reasoning which they [those from other cultural/ethical/philosophical traditions] can follow *(ibid.)*." O'Neill's view is that this can be achieved only by offering reasons in support of principles that have, in Kantian terms, "the form of law": principles which we believe our interlocutors "could adopt as principles of action (*ibid.*)."

scope of our moral concern, O'Neill proposes that we direct our attention to the web of assumptions that we regularly and for the most part, unconsciously, rely upon in our interactions with both near and distant strangers, including those so removed from our lives that we cannot individuate them.[27] As O'Neill observes, in many of our daily actions—in purchasing insurance or fair trade coffee, in posting a book review on a the website of an internet book vendor, or contributing an editorial change to a Wikipedia article—we behave as if such distant strangers were both subjects and agents. As O'Neill puts it, "we constantly assume that countless others who are strange and distant can produce and consume, trade and negotiate, translate and settle payments, pollute or protect the environment."[28]

Consequently, the operative distinction between the nearby and the distant stranger that determines the practical limits of the scope of our moral concern lies, not in any shortcoming of the distant other, but instead in our perceived inability to affect those distant others through our actions.

What O'Neill argues convincingly in her paper is that this perception of impotence is unjustified in a globalized world of instant communication and rapid transportation technologies. In fact, she observes, our collective actions can effect dramatic changes in the circumstances of distant strangers, and do, not least insofar as they structure the global economic order in a manner that systematically privileges the inhabitants of certain states and harms the inhabitants of others.[29] While our interactions with distant others are usually mediated through institutions, they remain interactions with real-world consequences, nonetheless. O'Neill argues that it is simply incorrect to suggest that an inability to affect distant others through our actions could serve as an adequate basis for limiting the scope of our moral concern for most people now living on the planet.

Thus, O'Neill's strategy involves describing what we do in our everyday condition of concernful coping—the unreflective ways in which we treat strangers both near and distant. Her act of description is meant to jar us into a thematized awareness of both these unreflective practices involving distant others, and the constellation of pre-political commitments and background understandings that they imply.

Invoking one of Habermas' more lyrical passages, we might say that O'Neill draws our attention to "the wound opened up in everyday practice by a truth claim that has become problematic."[30] The (un)truth claim in this case refers to our implicit assumption that we cannot make a difference in the circumstances of distant others—that there is no way for us to help, and therefore, in practical terms, those others reside beyond the outer limit of our moral concern.

27 *Ibid.* at 193.
28 *Ibid.* at 195–196.
29 *Ibid.* at 187.
30 Jürgen Habermas, *Truth and Justification*, ed. and trans. by Barbara Fultner (Cambridge, MA: MIT Press, 2005), at 101.

Implications of O'Neill's argument

The fact that we *can* make a difference in the lives of distant others is for O'Neill an undeniable feature of contemporary life in much of the world. O'Neill argues that this fact leads ineluctably to the conclusion that

> *if* we owe justice (or other forms of moral concern) to all whose capacities to act, experience and suffer we take for granted in acting we will owe it to strangers as well as to familiars, and to distant strangers as well as to those who are near at hand.[31]

This relational account of equal moral concern does not require agreement on any essential ground for moral standing. It is based upon nothing more than a demand for consistency[32] in our actions toward those whom we can affect. By refusing to commit herself to a "metaphysics of the person," O'Neill is thus able to develop an inter-culturally legitimizable basis for expanding the domain of our moral concern to include distant others.

The main consequence of O'Neill's view is that we cannot continue to regard distant others who are suffering or under threat of profound violations of their human security (whether through ethnic cleansing, genocide, or even systemic poverty) as, in Thomas Pogge's words, another "remote good cause alongside the spotted owl."[33]

The duty to assist and the responsibility to protect

It is pertinent to note that the relationship of moral concern identified and explored by O'Neill in her discussion of our responsibility to distant others is one that appears to animate an existing legal doctrine of the civil law tradition, which figures in the

31 O'Neill, *Bounds of Justice*, at 196. The proper scope of moral concern for O'Neill at first appears to include all those whom we treat as subjects and agents, in the sense that we treat them *as if* they were proper subjects of our moral concern—as if they could suffer, etc. However, it is quickly apparent that this cannot be O'Neill's intention, because such a criterion would include entities such as my daughter's favourite teddy bear, and the family cat—both beings who are treated, quite scrupulously, as proper subjects of moral concern by my daughter—but O'Neill clearly does not want to be *that* inclusive. Rather, O'Neill clearly means those whom we treat as subjects and agents *and* who have the capacity to be moved by the kinds of considerations in their practical reasoning activities (e.g., non-arbitrariness, accessible authority) that she appeals to in the effort at ethical guidance constituted by her paper.

32 O'Neill has nothing satisfying to say in defence of this principle of consistency, at least not in this article. I suspect that it would be possible to back up her demand for consistency, in the sense of treating like (distant subjects of our moral concern) as like (nearby subjects of our moral concern), by working within a Habermasian framework of communicative action. Within such a framework (which accords fairly well with O'Neill's other assumptions), the demand for consistency in the preceding sense could be described in terms of a rational reconstruction of the idealizing presuppositions of speech, when the purpose of such communicative exchange is to achieve mutual understanding for the purpose of action coordination.

33 Thomas Pogge, *World Poverty and Human Rights* (Cambridge: Polity Press, 2002), at 26.

penal codes of many European countries, as well as the American states of Vermont and Minnesota, and the Canadian province of Québec. This obligation of solidarity, often referred to the as the duty to assist or to rescue, sanctions those who do not come to the aid of a person who is unable to protect him or herself.[34] O'Neill's argument suggests that the responsibility to protect is most productively conceived as a transnational instantiation of the same constellation of moral commitments captured domestically by the duty to assist.

Looking at our practices of moral concern in the relational terms proposed by O'Neill provides a basis for the claim that we owe moral concern to far-flung others—one that is usefully non-culture-specific in its philosophical commitments. It also allows us to take the final step toward closing the logical gap in the ICISS report's claim that a moral relationship links "other" states with the inhabitants of a particular state: once an uncontroversial connection between distant *individual* strangers is established, the argument can be made that one way of expressing the moral concern that is implicit in that connection is through collective action manifested institutionally, in the policies and actions of the states that represent us as individuals.

But if we accept O'Neill's relational account of moral standing as a plausible basis for the claim that our moral communities could extend to all human individuals, then we must also accept that the vehicles of the collective action that such a claim calls forth cannot be restricted to the state. If we work out the inferences required by the very broadly drawn theoretical assertions of the ICISS approach, the most tenable and consistent argument that emerges is that *individuals*, firstly—and only secondarily, the collectivities or communities they form, including states—are the bearers of the responsibility to protect. On this view, the achievement of human security is best understood as one of the varied goals of organized communities, among which the state is not regarded as a favoured exception.

Agency and the responsibility to protect

Agency to be subject to the responsibility to protect must be twinned with agency to fulfil that self-same responsibility. This self-evident observation has implications for our understanding of current global governance practices around the responsibility to protect norm.

As the *travaux préparatoires* of the founding subcommittee on the UN's purposes and principles recognized, when foundational freedoms and human rights are "grievously outraged so as to create conditions which threaten peace or to obstruct the application of the provisions of the Charter, then they cease

34 See Mario Bettati, "The International Community and the Limits of Sovereignty," (1996) 44 *Diogenes* 91 at 103; Mitchell McInnes, "The Question of a Duty to Rescue in Canadian Tort Law," (1990) 13 *Dalhousie Law Journal* 85.

to be the sole concern of each state."[35] While the Security Council is charged with "primary responsibility for the maintenance of international peace and security,"[36] it is not clear that under the Charter, the Security Council possesses a monopoly upon the lawful use of international force[37]—although it is without doubt that all proponents of the responsibility to protect regard Security Council authorization of a use of force as by far the most desirable and authoritative course. One possible interpretation would allow for military intervention to be undertaken under certain circumstances without violation of Charter Article 2 (4)—which precludes "the threat or use of force against the territorial integrity or political independence of any state, or in any other manner inconsistent with the Purposes of the United Nations."[38] This argument builds upon Gelijn Molier's work on the relationship between the responsibility to protect and the *Draft Articles on State Responsibility* of the International Law Commission (ILC).[39]

Molier's work is based in part upon a sophisticated analysis of the defences mounted by the Belgian and UK governments regarding the international legality of their respective military interventions in the Congo (Belgium, 1960) and Kosovo (the U.K. and Belgium, 1999), which turned on the assertion that the customary international law principle of necessity can be invoked to justify the use of force. Molier follows the ILC's lead in adopting this approach. In support of her interpretation, she cites in particular the description of the circumstances under which the use of force might be employed without being classified as aggression provided in the ILC's 1980 Yearbook:

> the existence of grave and imminent danger to the State, to some of its nationals or simply to human beings—a danger of which the territory of the foreign State is either the theatre or the place of origin, and which the foreign State has a duty to avert by its own action, but which its unwillingness or

35 Doc. 723, I/1/A/19, Report of Rapporteur, Subcommittee I/1/A to Committee I/1 (Preamble, Purposes and Principles), Documents of the United Nations Conference on International Organization, San Francisco 1945, vol. 6, June 1, 1945 at 705; cited in UN Secretary-General Ban Ki-Moon, "Human Protection and the 21st Century United Nations," Cyril Foster Lecture, Oxford University (2 February 2011), online at www.un.org/sg/en/content/sg/speeches/2011-02-02/cyril-foster-lecture-oxford-university-human-protection-and-21st, at 8.

36 *Charter of the United Nations*, Art. 24.

37 It is important to distinguish the following argument from the legal theories of "*implied* authorization" developed during the initial efflorescence of international peace and security actions following the fall of the Berlin Wall. For a detailed account of this theoretical approach, which based claims of legality upon supposed instances of *post facto* authorization of multilateral actions (consonant with an idealized Security Council's decision-making model), see Craig Scott's "Interpreting Intervention," (2001) 39 *Canadian Yearbook of International Law* 333.

38 *Charter of the United Nations*, Art. 2(4).

39 International Law Commission, Draft Articles on Responsibility of States for Internationally Wrongful Acts, with Commentaries (2001), online at http://legal.un.org/ilc/texts/instruments/english/commentaries/9_6_2001.pdf, see Art. 25; Art. 26, para. 5; Art. 48, paras. 9, 10.

> inability to act allows to continue. Another common feature is the limited character of the actions in question, as regards both the duration and the means employed, in keeping with their purpose, which is restricted to eliminating the perceived danger.[40]

Molier deftly assembles the conflicting legal arguments concerning the breadth of application of the *jus cogens* [41] prohibition on the aggressive use of force recognized in Article 2(4) of the Charter, and makes a plausible case for regarding highly circumscribed violations of Article 2(4) as *not* constituting aggression,[42] and not, therefore, in violation of the *jus cogens* norm.[43] Activities that might be undertaken in compliance with the responsibility to protect criteria for military intervention but without Security Council approval, on the grounds of necessity, could constitute examples of such exceptions.

This, or a similar view of Article 2(4) is implied by the hesitant but unmistakable decision by the ICISS commissioners to leave room for invocation of the responsibility to protect as a legal justification in cases that meet all of the Commission's precautionary criteria, but *are not supported* by the Security Council.[44] In making its argument for the existence of this space for extraordinary, non-Security Council-authorized actions in fulfilment of the responsibility to protect, the ICISS approach refuses to forget the ugly history of *non*-interventions by the UN in recent memory, such as the shameful failures in Rwanda and Srebreniça in the years just preceding the Commission's creation. At the same time, ICISS underscores the profound undesirability of such a course of conduct, and emphasizes its potential for undercutting "the stature and credibility" of the UN.[45] The report's authors frankly admit that

> [i]t is a real question in these circumstances where lies the most harm: in the damage done to the international order if the Security Council is bypassed or in the damage to that order if human beings are slaughtered while the Security Council stands by.[46]

40 Molier, "Humanitarian Intervention," at 52–58.

41 *Jus cogens* norms are "peremptory norm[s] of general international law." They cannot be derogated from nor modified, except by "a subsequent norm of general international law having the same character" (*Vienna Convention on the Law of Treaties*, Art. 53, para. 2).

42 *Yearbook of the International Law Commission 1980*, vol. 2, part 2 (New York: UN, 1980), at 43–44.

43 An outline of the application of this argument to the case of Libya appears in Natalie Oman, "Could R2P Justify a No-Fly Zone in the Absence of Security Council Approval?" Guest Blog, Opinio Juris (17 March 2011), online at http://opiniojuris.org/2011/03/17/could-rtop-justify-a-no-fly-zone-in-the-absence-of-security-council-approval/

44 These early proposed criteria include just cause, right intention, last resort, proportional means, and reasonable prospects (ICISS, *The Responsibility to Protect* (Ottawa: International Development Research Centre, 2001), at 16, 32–37, 54, 55).

45 *Ibid.* at 55.

46 *Ibid.*

Unsurprisingly perhaps, the assertion that the responsibility to protect provides a legal basis for non-Security Council-authorized use of force under extremely limited and carefully-defined circumstances has been quietly ignored by the UN, and since (at least) the release of the 2004 *Report of the Secretary-General's High-Level Panel on Threats, Challenges and Change*, all official UN pronouncements on the responsibility to protect have described prospective military interventions under the principle as requiring Security Council approval.[47]

Undoubtedly, multilateralism and broad consultation—with scrupulous attention to the expressed will of those who are seen as being in need of protection and a transparent assessment of whether the evolving UN criteria for military intervention[48] are met—are most satisfyingly achieved under the auspices of the Security Council, or failing that, the General Assembly. However, any claim that the Security Council exercises exclusive legitimating authority for actions undertaken to fulfil the responsibility to protect can only rest upon an erroneous view of its current nature.

47 Beginning with the report of the Secretary-General's High-Level Panel on Threats, Challenges and Change (*A More Secure World: Our Shared Responsibility* (2004), online at www.unorg/secureworld/report2.pdf at paras. 201–203), the interpretation of the responsibility to protect developed under the auspices of the UN (the "RtoP" view) has arrogated to the Security Council alone the authority to invoke the principle as an internationally legal justification for intervention. This view was echoed not only in the followup report of then-Secretary-General Kofi Annan (*In Larger Freedom: Towards Security, Development, and Human Rights for All*, UNGAOR, 59th Sess. UN Doc. A/59/2005 (21 March 2005), at para. 135) and the World Summit Outcome Document (GA Res. 60/1, UN GAOR, 60th Sess., UN Doc. A/RES/60/1 (24 October 2005) at paras. 138–139), but also in public pronouncements by Secretary-General Ban Ki-moon ("Responsible Sovereignty: International Cooperation for a Changed World, " SG/SM/11701 (15 July 2008), online at www.un.org/News/Press/docs/2008/sgsm11701.doc.htm); and his 2009 Report to the General Assembly on the responsibility to protect (Implementing the Responsibility to Protect, A/63/67 (12 January 2009)), online at http://daccess-dds-ny.un.org/doc/UNDOC/GEN/N09/206/10/PDF/N0920610.pdf?OpenElement; and 2010 update to the General Assembly—"Early Warning, Assessment and the Responsibility to Protect," A/64/864 (14 July 2010), online at www.unrol.org/files/SGReportEarlyWarningandAssessmentA64864.pdf—as well as numerous speeches and writings by Special Adviser to the Secretary-General on the Responsibility to Protect Edward Luck (see for example, his Stanley Foundation policy brief—"The United Nations and the Responsibility to Protect" (August 2008), online at www.stanleyfoundation.org/publications/pab/LuckPAB808.pdf, at 7, his prepared remarks at the UN General Assembly Thematic Debate on the Responsibility to Protect, Press Release GA/10847 (23 July 2009), online at www.un.org/News/Press/docs/2009/ga10847.doc.htm, and "The Responsibility to Protect: Growing Pains or Early Promise?" 2010 *Ethics & International Affairs* 349 at 356. More latterly, comments in response to questions from the press by Secretary-General Ban concerning the possibility of a no-fly zone being imposed on Libya reiterated this position ("Off the Cuff" press conference, (23 February 2011), online at http://www.un.org/apps/sg/offthecuff.asp?nid=1733). Gelijn Molier is a keen observer of the implications of this break with the ICISS report's recommendations ("Humanitarian Intervention," at 50–51).

48 For discussion of recently-revived attention to these criteria under the leadership of Brazil and China, see Chapter 5.

On the still-prevailing deliberative democratic narrative that reflects the key commitments of global human rights culture, procedural legitimacy flows from the interdependence of the rule of law and popular sovereignty.[49] The feeling of *oughtness*—that law deserves our recognition—is in large part a function of the institutional realization of this interdependence through a process of constitutionalization.[50] But at the global level, this institutional expression is incomplete because of the undemocratic character of the Security Council. Because of the privileges of the veto and permanent membership enjoyed exclusively by five members—the People's Republic of China, the UK, the USA, France, and the Russian Federation—the Security Council cannot claim that the norms it recognizes or applications of those norms that it endorses enjoy procedural legitimacy. And (at least) until it does, the possibility of invoking the general principle of a responsibility to protect as a legal justification for military intervention that meets the atrocity crimes triggering threshold and the precautionary criteria outlined in the ICISS report will remain open, despite the dangers of selective application and abuse.[51] The uncertainty of this situation cannot be wished away,[52] and it remains a fraught and worrisome, but real option of last resort when politics fails at the level of the Security Council due to the threat, or the capricious use, of the veto.

49 I rely upon Habermas for this formulation. See for example, Jürgen Habermas, "Legitimation," at 112–118, and Jürgen Habermas, *The Inclusion of the Other*, ed. by Ciaran Cronin and Pablo De Greiff (Cambridge, MA: MIT Press, 1998), at 254–262.

50 For a largely complementary discussion of the sources of felt legitimacy of international norms, see Stephen Toope, "Powerful but Unpersuasive?" in Michael Byers and Georg Nolte, eds. *United States Hegemony and the Foundations of International Law* (West Nyack, NY: Cambridge University Press, 2003), at 303.

51 One way of limiting these dangers would be through the revival and development of a shelved Dutch proposal to create a "senatorial" chamber to serve as a check on the Security Council (cited in Thomas Franck). Endorsement by such a body, acting either within or beyond UN auspices, could serve as a neutral and credible means of addressing the legitimacy deficit that those proposing a non-UN Security Council-sanctioned action in fulfilment of the responsibility to protect would face. A model for such a body is the Elders—a group of global leaders retired from formal political office and chosen for their impeccable international reputations, who "promote the shared interests of humanity" (The Elders, online at www.theelders.org/).

52 Disturbingly, this seems to be the tactic employed by the Secretary-General's Special Adviser on the Responsibility to Protect, Edward Luck, in his reported assertions that it is a "tired canard" that the responsibility to protect has the character of a legal norm, and that the principle is "a political, not a legal, concept based [confusingly] on well-established international law and the provisions of the Charter" (United Nations, Press Release, GA/10847, "Summary of the Thematic Debate on the Responsibility to Protect" (23 July 2009), online at www.un.org/News/Press/docs/2009/ga10847.doc.htm). This approach also appears to be adopted in the comments of Secretary-General Ban regarding the responsibility to protect, in which he restricts himself to acknowledging the "*moral and political* responsibility to protect populations" borne by himself and other world leaders [emphasis added] (Ban, "Human Protection," at 2).

Recommendations and conclusions

The responsibility to protect and human security are best understood in terms of a Derridean "double gesture" that both affirms the desirability of the overt humanitarian goals of the responsibility to protect and human security policies, and reveals the hegemonic strategies that variants of these concepts can serve. Here, I have rehearsed and developed elements of arguments introduced earlier in this book to show that it is possible to limit the extent to which these emerging legal, moral, and policy principles can be incorporated into either liberal pluralist or liberal anti-pluralist legal agendas.

The larger purpose of these assembled articles has been to demonstrate that while the precise demarcation line between the core and penumbral elements of the responsibility to protect varies among interpretations, the foundational elements established by ICISS have come to enjoy broad recognition and indeed, have attained international legal status. In order to fulfil the aspirations associated with these core elements, this study suggests a number of priorities for action.

First, in the short term, a "thin" reading of human security will obstruct great power efforts to co-opt the human security and root cause/structural prevention concepts. This requires a clear assertion of the distinction between the legal norm of the responsibility to protect and the broader human protection agenda associated with human rights promotion.

Second, recognized risk factors for atrocity crimes should continue to be addressed urgently, but using already existing mechanisms enjoying a high degree of consensus. These include UN human rights and humanitarian programs such as the Human Rights up Front initiative, the existing UN template for protection of civilians in UN peace operations,[53] and culturally-specific efforts to pursue the 2030 Agenda for Sustainable Development.[54] The focal points regional network agendas should clearly reflect the distinction between the core concerns of the responsibility to protect (anti-escalation, imminent emergency, and atrocity crime responses) and pre-crisis conditions. At the national level, fact-based policy development to reduce domestic atrocity crime risk should be encouraged.

53 Sebastian von Einsiedel and Louise Bosetti, "How António Guterres Can Advance the UN's Protection Agenda," United Nations University Centre for Policy Research Occasional Paper 7 (November 2016, online at http://i.unu.edu/media/cpr.unu.edu/attachment/2247/OC_07-Guterres-Protection-Agenda.pdf), at 4–7.

54 The sustainable development goals (SDGs) marry a commitment to achieving prosperity with recognition of the urgent need to protect the global environment. and were unanimously endorsed by UN member states in 2015. SDGs #5 (gender equality), #10 (reduced inequalities), #13 (climate action), #16 (peace, justice and strong institutions), and #17 (partnerships for the goals) are especially relevant to addressing the structural conditions understood to give rise to atrocity crimes (UN Sustainable Development Goals Knowledge Platform, *Sustainable Development Goals*, online at https://sustainabledevelopment.un.org/sdgs).

Third, to facilitate this work, an international effort to support research on root causes and risk factors of atrocity crimes should be prioritized, with special attention to the differences among risk factors and processes of dynamic development among the distinct classes of war crimes, crimes against humanity, ethnic cleansing and genocide.

Fourth, initiatives proposed by theorists such as Robert Kagan to formalize the tacit historical practice of recognizing two tiers of states through the establishment of a league of democracies[55] should be vigorously resisted. Vigilant employment of the "detective aspect"[56] of human rights could help to curb the complacency that eliminates productive uncertainty and reflexivity about democratic constitutionalism's ends and means at both national and transnational levels. Every effort should be made to restructure the relations of recognition of jurisgenerative political (and other) communities in order to create an acknowledged space for normative orders that look different from the state-centric, western liberal democratic model that has dominated global affairs for much of the last century. The illusion that the normative order of the state is the only one that counts is especially dangerous in moments of rapidly shifting global power, because of its potential to distract attention from possibilities for building shared agreement on an account of human flourishing that might underpin an interculturally legitimate, thick definition of human security, and a positive solidarity.[57]

Fifth, and in the longer term, efforts to develop such a consensus on a rich reading of human flourishing must be pursued in new fora and with greater formal involvement by nonstate actors. Until more substantial and general agreement is achieved, the persistent fear that the responsibility to protect might be exploited as a rhetorical justification for great power military escapades cannot be fully answered. (As a stopgap, the UN has sought to address this worry by limiting the grounds for applying the principle to genocide, war crimes, ethnic cleansing, and crimes against humanity[58] and this modesty regarding the scope of the responsibility to protect appears to have been vindicated; in two post-Summit crises, attempts to apply the responsibility to protect beyond these core cases were unsuccessful.[59])

55 Robert Kagan, *The Return of History and the End of Dreams* (New York: Alfred Knopf, 2008), at 97.

56 Lutz Wingert, "Türöffner zu geschlossenen Gesellschaften" *Frankfurter Rundschau* (6 August 1995); cited in Habermas, *Postnational Constellation*, at 120.

57 Undeniably, such a suspension of judgement will be difficult in the face of a transforming global order characterized by threats to the multilateral institutions that recent relative (and unevenly distributed) global prosperity has depended upon. But it might also help to reveal the extraordinarily destructive and inequitable foundations of that prosperity for many of those not born into northern and western states or the more fortunate socio-economic groups within them, with constructive results.

58 Luck, "The United Nations," at 3.

59 As discussed in Chapter 5, the first of these incidents occurred when international humanitarian assistance was refused by the Myanmar/Burmese government following the devastation caused by Cyclone Nargis in 2008 and the French foreign minister of the day,

However, by most accountings, *exploitation* of the human protection rationale is a problem that continues to be overshadowed by the human cost of *inaction* regarding human security crises, as a litany of pronouncements by UN Secretaries-General, Special Rapporteurs, Security Council representatives, and GA members attest.[60] Consequently, the final urgent and predictable priority for action identified by this study is reconstitution of the UN's global governance mechanisms to make them more effective. A number of pragmatic measures have already been proposed to prevent inaction in the face of threatened atrocity crimes, most of which involve adapting the UN's collective security mechanism so that it better addresses intra-state crises. Because Chapter VII of the UN Charter establishes that the Security Council has "primary responsibility for the maintenance of international peace and security,"[61] it is that organ that is the subject of most of these proposed changes. As noted previously, these proposals include: the amendment of the Charter to eliminate Security Council vetoes for permanent members (P5); informal agreement among the P5 to restrict use of the veto where apparent atrocity crimes are under Security Council consideration;[62] Charter reform to make the Security Council's decisions subject to

Bernard Kouchner, proposed that the responsibility to protect be invoked to justify military delivery of the aid. The second instance took place when the Russian government attempted to invoke the responsibility to protect to rationalize its eight-day invasion of Georgia during the South Ossetia crisis in August 2008. (Interview of Sergey Lavrov, Minister of Foreign Affairs of the Russian Federation (8 August 2008) by BBC, online at www.mid.ru/ns-actt.nsf/c5506fd21677ea96c3257364003e3cf9/1be54297e3c d6e6fc32574a3002a6545?OpenDocument, and Speaking Notes of Sergey Lavrov, Minister of Foreign Affairs of the Russian Federation at the Carnegie Council on Foreign Relations (24 September 2008), online at www.cfr.org/russian-fed/prepared-rema rks-conversation-sergey-lavrov/p17335, at 7). In both of these cases, attempts to justify interventionary activity on responsibility to protect grounds were roundly rejected by the international community. (For a telling example of international rejection of Russia's position, see the Shanghai Cooperation Organization's response to the invasion in "Shanghai Cooperation Organisation Split on Georgia," *The Irrawaddy* (2 September 2008), online at www.irrawaddy.org/article.php?art_id=14141.)

60 Secretary-General Ban summarized the consequences of this indecision as follows: "historically, our chief failing as an international community has been the reluctance to act in the face of serious threats" (Address to the Stanley Foundation Conference on the Responsibility to Protect (R2P), 18 January 2012, New York). A UNGA resolution on the prevention of armed conflict in Syria serves as a representative example of authoritative pleas for action among the myriad available: "deploring the failure of the Security Council to agree on measures to ensure the compliance of Syrian authorities with its decisions … [the GA] [*d*]*emands* that all parties immediately and visibly implement Security Council resolutions 2042 (2012) and 2043 (2012) in order to achieve a cessation of armed violence in all its forms by all parties" (Draft resolution on the prevention of armed conflict (issued 31 July 2012), UN Doc. A/66/L.57). To appreciate the costs of inaction on atrocity crimes, one need look no further than the unprecedented humanitarian crises in Syria and Yemen in the late 2010, or the mass deaths and systematic abuse of human rights of civilians in Sri Lanka in 2008–2009.

61 *Charter of the United Nations*, Art. 24.

62 There are three major variants of this proposal, which originated in the ICISS report recommendations. They include the French government's attempt to galvanize a "responsibility not to veto" movement among UN members, the Accountability,

review, either by a newly-created senatorial chamber (perhaps modelled on the Elders) or by the ICJ; and the addition of regional, permanent or semi-permanent seats to the Security Council.

Other aspects of the UN's global governance systems also require modifications if inaction in the face of human security crises is to be prevented. These include multi-year protection of the core budgets of human rights monitoring bodies and units within the UN system,[63] restoration of the full suite of Dublin Process reforms to UN human rights treaty bodies aimed at enhancing nonstate actors' involvement,[64] formal representation of nonstate actors in key decision-making processes at the Security Council, General Assembly, Human Rights Council, and other important bodies, and enhanced opportunities for participation in human security-centred activities such as universal periodic review. Institutional support for such changes must take into account the disparity in resources and numbers that often exists between INGOs and other nonstate actors from the economic south and north.[65] Finally, the Uniting for Peace procedure needs to be championed so that global publics become aware of this potential conduit for translating the dictates of public conscience into concrete international action; and provision for including representation of nonstate political communities (such as indigenous peoples, the Kurds, the Sahrawi, etc.) and other actors in a renewed Uniting for Peace procedure must be explored.

If these remedies to the failures of the UN's global governance mechanisms to protect the most fundamental human rights continue to go unimplemented or are unsuccessful—the *sensus communis juris* that informs the responsibility to protect's status as a general principle of international law will still remain. Under such circumstances, the dangerous possibility of multilateral or even unilateral action to

Coherence and Transparency Group Code of Conduct initiative of 2015, and the Elders' call for P5 restraint. (See respectively, Geoffrey Johnston, "World Shirks Responsibility," *The Kingston Whig-Standard* (25 August 2016), online at www.thewhig.com/2016/08/25/world-shirks-responsibility/wcm/24168f9c-153f-c18e-036e-ef949b05f22e; Center for UN Reform, "fACT Sheet—The Accountability, Coherence and Transparency Group: Better Working Methods for Today's UN Security Council" (June 2015)," online at http://centerforunreform.org/sites/default/files/FACT%20SHEET%20ACT%20June%202015.pdf; and "Martti Ahtisaari Calls for UN Reform at Sciences Po Event in Paris," The Elders, online at https://theelders.org/news/martti-ahtisaari-calls-un-reform-sciences-po-event-paris).

63 See Colum Lynch, "At the U.N., China and Russia Score Win in War on Human Rights," *Foreign Policy* (26 March 2018), online at https://foreignpolicy.com/2018/03/26/at-the-u-n-china-and-russia-score-win-in-war-on-human-rights/. Ted Piccone makes a series of recommendations for countering campaigns by China and Russia to de-fund UN human rights bodies and reshape international practices around human rights monitoring in his "China's Long Game on Human Rights at the United Nations," Foreign Policy Paper Series on International Governance, The Brookings Institution (September 2018), online at www.brookings.edu/wp-content/uploads/2018/09/FP_20181009_china_human_rights.pdf

64 Broecker, "Human Rights Treaty Bodies."

65 On this issue see Makau Mutua, "Standard Setting in Human Rights: Critique and Prognosis," (2007) 29 *Human Rights Quarterly* 547 at 604–618.

fulfil the responsibility to protect without Security Council authorization, but within the limitations dictated by the evolving global deliberative consensus on the norm, remains at least a theoretical prospect.

Nonetheless, the responsibility to protect will *not* support what David Kennedy describes as the drift of humanitarianism toward becoming "the global ideology for the use of force,"[66] despite the inherent susceptibility of law to deployment for multiple purposes. The sustained efforts by the UN secretariat to develop a coherent and operationalizable responsibility to protect doctrine through the RtoP and UN-R2P initiatives are bearing fruit. The initial damage to the principle's credibility caused by regime-change in Libya that was precipitated by an unopposed Security Council vote in favour of targeted sanctions and a referral of the Libyan situation to the International Criminal Court in 2011[67] has actually enhanced its legal normativity. This apparent setback impelled a broader range of state actors to become involved in further developing practices of legality, and spurred a push for greater clarification of important elements of the principle's practical implementation. It is now undeniable that the responsibility to protect has achieved the status of a recognized, if evolving, norm within a global community of judgement. As Secretary-General Guterres stated in his 2017 report on implementation, "[t] he consensus on the purposes of the responsibility to protect spans every continent. There is no longer any question that the protection of populations from atrocity crimes is both a national and an international responsibility."[68]

The responsibility to protect norm is now the subject of an ongoing, pragmatic dialogue concerning evidence-based measures of risk, benefits and costs, and practical implementation strategies that is often guided by the UN, but not dictated by it. This deliberative conversation involves policy-makers, political elites, citizen journalists, humanitarian organizations, military planners, the global media, regional focal points networks, and members of threatened population themselves. Even if what Arendt terms a "boundary situation" should arise,[69] the complex scaffolding of decisions leading up to any consideration of military intervention in fulfilment of the responsibility to protect that occurred in the *absence* of Security Council approval would necessarily, now, be informed by this dialogue.

But while it is true that "global power shifts have brought new voices, new partners and new opportunities"[70] to this deliberative discourse, the rise of a multipolar geopolitical order appears to be, for the moment, reinforcing a state-centric reading of the norm by the UN. This is unsurprising, as China integrates

66 David Kennedy, *The Dark Sides of Virtue* (Princeton, NJ: Princeton University Press), at 337.

67 UN SC Res. 1970 (2011), UNSC, 26 February 2011, UN Doc. S/RES/1970 (2011), online at www.un.org/ga/search/view_doc.asp?symbol=S/RES/1970%20%282011%29

68 *Report of the Secretary-General, Implementing the Responsibility to Protect: Accountability for Prevention*, (10 August 2017), UN Doc. A/71/1016-S2017/556, para. 4.

69 Hannah Arendt, *The Life of the Mind* (New York: Harcourt, 1971), at 192.

70 Ban, "Human Protection," at 8.

further into the world market economy and positions itself as an international norm entrepreneur through its promotion of a global "community of shared future" while fortifying its military and economic position as a regional hegemon,[71] Russia reasserts itself militarily in Europe and the Middle East, and both states exercise a destabilizing impact on political and economic affairs beyond their borders through the sophisticated use of cyber-tools. These reassertions of state sovereignty only enhance a state-centric vision of international legal and political relationships as the USA withdraws from the post-WWII institutions of global governance, and regional powers like Brazil, South Africa, Turkey, and the Gulf Cooperation Council offer distinct perspectives on human rights, democracy, sovereignty, and the responsibility to protect.

Two consequent challenges arise for the UN in the coming years. The first will be to acknowledge that not only are the constituent elements of the responsibility to protect rooted in international law, but that the principle itself is one that enjoys direct international legal normativity as a general principle of international law, and perhaps also as developing customary international law.[72] The second will be to consider a further impact of those "new voices, new partners, and new opportunities" that have arisen because of the disaggregation of states under the impact of globalization. While states remain indispensable partners in global governance and international lawmaking, if a justificatory narrative that will make such endeavours legitimate to a global public is to be forged, the UN will need to craft an interpretation of international law formation that takes account of the changing role and capacities of states in a densely-populated, polycentric transnational arena.[73] In order to meet these challenges, the UN will have to confront the limitations of its commitment to preserve and strengthen the role of nation-states as the primary actors in international law, not least through its current interpretation of the responsibility to protect. ("Properly understood, RtoP is an ally of sovereignty, not an adversary.... By helping States meet one of their core

71 China's ambitions regarding the global human rights agenda are not limited to its "community of shared future" initiative. See Piccone "China's Long Game," and Ryan Mitchell, "Was the UN Human Rights Council Wrong to Back China's 'Shared Future" Resolution?'" (10 April 2018), online at www.ejiltalk.org/was-the-un-human-rights-council-wrong-to-back-chinas-shared-future-resolution/#more-16084

72 Such overlapping processes of norm affirmation are, of course, common in international law. Examples include the customary international legal process of norm-creation concerning treaties and the treaty-based process of norm-generation through the Vienna Convention on the Law of Treaties, as well as the complementary processes of norm generation that occurred in the Martens Clause in the preamble of the Hague Convention II (1899)—a text which relies upon both customary international legal and general principles of international law sources for the prohibition of inhuman warfare against civilians and combatants. (For a detailed discussion of divergent interpretations of the legal sources of the Martens Clause, see Antonio Cassese, "The Martens Clause: Half a Loaf or Simply Pie in the Sky?" (2000) 11 *EJIL* 188.)

73 On the evolving sources of *opinio juris* and state practice, see Achilles Skordas, "Hegemonic Custom?" in Michael Byers, ed., *United States Hegemony and the Foundations of International Law* (West Nyack, NY: Cambridge University Press, 2003), at 317.

responsibilities, RtoP seeks to strengthen sovereignty, not weaken it."[74]) By following its present path with respect to the norm, the UN continues to privilege "a certain set of knowledge and practices, which place the sovereign state at the foreground of the law, and a certain group of actors as principal lawmakers."[75] In doing so, it risks making itself irrelevant to the debate over transnational mechanisms of democratic participation and representation suited to the emerging reality of a horizontal and patchwork terrain of global governance.

The responsibility to protect's best immediate future is undoubtedly as a moral and political prod to action by members of the international community in the face of large-scale threats to human security.[76] Despite the shadow cast by subsequent events, the norm's potential to play this role was demonstrated decisively during the opening days of the 2011 Libyan revolution, when Libyan delegates to the UN made a formal statement asking the international community to act upon its "right to protect" in order to aid their fellow-citizens[77]—a clear reference to the responsibility to protect, urgently and authentically presented as a request for human protection in the most public of venues. Inclusive debate over the principle's core and penumbral elements following the Libyan intervention and parallel geopolitical shifts toward greater multipolarity have created conditions for the responsibility to protect to serve as a spur to collective action to prevent atrocity crimes in future. And the unexpected conclusion about the norm's character that emerges from this collection of papers, written over the course of the responsibility to protect's first two decades of evolution, helps to explain why. The responsibility to protect is not simply a moral and political doctrine. It is also a compelling legal principle, determined by and revealing of the process of *riconoscimento giuridico di esigenze della coscienza pubblica* that recognizes human rights and human rights protection norms, and invocable by a proliferating cast of transnational agents as an inevitable consequence of the contemporary search for a justificatory narrative of global law.

74 Ban Ki-moon, Press Release, "Secretary-General Defends, Clarifies 'Responsibility to Protect' at Berlin Event..." SG/SM/11701 (15 July 2008), online at www.un.org/News/Press/docs/2008/sgsm11701.doc.htm

75 Anne Orford, "A Jurisprudence of the Limit" in Anne Orford, ed., *International Law and Its Others* (Cambridge: Cambridge University Press, 2006), 1 at 12.

76 Alex J. Bellamy makes a parallel point when he writes that the norm can serve as a "speech act that provides [sic] catalyst for timely and decisive action in the face of emergencies" (*Global Politics and the Responsibility to Protect: From Words to Deeds* (Abingdon, UK: Routledge, 2011), at 89).

77 "Libyan UN Mission Asks UN to Probe Situation in Libya" (22 February 2011), online at http://english.cri.cn/6966/2011/02/22/2021s622000.htm

Bibliography

International agreements

African Charter on Human and Peoples' Rights (1986) 1520 UNTS 217.

American Convention on Human Rights (1969) 9 ILM 99.

Charter of the United Nations, 26 June 1945. Can. TS 1945 No. 7.

Constitutive Act of the African Union, 11 July 2000. Online: www.africa-union.org/root/au/AboutAU/Constitutive_Act_en.htm

Convention (II) with Respect to the Laws and Customs of War on Land and its Annex: Regulations Concerning the Laws and Customs of War on Land. The Hague, 29 July 1899. Online: ICRC, Treaties and States Parties to Such Treaties www.icrc.org/applic/ihl/ihl.nsf/Article.xsp?action=openDocument&documentId=9FE084CDAC63D10FC12563CD00515C4D

Convention (IV) with Respect to the Laws and Customs of War on Land and its Annex: Regulations Concerning the Laws and Customs of War on Land. The Hague, 18 October 1907. Online: ICRC, Treaties and States Parties to Such Treaties www.icrc.org/applic/ihl/ihl.nsf/0/1d1726425f6955aec125641e0038bfd6

European Convention for the Protection of Human Rights and Fundamental Freedoms (1953). 213 UNTS 221, ETS 5.

The Hague Conventions and Declarations of 1899 and 1907. Ed. by James Brown Scott. New York: Oxford University Press, 1918.

International Convention on the Protection of the Rights of All Migrant Workers and Members of their Families, 2220 UNTS, UN Doc. A/RES/45/158 (18 December 1990). Online: https://treaties.un.org/pages/ViewDetails.aspx?src=IND&mtdsg_no=IV-13&chapter=4&clang=_en

Rome Statute of the International Criminal Court (1998). 2187 UNTS 90, 37 ILM 999.

Statute of the International Court of Justice, 26 June 1945, Can. TS 1945 No. 7.

Statute of the Permanent Court of International Justice, 13 December 1920, 6 LNTS 170, 379.

Vienna Convention on the Law of Treaties (with Annex), 23 May 1969, 1155 UNTS 18232, 331.

Multilateral declarations and resolutions

American Declaration of the Rights and Duties of Man, 2 May 1948. OEA/Ser.L.V/II.71, at 17(1988).

The Bangkok Declaration, 1967. Online: www.aseansec.org/1212.htm

Cairo Declaration on Human Rights in Islam, 5 August 1990, Organization of the Islamic Conference. UNGAOR, World Conference on Human Rights, 4th Sess., UN Doc. A/CONF.157/PC/62/Add.18(1993).

Draft Resolution on the Prevention of Armed Conflict, UNGAOR, 66th Sess., UN Doc. A/66/L.57 (31 July 2012). Online: http://undocs.org/A/66/L.57

Follow-up to Paragraph 143 on Human Security of the 2005 World Summit Outcome. UNGAOR, 66th Sess. UN Doc. A/RES/66/290 (25 October 2012). Online: UN www.un.org/en/ga/search/view_doc.asp?symbol=%20A/RES/66/290&referer=www.un.org/depts/dhl/resguide/r66_resolutions_table_eng.htm&Lang=E

Resolution on Uniting for Peace, GA Res. 377, UNGAOR, 5th Sess., UN Doc. A/RES/5/377 (1950). Online: www.un-documents.net/a5r377.htm

Resolution 798, UNSC, 18 December 1992, UN Doc. S/RES/798. Online: https://undocs.org/S/RES/798(1992)

Resolution 808, UNSC, 22 February 1993, UN Doc. S/RES/808. Online: www.securitycouncilreport.org/wp-content/uploads/ICTY%20S%20RES%20808.pdf

Resolution 925, UNSC, 8 June 1994, UN Doc. S/RES/925. Online: http://unscr.com/en/resolutions/doc/925

Resolution 955, UNSC, 8 November 1994, UN Doc. S/RES/955. Online: http://unscr.com/en/resolutions/doc/955

Resolution 1970 (2011), UNSC, 26 February 2011, UN Doc. S/RES/1970(2011). Online: www.un.org/ga/search/view_doc.asp?symbol=S/RES/1970%20%282011%29

Resolution 1674 (2006), UNSC, 28 April 2006, UN Doc. S/RES/1674/2006. Online: www.un.org/ruleoflaw/files/S-Res-1674%20on%20protection%20civilians%20in%20armed%20conflict%20(28Apr06).pdf

Universal Declaration of Human Rights, GA Res. 217A (III), UNGAOR, UN Doc. A/810(1948).

World Summit Outcome Document, GA Res. 60/1, UNGAOR, 60th Sess., UN Doc. A/RES/60/1 (24 October, 2005). Online: www.who.int/hiv/universalaccess2010/worldsummit.pdf

Jurisprudence

Case Concerning Pulp Mills on the River Uruguay (Argentina v. Uruguay), Judgment. [2010] ICJ Rep. 11.

Certain Expenses of the United Nations. ICJ Rep. (1962) 151.

Chórzow Factory (Merits). PCIJ, Ser. A, no. 17.

Corfu Channel Case (United Kingdom v Albania), Merits. [1949] ICJ Rep 4.

Eastern Greenland [1933] PCIJ, Ser. A/B, no. 53.

Gabčíkovo-Nagymaros Project (Hungary v. Slovakia), Judgment. [1997] ICJ Rep. 7.

International Status of South-West Africa, Advisory Opinion. [1950] ICJ Rep. 128.

Legality of the Threat or Use of Nuclear Weapons Case, Advisory Opinion, [1996] ICJ Rep. 226.

Military and Paramilitary Activities in and against Nicaragua (Nicaragua v. United States of America), Merits. [1986] ICJ Rep. 39.

Legal Consequences for States of the Continued Presence of South Africa in Namibia (South West Africa) notwithstanding Security Council Resolution 276 (1970). Advisory Opinion (1971) ICJ Rep. 16.

Petroleum Development (Trucial Coast) Ltd. v. Sheikh of Abu Dhabi (1951) 18 ILR 144.

Prosecutor v. Dragoljub Kunarac, Radomir Kovac and Zoran Vukovic, Judgment. [Feb. 22, 2001] ICT Case No. IT-96–23/1- T.

South West Africa Cases (Ethiopia v. South Africa; Liberia v. South Africa); Second Phase, [1966] ICJ Rep. 6.

Western Sahara. Advisory Opinion (1975) ICJ Rep. 12.

Whaling in the Antarctic (Australia and New Zealand (intervening) v. Japan), Merits. [31 March 2014] ICJ Rep. 226.

United Nations documents

Secretary-General Reports

Early Warning, Assessment and the Responsibility to Protect. UNGAOR, 64th Sess. UN Doc. A/64/864 (14 July 2010). Online: UN http://undocs.org/A/64/864

Fulfilling Our Collective Responsibility: International Assistance and the Responsibility to Protect. UNGAOR 68th Sess. UN Doc. A/68/947-S/2014/449 (11 July 2014). Online: UN https://digitallibrary.un.org/record/775455?ln=en

Implementing the Responsibility to Protect. UNGAOR 63rd Sess. UN Doc. A/63/677 (12 January 2009). Online: UN http://undocs.org/A/63/677

Implementing the Responsibility to Protect: Accountability for Prevention. UNGAOR, 71st Sess. UN Doc. A/71/1016-S/2017/556 (10 August 2017). Online: UN http://undocs.org/A/71/1016-S/2017/556

In Larger Freedom: Towards Security, Development, and Human Rights for All. UNGAOR, 59th Sess. UN Doc. A/59/2005 (21 March 2005). Online: UN http://undocs.org/A/59/2005

Report of the Secretary-General, Pursuant to General Assembly Resolution 53/35: The Fall of Srebreniça. UNGAOR 54th Sess. UN Doc. A/54/549 (15 November 1999). Online: UN https://undocs.org/A/54/549

Responsibility to Protect: State Responsibility and Prevention. UNGAOR 67th Sess. UN Doc. A/67/929-S/2013/399 (9 July 2013). Online: UN https://digitallibrary.un.org/record/754122?ln=en

Responsibility to Protect: Timely and Decisive Response. UNGAOR 66th Sess. UN Doc. A/66/874-S/2012/578 (25 July 2012). Online: UN https://digitallibrary.un.org/record/732671?ln=en

A Vital and Enduring Commitment: Implementing the Responsibility to Protect. UNGAOR 69th Sess. UN Doc. A/69/981-S/2015/500 (15 July 2015). Online: UN https://digitallibrary.un.org/record/798795?ln=en.

International Law Commission materials

Draft Articles on Responsibility of States for Internationally Wrongful Acts, with Commentaries (2001). Online: ILC http://legal.un.org/ilc/texts/instruments/english/commentaries/9_6_2001.pdf

Report of the International Law Commission on the work of its sixty-eighth session, resolution adopted by the GA. UNGAOR, 71st Sess. UN Doc. A/RES/71/140 (13 December 2016).

Report on the Fifty-Third Session. UNGAOR, 66th Sess., Supp. No. 10 (A/56/10), chap. IV. E. 1.

Summaries of the Work of the International Law Commission. Identification of Customary International Law. Online: UN http://legal.un.org/ilc/summaries/1_13.shtml

Yearbook of the International Law Commission 1980. Vol. 2, part 2. New York: UN, 1980. Online: http://legal.un.org/ilc/publications/yearbooks/english/ilc_1980_v2_p2.pdf

Other UN documents

Commission on Human Security. *Human Security Now*. (2003). Online: UN Human Security Unit https://reliefweb.int/sites/reliefweb.int/files/resources/91BAEEDBA50C6907C1256D19006A9353-chs-security-may03.pdf

Framework of Analysis for Atrocity Crimes: A Tool for Prevention (July 2014). Online: UN www.un.org/en/genocideprevention/documents/about-us/Doc.3_Framework%20of%20Analysis%20for%20Atrocity%20Crimes_EN.pdf

General Assembly Thematic Debate on Human Security. President of the 62nd Session United Nations General Assembly. (22 May 2008). Online: UN www.un.org/ga/president/62/ThematicDebates/humansecurity.shtml

General Assembly Thematic Debate on the Responsibility to Protect. Press Release GA/10847 (23 July 2009). Online: UN www.un.org/News/Press/docs/2009/ga10847.doc.htm

Human Rights Council. "Documents and Resolutions." Online: UNHRC www.ohchr.org/EN/HRBodies/HRC/Pages/Documents.aspx

"Human Rights up Front: A Summary for Staff." Online: UN www.un.org/News/dh/pdf/english/2016/Human-Rights-up-Front.pdf

Letter dated 28 November 2007 from the Secretary-General addressed to the President of the Security Council. UNSC, UN Doc. S/2007/753 (21 December 2007). Online: UN http://undocs.org/S/2007/753

Letter Dated 9 November 2011 from the Permanent Representative of Brazil to the United Nations Addressed to the Secretary-General. UNSC, UN Doc. A/66/551–S/2011/701 (9 November 2011). Online: www.securitycouncilreport.org/atf/cf/%7B65BFCF9B-6D27-4E9C-8CD3-CF6E4FF96FF9%7D/POC%20S2011%20701.pdf

Report of Rapporteur, Subcommittee I/1/A to Committee I/1 (Preamble, Purposes and Principles). Documents of the United Nations Conference on International Organization, San Francisco 1945, vol. 6, June 1, 1945, Doc. 723, I/1/A/19, 705.

Report of the Secretary-General's High-Level Panel on Threats, Challenges and Change, A More Secure World: Our Shared Responsibility. UNGAOR 59th Sess. UN Doc. A/59/565 (2 December 2004). Online: www.unog.ch/80256EDD006B8954/(httpAssets)/C9B1B6D819968E83C1256F5E00597208/$file/Report+of+the+High-level+Panel+on+Threats+Challenges+and+Change.pdf

Second Interim Report of the Commission of Experts Established Pursuant to Security Council Resolution 780. UNSC, 6 October 1993, UN Doc. S26545.

Special Adviser to the UN Secretary-General Edward Luck. "Remarks to the General Assembly on the Responsibility to Protect: Thematic Debate on the Responsibility to Protect" (23 July 2009). Online: UN www.un.org/ga/president/63/interactive/protect/luck.pdf

Special Adviser to the UN Secretary-General Edward Luck. "The United Nations and the Responsibility to Protect" (August 2008). Online: Stanley Foundation www.stanleyfoundation.org/publications/pab/LuckPAB808.pdf

United Nations. *Human Rights: A Compilation of International Instruments*. United Nations Publications, 1993.

United Nations Department of Public Information. "Demanding that Lord's Resistance Army End All Attacks, Security Council Calls for Full Implementation of Regional Strategy in Central Africa." UN Doc. SC/11018, (29 May 2013). Online: UN www.un.org/News/Press/docs/2013/sc11018.doc.htm

United Nations Department of Public Information. *Outreach Programme on the Rwanda Genocide and the United Nations* (March 2014). Online: United Nations www.un.org/en/preventgenocide/rwanda/about/bgresponsibility.shtml

United Nations Department of Public Information. "Deputy Secretary-General Addresses Panel on Human Security Marking Twentieth Anniversary of Vienna International Centre." UN Doc. DSG/SM/70, (12 October 1999). Online: UN www.un.org/News/Press/docs/1999/19991012.dsgsm70.doc.html

United Nations Department of Public Information. "Secretary-General Defends, Clarifies 'Responsibility to Protect' at Berlin Event on Responsible Sovereignty: International Cooperation for a Changed World." UN Doc. SG/SM/11701, (15 July 2008). Online: UN www.un.org/News/Press/docs/2008/sgsm11701.doc.htm

United Nations Development Programme. *Human Development Report, 1993*. New York/Oxford: Oxford University Press, 1993. Online: http://hdr.undp.org/en/reports/global/hdr1993/

United Nations Development Programme. *Human Development Report, 1994*. New York/Oxford: Oxford University Press, 1994. Online: http://hdr.undp.org/en/reports/global/hdr1994/

United Nations Development Programme. *Human Development Report, 1995*. New York/Oxford: Oxford University Press, 1995. Online: http://hdr.undp.org/en/reports/global/hdr1995/

United Nations Development Programme. *Human Development Report, 1996*. New York/Oxford: Oxford University Press, 1996. Online: http://hdr.undp.org/en/reports/global/hdr1996/

United Nations Development Programme. *Human Development Report, 1997*. New York/Oxford: Oxford University Press, 1997. Online: http://hdr.undp.org/en/reports/global/hdr1997/

United Nations Development Programme. *Putting Human Rights up Front*. (7 August 2018). Online: https://stories.undp.org/putting-human-rights-up-front

United Nations Group of Experts. *Report on the Situation of Human Rights in Darfur, prepared by the Group of Experts mandated by Human Rights Council resolution 4/8*. (8 June 2007), UN Doc. A/HRC/5/6. Online: https://digitallibrary.un.org/record/601301?ln=en

United Nations Information Centre. "Security Council Considers Protection of Civilians in Armed Conflict and Stronger Peacekeeping Mandates." Summary of Open Debate of the United Nations Security Council on Protection of Civilians in Armed Conflict. (29 August 2013). Online: https://un.org.au/2013/08/29/security-council-considers-protection-of-civilians-in-armed-conflict-and-stronger-peacekeeping-mandates/

United Nations Information Service, Vienna. "Secretary-General Salutes International Workshop on Human Security in Mongolia." UN Doc. UNIS/SG/2555 (9 May 2000). Online: UNIS www.unis.unvienna.org/unis/pressrels/2000/sg2555.html

United Nations, Meetings Coverage and Press Releases. "'Responsibility to Protect' Remains Worthy, yet Elusive, Concept in Decade after World Leaders Pledge to End Atrocities, General Assembly Hears." Summary of Thematic Panel meetings. UN Doc. GA/11764, (26 February 2016). Online: UN www.un.org/press/en/2016/ga11764.doc.htm

United Nations Office of the President of the General Assembly. *Concept Note on Responsibility to Protect Populations from Genocide, War Crimes, Ethnic Cleansing and Crimes Against Humanity*, 2009. Online: www.un.org/ga/president/63/interactive/protect/conceptnote.pdf

United Nations Office on Genocide Prevention and the Responsibility to Protect. Online: www.un.org/en/genocideprevention/index.html#

United Nations Secretary-General António Guterres. *Secretary-General's Remarks to the General Assembly Debate on the Responsibility to Protect* [as delivered] (25 June 2018).

Online: UN www.un.org/sg/en/content/sg/statement/2018-06-25/secretary-generals-remarks-general-assembly-debate-responsibility

United Nations Secretary-General Ban Ki-Moon. "Human Protection and the 21st Century United Nations." Cyril Foster Lecture, Oxford University (2 February 2011). Online: UN www.un.org/sg/en/content/sg/speeches/2011-02-02/cyril-foster-lecture-oxford-university-human-protection-and-21st

United Nations Secretary-General Ban Ki-Moon. "Off the Cuff." Press Conference (23 February 2011). Online: UN www.un.org/apps/sg/offthecuff.asp?nid=1733

United Nations Secretary-General Ban Ki-Moon. "Responsible Sovereignty: International Cooperation for a Changed World." Address delivered in Berlin (15 July 2008). UN Doc. SG/SM/11701 (15 July 2008). Online: UN www.un.org/News/Press/docs/2008/sgsm11701.doc.htm

United Nations Secretary-General Kofi Annan. *We the Peoples: The Role of the United Nations in the 21st Century*. New York, NY: United Nations Department of Public Information, 2000. Online: UN www.un.org/en/events/pastevents/pdfs/We_The_Peoples.pdf

United Nations Secretary-General Kofi Annan. "Secretary-General Salutes International Workshop on Human Security in Mongolia." Address delivered at a two-day session in Ulaanbaatar (May 2000). Online: United Nations www.un.org/News/Press/docs/2000/200000508.sgsm7382.doc.html

United Nations Secretary-General Kofi Annan. "Two Concepts of Sovereignty." (6 September 1999) 352 *The Economist* 49.

Books, articles, and reports

Agamben, Giorgio. *Homo Sacer: Sovereign Power and Bare Life*. Trans. by Daniel Heller-Roazen. Stanford: Stanford University Press, 1998.

Agamben, Giorgio. *State of Exception*. Trans. by Kevin Attell. Chicago: University of Chicago Press, 2005.

Agné, Hans. "Is Successful Democracy Promotion Possible? The Conceptual Problem." (2014) 21 *Democratization* 49.

Alland, Denis. "Countermeasures of General Interest." (2002) 13 *European Journal of International Law* 1221.

Alston, Philip. "The Myopia of the Handmaidens." (1997) 8 *European Journal of International Law* 435.

Alston, Philip, ed. *People's Rights*. Oxford: Oxford University Press, 2001.

Alston, Philip. "Resisting the Merger and Acquisition of Human Rights by Trade Law: A Reply to Petersmann." (2002) 13 *European Journal of International Law* 815.

Alvarez, José E. "Do Liberal States Behave Better?" (2001) 12 *European Journal of International Law* 183.

Alvarez, José E. "Hegemonic International Law Revisited." (2003) 87 *American Journal of International Law* 873.

Alvarez, José E. *International Organizations as Law-makers*. Oxford: Oxford University Press, 2005.

Amnesty International. *Bosnia-Herzegovina: Rape and Sexual Abuse by Armed Forces* (January, 1993). Online: Amnesty International www.amnesty.org/download/Documents/188000/eur630011993en.pdf

Aman, Kenneth, ed. *Ethical Principles for Development*. Upper Montclair: Institute for Critical Thinking, 1991.

Anghie, Antony. *Imperialism, Sovereignty and the Making of International Law*. Cambridge: Cambridge University Press, 2005.

An-Na'im, Abdullahi Ahmed, ed. *Human Rights in Cross-Cultural Perspectives*. Philadelphia: University of Pennsylvania Press, 1992.

Appiah, Kwame Anthony. *Cosmopolitanism*. New York: Norton & Company, 2006.

Arendt, Hannah. *Between Past and Future*. New York: Penguin Books, 1968.

Arendt, Hannah. "Civil Disobedience." In *Crises of the Republic*. San Diego: Harcourt Brace & Company, 1972.

Arendt, Hannah. *Eichmann in Jerusalem: A Report on the Banality of Evil*. Revised and enlarged edition. New York, NY: Penguin Books, 1965, 1994.

Arendt, Hannah. *The Human Condition*. Chicago: University of Chicago Press, 1958.

Arendt, Hannah. *Lectures on Kant's Political Philosophy*. Ed. by Ronald Beiner. Chicago: University of Chicago Press, 1982.

Arendt, Hannah. *The Life of the Mind*. New York: Harcourt, 1971.

Arendt, Hannah. *Men in Dark Times*. San Diego: Harcourt Brace & Company, 1968.

Arendt, Hannah. *On Revolution*. New York: Penguin Books, 2006.

Arendt, Hannah. *Rahel Varnhagen*. Rev. edn. New York: Harcourt Brace Jovanovich, 1974.

Arendt, Hannah. *Responsibility and Judgment*. Ed. by Jerome Kohn. New York: Schocken Books, 2003.

Arendt, Hannah. *The Origins of Totalitarianism*. San Diego: Harcourt, 1968.

Arendt, Hannah. *The Portable Hannah Arendt*. Ed. by Peter Baehr. London and New York: Penguin, 2005.

Aristotle. *The "Art" of Rhetoric*. Trans. by John Henry Freese. Cambridge, MA: Harvard University Press, 1926.

Aristotle. *Politics*. Trans. by C.D.C. Reeve. Indianapolis, IN: Hackett Publishing, 1998.

Aristotle. *The Politics*. Ed. and trans. by Ernest Barker. Oxford: Oxford University Press, 1946.

Avaaz. Online: Avaaz www.avaaz.org/en/about.php

Axworthy, Lloyd. *Navigating a New World*. Toronto: A.A. Knopf Canada, 2003.

Balsamo, Michael. "A Look at Interference in the 2018 US Midterm Elections." *The Washington Post* (22 October 2018). Online: The Washington Post www.washingtonpost.com/politics/a-look-at-interference-in-the-2018-us-midterm-elections/2018/10/22/cb621a84-d5be-11e8-8384-bcc5492fef49_story.html?utm_term=.82e228cf2d97

Bartholomew, Amy, ed. *Empire's Law*. London: Pluto Press, 2006.

Baxi, Upendra. *The Future of Human Rights*. 2nd edn. Oxford: Oxford University Press, 2002, 2006.

Baxi, Upendra. "Voices of Suffering and the Future of Human Rights." (1998) 8 *Transnational Law and Contemporary Problems* 125.

Beck, Ulrich and Natan Sznaider. "A Literature on Cosmopolitanism: An Overview." (2006) 57 *The British Journal of Sociology* 153.

Beiner, Ronald. "Rereading Hannah Arendt's Kant Lectures." In Ronald Beiner and Jennifer Nedelsky, eds. *Judgment, Imagination, and Politics*. Lanham, Maryland: Rowman & Littlefield, 2001.

Beiner, Ronald and Jennifer Nedelsky, eds. *Judgment, Imagination, and Politics*. Lanham, Maryland: Rowman & Littlefield, 2001.

Bellamy, Alex J. *Global Politics and the Responsibility to Protect*. Abingdon, UK: Routledge, 2011.

Bellamy, Alex J. *Responsibility to Protect*. Cambridge: Polity Press, 2009.

Benhabib, Seyla. *Another Cosmopolitanism*. Ed. by Robert Post. Oxford: Oxford University Press, 2006.

Benhabib, Seyla. "Kantian Questions, Arendtian Answers: Statelessness, Cosmopolitanism, and the Right to Have Rights." In Seyla Benhabib and Nancy Fraser, eds. *Pragmatism, Critique, Judgment: Essays for Richard J. Bernstein*. Cambridge, MA: MIT Press, 2004.

Benhabib, Seyla. *The Reluctant Modernism of Hannah Arendt*. Lanham, MD: Rowman & Littlefield, 2003.

Benhabib, Seyla. *The Rights of Others*. Cambridge: Cambridge University Press, 2004.

Benhabib, Seyla. *Situating the Self*. Cambridge: Polity Press, 1992.

Benner, Thorsten. "Brazil as a Norm Entrepreneur: The 'Responsibility while Protecting' Initiative." GPPi working paper (March 2013). Online: www.gppi.net/fileadmin/user_upload/media/pub/2013/Benner_2013_Working-Paper_Brazil-RWP.pdf

Benvenisti, Eyal. "Upholding Democracy Amid the Challenges of New Technology: What Role for the Law of Global Governance?" (2018) 29*European Journal of International Law* 9.

Berman, Nathaniel. "Sovereignty in Abeyance: Self-Determination in International Law." In Robert McCorquodale, ed. *Self-Determination in International Law*. Aldershot, UK: Dartmouth Publishing, 2000.

Berry, David S. *Caribbean Integration Law*. Oxford: Oxford University Press, 2014.

Bettati, Mario. "The International Community and the Limits of Sovereignty." (1996) 44 *Diogenes* 91.

Bhargava, Rajeev. "How Should We Respond to the Cultural Injustices of Colonialism?" In Jon Miller and Rahul Kumar, eds. *Reparations: Interdisciplinary Inquiries*. Oxford: Oxford University Press, 2007.

Bin, Cheng. *General Principles of Law as Applied by International Courts and Tribunals*. Cambridge: Grotius Publications Ltd., 1987.

Bishara, Marwan. "West Overzealous on Libya." Opinion, Al Jazeera English (18 March 2011). Online: Al Jazeera English http://english.aljazeera.net/indepth/opinion/2011/03/2011318132217965513.html

Bismark, David. "E-voting Without Fraud." Lecture, TEDGlobal, July 2010. Online: TED www.ted.com/talks/david_bismark_e_voting_without_fraud.html

Bohman, James. *Democracy Across Borders*. Cambridge, MA: Massachusetts Institute of Technology Press, 2007.

Bohman, James. "Republican Cosmopolitanism." (2004) 12 *Journal of Political Philosophy* 335.

Borgen, Christopher J. "The Language of Law and the Practice of Politics: Great Powers and the Rhetoric of Self-Determination in the Cases of Kosovo and South Ossetia." (Summer 2009) 1*Chicago Journal of International Law* 1.

Borrows, John. *Recovering Canada: The Resurgence of Indigenous Law*. Toronto: University of Toronto Press, 2002.

Brammertz, Serge and Michelle Jarvis, eds. *Prosecuting Conflict-Related Sexual Violence*, Oxford: Oxford University Press, 2016.

Brown, Michael E. *Debating the Democratic Peace*. Ed. by Sean M. Lynn-Jones and Steven E. Miller. Cambridge, MA: MIT Press, 1996.

Brown, Wendy. "Suffering the Paradoxes of Rights." In Wendy Brown and Janet Halley, eds. *Left Legalism/Left Critique*. Durham, NC: Duke University Press, 2002.

Brownlie, Ian. *Principles of Public International Law*, 4th edn. Oxford: Oxford University Press, 1990.

Brunkhorst, Hauke. *Solidarity: From Civic Friendship to a Global Legal Community*. Cambridge, MA: Massachusetts Institute of Technology Press, 2005.

Brunnée, Jutta and Stephen J. Toope, "International Law and Constructivism: Elements of an Interactional Theory of International Law." (2000) 39 *Columbia Journal of Transnational Law*19.

Brunnée, Jutta and Stephen Toope. *Legitimacy and Legality in International Law: An Interactional Account.* Cambridge: Cambridge University Press, 2010.

Buchanan, Allen and Robert O. Keohane. "The Preventive Use of Force: A Cosmopolitan Institutional Proposal." (2004) 18*Ethics and International Affairs* 1.

Burai, Erna. "Parody as Norm Contestation: Russian Normative Justifications in Georgia and Ukraine and Their Implications for Global Norms." (2016) 30 *Global Society* 67.

Burley, Anne-Marie. "Law among Liberal States: Liberal Internationalism and the Act of State Doctrine." (1992) 92 *Columbia Law Review* 1907.

Byers, Michael. *Custom, Power, and the Power of Rules.* Cambridge: Cambridge University Press, 1999.

"Cairo's Biggest Protest Yet Demands Mubarak's Immediate Departure", *The Guardian* (5 February 2011). Online: The Guardian www.theguardian.com/world/2011/feb/05/egypt-protest-demands-mubarak-departure

Calhoun, Craig. "Plurality, Promises and Public Spaces." In Craig Calhoun and John McGowan, eds. *Hannah Arendt and The Meaning of Politics.* Minneapolis: University of Minnesota Press, 1997.

Card, Orson Scott. *Speaker for the Dead.* New York: Tom Doherty Associates, 1986.

Cassese, Antonio. *International Law in a Divided World.* Oxford: Clarendon Press, 1986.

Cassese, Antonio. "The Martens Clause: Half a Loaf or Simply Pie in the Sky?" (2000) 11*European Journal of International Law* 188.

Charter 08. Online: Charter 08 https://archive.is/20130119092014/www.charter08.com/.

Chen, Zheng. "China and the Responsibility to Protect." (April 2016) 25*Journal of Contemporary China* 686.

Clark, Ian. *Hegemony in International Society.* Oxford: Oxford University Press, 2011.

Cohen, Jean L. "Rethinking Human Rights, Democracy and Sovereignty in the Age of Globalization." (August 2008) 36*Political Theory* 599.

Cohen, Jean L. "The Role of International Law in Post-Conflict Constitution-Making." (2006/2007) 51*New York Law School Law Review* 497.

Cohen, Jean L. "Whose Sovereignty? Empire Versus International Law," (2004) 18*Ethics and International Affairs* 1.

Cohen, Roberta and Francis M. Deng. *Masses in Flight: The Global Crisis of Internal Displacement.* Washington DC: Brookings Institution Press, 1998.

Cohen, Roger. "How Kofi Annan Rescued Kenya." *New York Review of Books* (14 August 2008). Online: NYRB www.nybooks.com/articles/2008/08/14/how-kofi-annan-rescued-kenya/

"A Commentary on 'Renewing the United Nations: A Programme for Reform.'" A policy brief prepared by the South Centre at the request of the Group of 77. Online at https://www.g77.org/doc/policy%20brief.htm#What%20role%20for%20the%20UN

Correlates of War (COW) Project. Online: www.umich.edu/ cowproj/

Crawford, James. "Democracy and the Body of International Law." In Gregory H. Fox and Brad R. Roth, eds. *Democratic Governance and International Law.* Cambridge: Cambridge University Press, 2000.

Currie, John H. *Public International Law.* Toronto, Canada: Irwin Law, 2008.

d'Aspremont, Jean. "Customary International Law as a Dance Floor: Part I." EJIL:Talk!, April 2014. Online: EJIL www.ejiltalk.org/customary-international-law-as-a-dance-floor-part-i/

d'Aspremont, Jean. *Formalism and the Sources of International Law*. Oxford and New York: Oxford University Press, 2011.

Declaration of Charter 77. Online: http://chnm.gmu.edu/1989/archive/files/declaration-of-charter-77_4346bae392.pdf

De Sousa Santos, Boaventura. "Beyond Neoliberal Governance." In Boaventura De Sousa Santos and César A. Rodriguez-Garavito, eds. *Law and Globalization from Below*. Cambridge: Cambridge University Press, 2005.

Deng, Francis M. *A Challenge for the International Community*. Washington, DC: The Brookings Institution Press, 1993.

Deng, Francis M. *Protecting the Dispossessed*. Washington, DC: The Brookings Institution Press, 1993.

Derrida, Jacques. *Interventions*. Stanford: Stanford University Press, 2002.

Derrida, Jacques. "The Principle of Reason: The University in the Eyes of its Pupils." Trans. by C. Porter and E. P. Morris. (1983) 13 *Diacritics* 3.

Disch, Lisa. *Hannah Arendt and the Limits of Philosophy*. Ithaca, NY: Cornell University Press, 1994.

Disch, Lisa. "Please Sit Down, But Don't Make Yourself at Home: Arendtian 'Visiting' and the Prefigurative Politics of Consciousness-Reading." In Craig Calhoun and John McGowan, eds. *Hannah Arendt and The Meaning of Politics*. Minneapolis: University of Minnesota Press, 1997.

Disch, Lisa Jane. "More Truth Than Fact: Storytelling as Critical Understanding in the Writings of Hannah Arendt." (1993) 21 *Political Theory* 665.

Donnelly, Jack. "The Relative Universality of Human Rights." (2007) 29 *Human Rights Quarterly* 281.

Donnelly, Jack. "State Sovereignty and International Intervention." In Gene M. Lyons and Michael Mastanduno, eds. *Beyond Westphalia?* Baltimore, MD: Johns Hopkins, 1995.

Donnelly, Jack. *Universal Human Rights in Theory and Practice*, 2nd edn. Ithaca, NY: Cornell University Press, 2003.

Douzinas, Costas. "Postmodern Just Wars and the New World Order." (2006) 5 *Journal of Human Rights* 355.

Doyle, Michael W. "Kant & Liberal Internationalism." In Pauline Kleingeld, ed. *Toward Perpetual Peace & Other Writings on Politics, Peace, & History*. Binghamton, NY: Vail-Ballou Press, 2006.

Doyle, Michael W. "Kant, Liberal Legacies and Foreign Affairs." (1983) 12 *Philosophy and Public Affairs* 205.

Dupuy, Pierre-Marie. "Les 'considérations élémentaires d'humanité' dans la jurisprudence de la Cour Internationale de Justice." In René-Jean Dupuy and L.A. Sicilianos, eds. *Mélanges en l'honneur de N. Valticos*. Paris: Pédone, 1999.

Eckert, Amy E. "Free Determination or the Determination to be Free?" (1999) 4 *UCLA Journal of International Law and Foreign Affairs* 55.

Elbe, Stefan. "Should HIV/AIDS be Securitized?" (2006) 50 *International Studies Quarterly* 119.

Falk, Richard A. *The Costs of War: International Law, the UN, and World Order After Iraq*. New York: Routledge, 2008.

Falk, Richard A. "Kicking the Intervention Habit." Opinion, Al Jazeera English (10 March 2011). Online: Al Jazeera English http://english.aljazeera.net/indepth/opinion/2011/03/2011381434487866 61.html

Falk, Richard A. "The New Interventionism and the Third World." (1999) 98 *Current History* 370.

Fine, Robert. "Cosmopolitanism and Violence: Difficulties of Judgment." (2006) 57 *The British Journal of Sociology* 49.

Fitzmaurice, Sir Gerald. *The Law and Procedure of the International Court of Justice*, Vol. I, Grotius: Cambridge University Press, 1986.

Forst, Rainer. "Towards a Critical Theory of Transnational Justice." In Thomas W. Pogge, ed. *Global Justice*. Oxford: Blackwell, 2001.

Franck, Thomas. "The Emerging Right to Democratic Governance." (1992) 86 *American Journal of International Law* 46.

Franck, Thomas. "Legality and Legitimacy in Humanitarian Intervention." Paper presented to the American Political Science Association Annual Meeting, Boston, 2002 [Unpublished].

Fraser, Nancy. "Rethinking the Public Sphere." In Craig Calhoun, ed. *Habermas and the Public Sphere*. Cambridge, MA: MIT Press, 1992.

Fukuyama, Francis. 'The End of History?' (Summer, 1989) 16 *The National Interest* 3.

Fukuyama, Francis. *The End of History and the Last Man*. New York: Macmillan, 1992.

Fuller, Lon L. *The Morality of Law*, rev. edn. New Haven, CT: Yale University Press, 1969.

Gadamer, Hans-Georg. "The Principle of Effective History." In Kurt Mueller-Volmer, ed. *The Hermeneutics Reader*. Trans. by Garrett Barden and John Cumming. New York: Continuum, 1985.

Gadamer, Hans-Georg. "The Rehabilitation of Authority and Tradition." In Kurt Mueller-Volmer, ed. *The Hermeneutics Reader*. Trans. by Garrett Barden and John Cumming. New York: Continuum, 1985.

Galtung, Johan. "Violence, Peace and Peace Research." (1969) 6 *Journal of Peace Research* 167.

Garwood-Gowers, Andrew. "China's 'Responsible Protection' Concept." (2016) 6 *Asian Journal of International Law* 89.

Geertz, Clifford. "From the Native's Point of View." In *Local Knowledge*. New York: Basic Books, 1983.

Geertz, Clifford. "Thick Description: Toward an Interpretive Theory of Culture." In *The Interpretation of Cultures*. New York: Basic Books, 1973.

Geertz, Clifford. "The Uses of Diversity." (1986) 25 *Michigan Quarterly Review* 105.

Global Centre for the Responsibility to Protect. *About R2P*. Online: www.globalr2p.org/about_r2p

Global Centre for the Responsibility to Protect. *UN General Assembly Resolutions Referencing R2P*. Online: www.globalr2p.org/resources/1133

Government of Canada. *Foreign Policy*. Online: Foreign Affairs and International Trade Canada http://geo.international.gc.ca/cip-pic/cip-pic/aboutthegbp-en.aspx

Government of Canada. *Human Security Program Policy Statement*, 2005. Online: Government of Canada www.humansecurity.gc.ca/psh-en.asp

Government of Japan. *Diplomatic Bluebook*, 1999. Ministry of Foreign Affairs. Online: Government of Japan www.mofa.go.jp

Government of Japan. *Human Security*, 2007. Ministry of Foreign Affairs. Online: Government of Japan www.mofa.go.jp/policy/oda/sector/security/action.html

Gray, Christine. "From Unity to Polarization: International Law and the Use of Force in Iraq." (2002) 13 *European Journal of International Law* 1.

Guttman, Amy. "Introduction." In Michael Ignatieff, ed. *Human Rights as Politics and Idolatry*. Princeton, NJ: Princeton University Press, 2001.

Habermas, Jürgen. *The Divided West*. Cambridge, MA: Polity Press, 2006.

Habermas, Jürgen. *Time of Transitions*. Trans. and ed. by Ciaran Cronin and Max Pensky. Cambridge: Polity, 2006.

Habermas, Jürgen. *Truth and Justification*. Trans. and ed. by Barbara Fultner. Cambridge, MA: Massachusetts Institute of Technology Press, 2003.

Habermas, Jürgen. *The Postnational Constellation*. Trans. and ed. by Max Pensky. Cambridge, MA: MIT Press, 2001.

Habermas, Jürgen. "Bestiality and Humanity: A War on the Border between Legality and Morality." (1999) 6 *Constellations* 263.

Habermas, Jürgen. *The Inclusion of the Other*. Ed. by Ciaran Cronin and Pablo De Greiff. Cambridge, MA: MIT Press, 1998.

Habermas, Jürgen. *On the Pragmatics of Communication*. Ed. by Maeve Cooke. Cambridge, MA: MIT Press, 1998.

Habermas, Jürgen. *Between Facts and Norms*. Trans. by Wilhelm Rehg. Cambridge, MA: Massachusetts Institute of Technology Press, 1996.

Habermas, Jürgen, Jacques Derrida and Giovanna Borradori. Philosophy in a Time of Terror. Chicago: University of Chicago Press, 2003.

Habermas, Jürgen. *Justification and Application*. Trans. by Ciaran P. Cronin. Cambridge, MA: MIT Press, 1993.

Habermas, Jürgen. *Moral Consciousness and Communicative Action*. Trans. by Christian Lernhardt and Shierry Weber Nicholsen. Cambridge, MA: Massachusetts Institute of Technology Press, 1990.

Habermas, Jürgen. Jacques Derrida and Giovanna Borradori. *Philosophy in a Time of Terror*. Chicago: University of Chicago Press, 2003.

Hale, Thomas. "Barack Obama and the Deepening of Democracy." (2008) 15 *Democratiya*53.

Handley, Keith. "Res Judicata: General Principles and Recent Developments." (1999) 18 *Australian Bar Review* 214.

Hardt, Michael and Antonio Negri. *Empire*. Cambridge, MA: Harvard University Press, 2000.

Hardt, Michael and Antonio Negri. *Multitude*. New York: Penguin Press, 2004.

Hart, H.L.A. "Positivism and the Separation of Law and Morals." (1958) 71 *Harvard Law Review* 593.

Hehir, Aidan. "Assessing the Influence of the Responsibility to Protect on the UN Security Council during the Arab Spring." (2016) 51 *Cooperation and Conflict* 2.

Hehir, Aidan. "From Human Security to the Responsibility to Protect: The Co-option of Dissent." (2015) 23 *Michigan State International Law Review* 675.

Hehir, Aidan. "NATO's 'Humanitarian Intervention' in Kosovo: Legal Precedent or Aberration?" (2009) 8 *Journal of Human Rights* 245.

Heieck, John. *A Duty to Prevent Genocide: Due Diligence Obligations Among the P5*. Cheltenham, UK: Edward Elgar, 2018.

Hobbes, Thomas. *Leviathan: or, the Matter, Forme and Power of a Commonwealth*. Ed. by Michael Oakeshott. New York: Macmillan, 1962.

Hollis, Martin and Steven Lukes, eds. *Rationality and Relativism*. Cambridge, MA: Massachusetts Institute of Technology Press, 1982.

Honig, Bonnie. "Another Cosmopolitanism? Law and Politics in the New Europe." In Robert Post, ed. *Another Cosmopolitanism*. Oxford: Oxford University Press, 2006.

Honig, Bonnie. *Political Theory and the Displacement of Politics*. Ithaca, NY: Cornell University Press, 1993.

Howard, Rhoda E. *Human Rights in Commonwealth Africa*. Totowa, NJ: Rowman & Littlefield, 1986.

Howse, Robert and Makau wa Mutua. *Protecting Human Rights in a Global Economy: Challenges for the World Trade Organization*. Montréal: Right and Democracy, International Centre for Human Rights and Democratic Development, 2000. Online: www.dd-rd.ca/site/publications/index.php?id=1271&page=3&subsection=catalogue

Hubert, Don and Ariela Blätter. "The Responsibility to Protect as International Crimes Prevention." (2012) 4 *Global Responsibility to Protect* 33.

Hurrell, Andrew. *On Global Order: Power, Values, and the Constitution of International Society*. Oxford: Oxford University Press, 2007.

Ignatieff, Michael. *Empire Lite*. Toronto: Penguin Press, 2003.

Ignatieff, Michael. *Human Rights as Politics and Idolatry*. Princeton, NJ: Princeton University Press, 2001.

International Coalition for the Responsibility to Protect. Online: www.responsibilitytoprotect.org

International Commission on Intervention and State Sovereignty. *The Responsibility to Protect*. Ottawa, Canada: International Development Research Centre, 2001.

International Commission on Intervention and State Sovereignty. *The Responsibility to Protect: Research, Bibliography, Background: Supplementary Volume to the Report of the International Commission on Intervention and State Sovereignty*. Ottawa: International Development Research Centre, 2001.

Jackson, John H. *World Trade and the Law of GATT*. New York: Bobbs-Merrill, 1969.

Kagan, Robert. *The Return of History and the End of Dreams*. New York: Alfred A. Knopf, 2008.

Kanetake, Machiko. *The UN Security Council and Domestic Actors: Distance in International Law*. London: Routledge, 2015.

Kant, Immanuel. *Critique of Judgement*. Trans. and with an introduction by J.H. Bernard. New York: Hafner Publishing, 1951.

Kant, Immanuel. *Grounding for the Metaphysics of Morals*. 1785. Trans. by J.W. Ellington. Indianapolis, IN: Hackett Publishing, 1981.

Kant, Immanuel. *Kant Selections*. The Great Philosophers. Paul Edwards, general editor. New York: Macmillan Publishing, 1988.

Kant, Immanuel. *Perpetual Peace and Other Essays on Politics, History, and Morals*. Trans. and ed. by Ted Humphrey. Indianapolis, IN: Hackett Publishing, 1983.

Kant, Immanuel. "Toward Perpetual Peace." In Pauline Kleingeld, ed. *Toward Perpetual Peace & Other Writings on Politics, Peace, & History*. Binghamton, NY: Vail-Ballou Press, 2006.

Kant, Immanuel. *Toward Perpetual Peace and Other Writings on Politics, Peace, and History*. Trans. by D. L. Colclasure. Ed. by Pauline Kleingeld. New Haven, CT: Yale University Press, 2006.

Keeble, Edna. "Canadians and Global Beneficence." In Susan Sherwin and Peter Schotch, eds. *Engaged Philosophy: Essays in Honor of David Braybrooke*. Toronto: University of Toronto Press, 2007.

Kennedy, David. *The Dark Sides of Virtue*. Princeton, NJ: Princeton University Press, 2004.

Kennedy, David. "The International Human Rights Movement: Part of the Problem?" (2002) 15 *Harvard Human Rights Journal* 101.

Klein, Pierre. "Responsibility for Serious Breaches of Obligations Deriving from Peremptory Norms of International Law and United Nations Law." (2002) 13 *European Journal of International Law* 1241.

Koskenniemi, Martti. "Carl Schmitt, Hans Morgenthau, and the Image of Law in International Relations." In Michael Byers, ed. *The Role of Law in International Politics.* by. Oxford: Oxford University Press, 2000.

Koskenniemi, Martti. *From Apology to Utopia: The Structure of International Legal Argument.* Cambridge: Cambridge University Press, 2005.

Koskenniemi, Martti. *The Gentle Civilizer of Nations: The Rise and Fall of International Law 1870–1960.* Cambridge: Cambridge University Press, 2004.

Koskenniemi, Martti. "Hierarchy in International Law: A Sketch." (1997) 8 *European Journal of International Law* 566.

Koskenniemi, Martti. "International Law and Hegemony: A Reconfiguration." (July 2004) 17 *Cambridge Review of International Affairs* 198.

Koskenniemi, Martti. "International Law in Europe: Between Tradition and Renewal." (2005) 16 *European Journal of International Law* 116.

Koskenniemi, Martti. "'Intolerant Democracies': A Reaction." (1996) 37 *Harvard International Law Journal* 231.

Koskenniemi, Martti. "The Police in the Temple. Order, Justice and the UN." (1995) 6 *European Journal of International Law* 325.

Koskenniemi, Martti. "The Politics of International Law." (1990) 1 *European Journal of International Law* 4.

Kotuby, Jr., Charles T. and Luke A. Sobota. *General Principles of Law and International Due Process.* Oxford: Oxford University Press, 2017.

Krasner, Stephen D. *Sovereignty.* Princeton, NJ:Princeton University Press, 1999.

Kratochwil, Friedrich. "Sovereignty as Dominium." In Gene M. Lyons and Michael Mastanduno, eds. *Beyond Westphalia?* Baltimore, MD: Johns Hopkins, 1995.

Kunadt, Nadja. "The Responsibility to Protect as a General Principle of International Law." (2011) 11 *Anuario Mexicano de Derecho Internacional* 187.

Kurtz, Geritt and Madhan Mohan Jaganathan. "Protection in Peril: Counterterrorism Discourse and International Engagement in Sri Lanka in 2009." (2016) 30 *Global Society* 94.

Kurtz, Gerrit and Philipp Rotmann. "The Evolution of Norms of Protection." (2016) 30 *Global Society* 13.

Layne, Christopher. "Kant or Cant." In Michael E. Brown, Sean M. Lynn-Jones and Steven E. Miller, eds. *Debating the Democratic Peace.* Cambridge, MA: MIT Press, 1996.

"Libyan UN Mission Asks UN to Probe Situation in Libya." (22 February 2011). Online: Cri.English.com http://english.cri.cn/6966/2011/02/22/2021s622000.htm.=

Löwenheim, Oded. "'Do Ourselves Credit and Render A Lasting Service to Mankind': British Moral Prestige, Humanitarian Intervention, and the Barbary Pirates" (2003) 47*International Studies Quarterly* 23.

Luck, Edward. "The Responsibility to Protect: Growing Pains or Early Promise?" (2010) *Ethics and International Affairs* 349.

Luers, William H. "Czechoslovakia: Road to Revolution" (1990) 69 *Foreign Affairs* 77.

Luhmann, Niklas. *Die Gesellschaft der Gesellschaft.* Vol. 2. Frankfurt/Main: Suhrkamp Verlag, 1997.

Lynch, Colum. "At the U.N., China and Russia Score Win in War on Human Rights." *Foreign Policy* (26 March 2018). Online at https://foreignpolicy.com/2018/03/26/at-the-u-n-china-and-russia-score-win-in-war-on-human-rights/

Macedo, Stephen. "The Law of Peoples: What Self-Governing Peoples Owe to One Another." (2004) LXXII *Fordham Law Review* 1721.

Macpherson, C.B. *The Life and Times of Liberal Democracy*. Oxford: Oxford University Press, 1977.
Malone, David and Simon Chesterman. "It's Our Duty to Act." *Globe and Mail* (18 December 2001), A19.
Manning, Carrie. "Local Level Challenges to Post-Conflict Peacebuilding" (2003) 10 *International Peacekeeping* 25.
Marks, Susan. "The End of History?: Reflections on Some International Legal Theses." (1997) 8 *European Journal of International Law* 449.
Marks, Susan. *The Riddle of all Constitutions: International Law, Democracy and the Critique of Ideology*. Oxford: Oxford University Press, 2000.
Martin, Rex and David A. Ready, eds. *Rawls' Law of Peoples*. Malden, MA: Blackwell, 2006.
Mayer, Ann E. *Islam and Human Rights*, 2nd edn. Boulder, CO: Westview Press, 1999.
Mayer, Ann E. "Review of Human Rights in Cross-Cultural Perspectives: A Quest for Consensus. Ed. by Abdullahi Ahmed An-Na'im." (1992) 14 *Human Rights Quarterly* 527.
Mbeoji, Ikechi. *Collective Insecurity: The Liberian Crisis, Unilateralism, and the Global Order*. Vancouver: UBC Press, 2003.
McInnes, Mitchell. "The Question of a Duty to Rescue in Canadian Tort Law." (1990) 13 *Dalhousie Law Journal* 85.
Mearsheimer, John J. "Back to the Future." (1990) 15 *International Security* 5.
Mehta, Pratap Bhanu. "From State Sovereignty to Human Security (Via Institutions?)." Paper presented at the American Political Science Association Annual Meeting, Boston, 2002.
Meiland, Jack W. and Michael Krausz, eds. *Relativism: Cognitive and Moral*. Notre Dame: University of Notre Dame Press, 1982.
Michelman, Frank I. "Parsing a 'Right to Have Rights.'" (1996) 3 *Constellations* 200.
Minister of Foreign Affairs of the Russian Federation, Sergey Lavrov. Interview with BBC, 8 August 2008. Online: https://argentina.mid.ru/news/2008/-/asset_publisher/xN4dOI7LPB79/content/09-08-2008-interview-by-minister-of-foreign-affaires-of-the-russian-federation-sergey-lavrov-to-bbc-moscow-august-9-2008
Minister of Foreign Affairs of the Russian Federation, Sergey Lavrov. "A Conversation with Sergey Lavrov." Speaking at the Carnegie Council on Foreign Relations, New York, NY, 24 September 2008. Online: Carnegie Council on Foreign Relations www.cfr.org/event/conversation-sergey-lavrov
Ministry of Foreign Affairs of Japan. *Human Security*, (2007). Online: www.mofa.go.jp/policy/oda/sector/security/action.html
Minnich, Elizabeth. "To Judge in Freedom: Hannah Arendt on the Relation of Thinking and Morality." In Gisela T. Kaplan and Clive S. Kessler, eds. *Hannah Arendt: Thinking, Judging, Freedom*. Sydney, Australia: Allen & Unwin, 1989.
Mitchell, Ryan. "Was the UN Human Rights Council Wrong to Back China's 'Shared Future' Resolution?" EJILTalk! (10 April 2018). Online: ejiltalk.org/was-the-un-human-rights-council-wrong-to-back-chinas-shared-future-resolution/
Molier, Gelijn. "Humanitarian Intervention and the Responsibility to Protect After 9/11." (2006) 53 *Netherlands International Law Review* 37.
Moon, Donald J. "Practical Discourse and Communicative Ethics." In Steven K. White, ed. *The Cambridge Companion to Habermas*. Cambridge: Cambridge University Press, 1995.
Moore, Alison. "A New Angle on Public Involvement." *Health Service Journal* (22 August 2014). Online: HSJ www.hsj.co.uk/resource-centre/supplements/a-new-angle-on-public-involvement/5073601.article

Moravcsik, Andrew M. "Liberalism and International Relations Theory." Center for International Affairs, Harvard University, Working Paper No. 92–96, 1992.

Morawetz, Thomas. "The Epistemology of Judging." In Dennis Patterson, ed. *Wittgenstein and Legal Theory*. Boulder, CO: Westview Press, 1992.

Morawetz, Thomas. *Wittgenstein and Knowledge*. Amherst: University of Massachusetts Press, 1978.

Moynihan, Colin. "Libya's UN Diplomats Break With Qaddafi." *The New York Times* (21 February 2011). Online: NYT www.nytimes.com/2011/02/22/world/africa/22nations.html?_r+0

Mutua, Makau. *Human Rights: A Political and Cultural Critique*. Philadelphia: University of Pennsylvania Press, 2002.

Mutua, Makau. "Politics and Human Rights: An Essential Symbiosis." In Michael Byers, ed. *The Role of Law in International Politics*. Oxford: Oxford University Press, 2000.

Mutua, Makau. "Savages, Victims, and Saviors: The Metaphor of Human Rights." (2001) 42 *Harvard International Law Journal* 201.

Mutua, Makau. "Standard Setting in Human Rights: Critique and Prognosis." (2007) 29 *Human Rights Quarterly* 547.

Nagel, Thomas. *The View from Nowhere*. Oxford: Oxford University Press, 1986.

Nedelsky, Jennifer. "Communities of Judgment and Human Rights." (2000) 1 *Theoretical Inquiries in Law* 1.

Nedelsky, Jennifer. "Relations of freedom and law's relations." (2012) 8 *Politics and Gender* 231.

Nussbaum, Martha C. *Women and Human Development*. Cambridge: Cambridge University Press, 2000.

Nussbaum, Martha C. "In Defense of Universal Values." (2000) 36 *Idaho Law Review* 379.

Nussbaum, Martha C. *Sex and Social Justice*. New York: Oxford University Press, 1999.

Nussbaum, Martha C. "Human Functioning and Social Justice: In Defense of Aristotelian Essentialism." (1992) 20 *Political Theory* 202.

Nussbaum, Martha C. "Aristotelian Social Democracy." In R. Bruce Douglass, Gerald Wara, and Henry Richardson, eds. *Liberalism and the Good*. London: Routledge, 1990.

Nussbaum, Martha C. "Nature, Function, and Capability: Aristotle on Political Distribution." WIDER Working Papers. Helsinki: World Institute for Development Economics Research, 1988.

Nussbaum, Martha C. "Non-Relative Virtues: An Aristotelian Approach." (1988) 13 *Midwest Studies in Philosophy* 32.

Nussbaum, Martha C. and Jonathan Glover, eds. *Women, Culture and Development*. Oxford: Clarendon Press, 1995.

Obama, Barack, David Cameron and Nicolas Sarkozy. "Libya's Pathway to Peace." Opinion, *New York Times* (11 April 2011). Online: New York Times www.nytimes.com/2011/04/15/opinion/15iht-edlibya15.html

Okafor, Obiora Chinedu. "Newness, Imperialism, and International Legal Reform in Our Time: A TWAIL Perspective." (2005) 43 *Osgoode Hall Law Journal* 171.

Oman, Natalie. "Could R2P Justify a No-Fly Zone in the Absence of Security Council Approval?" Guest Blog, Opinio Juris (17 March 2011). Online: Opinio Juris http://opiniojuris.org/2011/03/17/could-rtop-justify-a-no-fly-zone-in-the-absence-of-security-council-approval/

Oman, Natalie. *Final Report on Drivers and Recommendations for Prevention of Atrocity Crimes Targeting Indigenous Peoples in Latin America, prepared on behalf of the UN*

Office of the Special Advisers on Genocide Prevention and on the Responsibility to Protect. December 2016. [Unpublished]

Oman, Natalie. "Paths to Intercultural Understanding: Feasting, Shared Horizons, and Unforced Consensus." In Catherine Bell and David Kahane, eds. *Intercultural Dispute Resolution in Aboriginal Contexts.* Vancouver, BC: UBC Press, 2004.

Oman, Natalie. "Private Ordering and Transnational Social Justice: The Forest Stewardship Council's Advocacy of Free, Prior and Informed Consent." In Stepan Wood, et al., eds. *Transnational Business Governance Interactions: Empowering Marginalized Actors and Enhancing Regulatory Quality.* Cheltenham, UK: Edward Elgar, 2019.

Oman, Natalie. "Sharing Horizons: A Paradigm for Political Accommodation in Intercultural Settings." PhD diss., McGill University, 1997. [Unpublished]

O'Neill, Onora. "Agents of Justice." (2001) 32 *Metaphilosophy* 180.

O'Neill, Onora. *Bounds of Justice.* Cambridge: Cambridge University Press, 2000.

Onuf, Nicholas. "Intervention for the Common Good." In G. M. Lyons and M. Mastanduno, eds. *Beyond Westphalia?* Baltimore, MD: Johns Hopkins, 1995.

Onuf, Nicholas. *The Republican Legacy in International Thought.* Cambridge: Cambridge University Press, 1998.

Onuf, Nicholas. "'Tainted by Contingency': Retelling the Story of International Law." In Richard Falk, et al., eds. *Reframing the International.* New York: Routledge, 2002.

Onuma, Yasuaki. *A Transcivilizational Perspective on International Law.* Leiden: Brill/ Nijhoff, 2010.

Oren, Ido. "The Subjectivity of the 'Democratic' Peace." In Michael Edward Brown, Sean M. Lynn-Jones and Steven E. Miller, eds. *Debating the Democratic Peace.* Cambridge, MA: Massachusetts Institute of Technology Press, 1996.

Orford, Anne. "A Jurisprudence of the Limit." In Anne Orford, ed. *International Law and Its Others.* Cambridge: Cambridge University Press, 2006.

Oved, Marco Chown. "In Côte d'Ivoire, a Model of Successful Intervention." *The Atlantic* (9 June 2011). Online: www.theatlantic.com/international/archive/2011/06/in-c-te-divoire-a-model-of-successful-intervention/240164/

Owen, John M. "How Liberalism Produces Democratic Peace." In Michael Edward Brown, Sean M. Lynn-Jones and Steven E. Miller, eds. *Debating the Democratic Peace.* Cambridge, MA: Massachusetts Institute of Technology Press, 1996.

Parekh, Bhikhu. "The Cultural Particularity of Liberal Democracy." In David Held, ed. *Prospects for Democracy.* Stanford, CA: Stanford University Press, 1993.

Parekh, Serena. *Hannah Arendt and the Challenge of Modernity: A Phenomenology of Human Rights.* New York: Routledge, 2008.

Passavant, Paul A. "The Contradictory State of Giorgio Agamben." (2007) 35 *Political Theory* 147.

Pattison, James. *Humanitarian Intervention and the Responsibility to Protect: Who Should Intervene?* Oxford: Oxford University Press, 2010.

Permanent Court of International Justice, Advisory Committee of Jurists. *Documents Presented to the Committee Relating to Existing Plans for the Establishment of a Permanent Court of International Justice, 1920.* Online: www.icj-cij.org/pcij/serie_D/D_documents_to_comm_existing_plans.pdf

Permanent Court of International Justice, Advisory Committee of Jurists. *Procès-verbaux of the Proceedings of the Committee, June 16-July 24, 1920, with Annexes.* The Hague: Van Langenhuysen Brothers, 1920. Online: https://archive.org/stream/procsverbauxof00leaguoft#page/ii/mode/2up

Petersmann, Ernst-Ulrich. "Time for a United Nations 'Global Compact' for Integrating Human Rights into the Law of Worldwide Organizations." (2002) 13 *European Journal of International Law* 621.

Pettit, Philip. *Republicanism: A Theory of Freedom and Government.* Oxford: Oxford University Press, 1998.

Piccone, Ted. "China's Long Game on Human Rights at the United Nations." Foreign Policy Paper Series on International Governance, The Brookings Institution (September 2018). Online: www.brookings.edu/wp-content/uploads/2018/09/FP_20181009_china_human_rights.pdf

Pogge, Thomas. "'The Incoherence Between Rawls' Theories of Justice." (2004) LXXII *Fordham Law Review* 1739.

Pogge, Thomas. *World Poverty and Human Rights.* Cambridge: Polity Press, 2002.

Popovski, Vesselin. "Development of the Ethical Principles of Intervention through UN Security Council Resolutions." Paper presented at the Ethics of Intervention workshop, Key Centre, Griffith University, Brisbane, Australia, December 2004. [Unpublished].

"#R2P: Reflections on the Responsibility to Protect at 10, Part 1: A Norm for Our Times." Protection Gateway (24 April 2018). Online: Protection Gateway https://protectiongateway.com/2015/04/22/r2p-reflections-on-the-responsibility-to-protect-at-10-part-1-a-norm-for-our-times/

Rajagopal, Balakrishnan. *International Law from Below.* Cambridge: Cambridge University Press, 2003.

Rawls, John. "The Law of Peoples." (1993, essay version). In Samuel Freedman, ed. *John Rawls: Collected Papers.* Cambridge, MA: Harvard University Press, 1999.

Rawls, John. *The Law of Peoples with The Idea of Public Reason Revisited.* Cambridge, MA: Harvard University Press, 2001.

Rawls, John. *Political Liberalism.* 2nd edn. New York: Columbia University Press, 1993, 1996.

The Registrar of the ICJ. *International Court of Justice Handbook.* 5th edn. The Hague, Netherlands: ICJ, 2004, 2013. Online: ICJ www.icj-cij.org/files/publications/handbook-of-the-court-en.pdf.

Reisman, W. Michael. "Sovereignty and Human Rights in Contemporary International Law." (1990) 84 *American Journal of International Law* 866.

Report of the International Committee of Jurists, League of Nations Official Journal, Special Supplement no. 3, October 1920.

Reus-Smit, Christian. "The Strange Death of Liberal International Theory." (2001) 12 *European Journal of International Law* 573.

Rousseau, Jean-Jacques. *On the Social Contract.* Trans. by D.A. Cress. Indianapolis, IN: Hackett Publishing, 1987.

Russett, Bruce. *Grasping the Democratic Peace.* Princeton, NJ: Princeton University Press, 1993.

"Russian Twitter Trolls Meddled in the Brexit Vote. Did They Swing It?" *The Economist* (23 November 2017). Online: Economist www.economist.com/britain/2017/11/23/russian-twitter-trolls-meddled-in-the-brexit-vote-did-they-swing-it

Ryan, Alan. "Hobbes' Political Philosophy." In Tom Sorell, ed. *The Cambridge Companion to Hobbes.* Cambridge, United Kingdom: Cambridge University Press, 1996.

Sachs, Jeffrey D. "Institutions Don't Rule: Direct Effects of Geography on Per Capita Income." National Bureau of Economic Research, NBER Working Paper No. 9490 (2003). Online: National Bureau of Economic Research www.nber.org/papers/w9490

Sassen, Saskia. "The State and the New Geography of Power." In *Losing Control? Sovereignty in an Age of Globalization.* New York: Columbia University Press, 1996.

Sceats, Sonya. "Guest Post: China as a Shaper of International Norms," Opinio Juris (17 March 2015). Online: http://opiniojuris.org/2015/03/17/guest-post-china-as-a-shaper-of-international-law/?utm_source=feedburner&utm_medium=email&utm_campaign=Feed%3A+opiniojurisfeed+%28Opinio+Juris%29

Schachter, Oscar. *International Law in Theory and Practice.* Dordrecht: Martinus Nijhoff, 1991.

Schmitt, Carl. *The Concept of the Political.* Trans. and with an introduction by George Schwab, expanded edn. Chicago and London: The University of Chicago Press, 1996.

Schmitt, Carl. *The Nomos of the Earth in the International Law of the Jus Publicum Europaeum.* Trans. by G. L. Ulmen. New York: Telos Press, 2003.

Schreuer, Christopher. "The Waning of the Sovereign State: Towards a New Paradigm for International Law?" (1993) 4 *European Journal of International Law* 447.

Scobbie, Iain. "The Invocation of Responsibility for the Breach of Obligations under Peremptory Norms of General International Law." (2002) 13 *European Journal of International Law* 1201.

Scott, Craig. "Interpreting Intervention" (2001) 39 *Canadian Yearbook of International Law* 333.

Sen, Amartya. *Development as Freedom.* New York: Alfred A. Knopf, 1999.

Sen, Amartya. *On Rethinking the Third World.* New York: Alfred A. Knopf, 1999.

Sen, Amartya. "More than 100 Million Women are Missing." (1990) 37 *New York Review of Books* 61.

Shanghai Cooperation Organization."Shanghai Cooperation Organisation Split on Georgia" (2 September 2008). Online: The Irrawaddy www.irrawaddy.org/article.php?art_id=14141

Shue, Henry. *Basic Rights: Subsistence, Affluence, and U.S. Foreign Policy.* Princeton, NJ: Princeton University Press, 1980.

Simma, Bruno and Philip Alston. "The Sources of Human Rights Law: Custom, Jus Cogens, and General Principles." (1988–1989) 12 *Australian Year Book of International Law* 82.

Simpson, Gerry J. *Great Powers and Outlaw States.* Cambridge: Cambridge University Press, 2004.

Skordas, Achilles. "Hegemonic Custom?" In Michael Byers, ed. *United States Hegemony and the Foundations of International Law.* West Nyack, NY: Cambridge University Press, 2003.

Slaughter, Anne-Marie. "International Law in a World of Liberal States" (1995) 6 *European Journal of International Law* 503.

Slaughter, Anne-Marie. *A New World Order.* Princeton, NJ:Princeton University Press, 2004.

Smith, William. "Anticipating a Cosmopolitan Future: The Case of Humanitarian Military Intervention." (2007) 44 *International Politics* 72.

Spears, Ian S. "Debating Secession and the Recognition of New States in Africa" (2004) 13 *African Security Review* 35.

Sperduti, Giuseppe. *Lezioni di diritto internazionale.* Milano: A. Giuffrè, 1958.

Spiro, David E. "The Insignificance of the Liberal Peace." In Michael Edward Brown, Sean M. Lynn-Jones and Steven E. Miller, eds. *Debating the Democratic Peace.* Cambridge, MA: Massachusetts Institute of Technology Press, 1996.

Stahn, Carsten. "Responsibility to Protect: Political Rhetoric or Emerging Legal Norm?" (2007) 101 *American Journal of International Law* 99.

Statement on behalf of the Group of Friends of the Responsibility to Protect, delivered by Her Excellency Ambassador Alya Ahmed S. Al-Thani, Permanent Representative of the State of Qatar to the United Nations before the Open Debate of the United Nations Security Council on Women, Peace and Security: Sexual Violence in Conflict (23 April

2019). Online: www.globalr2p.org/media/files/final-version-gof-r2p-statement-open-debate-unsc-sexual-violence-in-conflict.pdf

Steiner, Henry J. and Philip Alston, eds. *International Human Rights in Context.* Oxford: Oxford University Press, 2000.

Stiglmayer, Alexandra, ed. *Mass Rape: The War Against Women in Bosnia-Herzegovina.* Trans. by Marion Faber. Lincoln, NE: University of Nebraska Press, 1994.

"Stop the Clash of Civilizations." Online: Avaaz www.youtube.com/watch?v=WWyJJQbFago

Strange, Susan. *The Retreat of the State: The Diffusion of Power in the World Economy.* Cambridge: Cambridge University Press, 1996.

Summaries of UN General Assembly Debates and Interactive Dialogues on R2P, Global Centre for the Responsibility to Protect. Online: www.globalr2p.org/resources/897

Suzuki, Susumu, Volker Krause and J. David Singer. "The Correlates of War Project: A Bibliographic History of the Scientific Study of War and Peace, 1964–2000." (2002) 19 *Conflict Management and Peace Studies* 67.

Tams, Christian J. "Do Serious Breaches Give Rise to Any Specific Obligations of the Responsible State?" (2002) 13 *European Journal of International Law* 1161.

Taylor, Charles. "Conditions of an Unforced Consensus on Human Rights." Paper presented to the Cultural Sources of Human Rights in East Asia Conference, Chulalongkorn University, 1996.

Taylor, Charles. "Modernity, Faith, and Morality." Paper presented in the Sprole Lectures Series, Faculty of Religious Studies, McGill University, Montréal, 1992. [Unpublished].

Taylor, Charles. "The Politics of Recognition." In *Philosophical Arguments.* Cambridge, MA: Harvard University Press, 1995.

Taylor, Charles. "What is Human Agency?" In *Philosophical Papers: Human Agency and Language*, Vol. 1. Cambridge: Cambridge University Press, 1985.

Taylor, Charles. "Understanding and Ethnocentricity." In *Philosophical Papers: Philosophy and the Human Sciences*, Vol. 2. Cambridge: Cambridge University Press, 1985.

Teitel, Ruti G. *Humanity's Law.* Oxford and New York: Oxford University Press, 2011.

Téson, Fernando. *Humanitarian Intervention.* Dobbs Ferry, NY: Transnational, 1988.

Téson, Fernando . *A Philosophy of International Law.* Boulder, CO: Westview Press, 1998.

Teubner, Gunther. *Constitutional Fragments: Societal Constitutionalism and Globalization.* Oxford: Oxford University Press, 2012.

Teubner, Gunther. *Global Law Without a State.* Aldershot, UK: Dartmouth Publishing, 1997.

The Elders. Online: The Elders www.theelders.org/

Todorov, Tzvetan. "Right to Intervene or Duty to Assist?" In Nicolas Owen, ed. *Human Rights, Human Wrongs: The Oxford Amnesty Lectures 2001.* Oxford: Oxford University Press, 2003.

Tomaševski, Katarina. *Responding to Human Rights Violations, 1946–1999.* The Hague: Martinus Nijhoff, 2000.

Toope, Stephen. "Powerful but Unpersuasive?" In Michael Byers and Georg Nolte, eds. *United States Hegemony and the Foundations of International Law.* West Nyack, NY: Cambridge University Press, 2003. P. 303.

Tourinho, Marcos, Oliver Stuenkel, and Sarah Brockmeier, "'Responsibility while Protecting': Reforming R2P Implementation." (2016) 30 *Global Society* 144.

Tully, James. "On Law, Democracy and Imperialism." Paper presented at the Twenty-First Annual Public Lecture, Centre for Law and Society. University of Edinburgh, 2005. Online: University of Victoria www.law.uvic.ca/demcon/documents/Tully%20Presem%20-%20Edinburgh%20draft%20criculation%20paper.doc.

Vagts, Detlev F. "Hegemonic International Law." (2001) 95 *American Journal of International Law* 843.

van Boven, Theo. "Human Rights and the Rights of Peoples." (1995) 6 *European Journal of International Law* 461.

Van der Burg, Wibren. "The Morality of Aspiration." In Willem J. Witteveen and Wibren Van der Burg, eds. *Rediscovering Fuller*. Amsterdam: Amsterdam University Press, 1999.

Wa, Gisday and Delgam Uukw. *The Spirit in the Land*. Gabriola, BC: Reflections, 1989, 1992.

Walbel, Michael. "Book Symposium: The Rise of Interpretive Communities in Treaty Interpretation." (7 April 2015). Online, Opinio Juris http://opiniojuris.org/2015/04/07/book-symposium-the-rise-of-interpretive-communities-in-treaty-interpretation/

Waltz, K. "America as a Model for the World? A Foreign Policy Perspective" (1991) 24 *PS: Political Science and Politics* 667.

Webber, Jeremy. "Relations of Force and Relations of Justice: The Emergence of Normative Community Between Colonists and Aboriginal Peoples." (1995) 33 *Osgoode Hall Law Journal* 623.

Webster's Ninth New Collegiate Dictionary. Springfield, MA: Merriam-Webster, Inc., 1987.

Weiss, Thomas G. and Jarat Chopra. "Sovereignty Under Siege." In Gene M. Lyons and Michael Mastanduno, eds. *Beyond Westphalia?: State Sovereignty and International Intervention*. Baltimore, MD: Johns Hopkins, 1995.

Welsh, Jennifer, Patrick Quinton-Brown and Victor MacDiarmid. "Brazil's 'Responsibility While Protecting' Proposal: A Canadian Perspective." (12 July 2013) Canadian Consortium on the Responsibility to Protect. Online: CCR2P http://ccr2p.org/publications-3

Wesley, Michael. "Towards a Realist Ethics of Intervention." (2005) 19 *Ethics and International Affairs* 55.

Wheeler, Nicholas. *Saving Strangers: Humanitarian Intervention in International Society*. Oxford: Oxford University Press, 2003.

Willett, Susan. "A Global Security, the Liberal Peace, and Human Security." (2006) 18 *Economists for Peace and Security Quarterly* 1.

Willett, Susan. "Insecurity, Conflict and the New Global Disorder." (2001) 32 *Institute of Development Studies Bulletin* 35.

Willett, Susan. "New Barbarians at the Gate: Losing the Liberal Peace in Africa." (2005) 32 *Review of African Political Economy*, 569.

Wingert, Lutz. "Türöffner zu geschlossenen Gesellschaften." *Frankfurter Rundschau* (6 August 1995).

Winston, K. "The Ideal Element in a Definition of Law." (1986) 5 *Law and Philosophy* 89.

Wittgenstein, Ludwig. *On Certainty*. Ed. by G.E.M. Anscombe and G.H. von Wright. Trans. by Dennis Paul and G.E.M. Anscombe. New York: Harper Torchbooks, 1969.

Wittgenstein, Ludwig. *Philosophical Investigations*, 3rd edn. Trans. by G.E.M. Anscombe. New York: Macmillan Publishing Co., 1958.

Woocher, Lawrence. "The Responsibility to Prevent: Toward a Strategy." In W. Andy Knight and Frazer Egerton, eds. *The Routledge Handbook of the Responsibility to Protect*. London and New York: Routledge, 2012.

Wu, Tim. *The Master Switch: The Rise and Fall of Information Empires*. New York: Vintage Books, 2010, 2011.

Yannis, Alexandros. "The Concept of Suspended Sovereignty in International Law." (2002) 13 *European Journal of International Law* 1037.

Young, Iris Marion. "Asymmetrical Reciprocity: On Moral Respect, Wonder, and Enlarged Thought." (1997) 1 *Constellations* 1.

Young, Iris Marion. "Communication and the Other: Beyond Deliberative Democracy." In Seyla Benhabib, ed. *Democracy and Difference: Contesting the Boundaries of the Political.* Princeton, NJ: Princeton University Press, 1996.

Young, Iris Marion. *Justice and the Politics of Difference.* Princeton, NJ: Princeton University Press, 1990.

Zagor, Matthew. "Elementary Considerations of Humanity." In Karine Bannelier, et al., eds. *The ICJ and the Evolution of International Law: The Enduring Impact of the Corfu Channel Case.* London, UK: Routledge, 2012.

Zolo, Danilo. *Invoking Humanity.* London: Continuum, 2002.

Zongze, Ruan. "Responsible Protection." *China Daily News* (15 March 2012). Online: China Daily News www.usa.chinadaily.com.cn/opinion/2012-03/15/content_14838556.htm

Zongze, Ruan. "Responsible Protection: Building a Safer World." China Institute of International Studies (15 June 2012). Online: China Institute of International Studies www.ciis.org.cn/english/2012-06/15/content_5090912.htm

Index

Note: Page numbers followed by 'n' refer to notes.

For Product Safety Concerns and Information please contact our EU
representative GPSR@taylorandfrancis.com
Taylor & Francis Verlag GmbH, Kaufingerstraße 24, 80331 München, Germany

www.ingramcontent.com/pod-product-compliance
Ingram Content Group UK Ltd.
Pitfield, Milton Keynes, MK11 3LW, UK
UKHW011013180926
475701UK00004B/710

* 9 7 8 1 0 3 2 0 8 3 2 4 7 *